T0271295

CLIMATE POLICY FOUNDATIONS

This book provides a thorough grounding in the science and economics of climate policy issues and draws key lessons from the longer experiences of central banks in grappling with related challenges. Findings and controversies of climate history and the effects of human activities on climate are reviewed. The author describes similarities in risk management approaches for climate and monetary policy. Overall goals and frameworks for addressing climate change risks are assessed. Command-and-control and market-based options are compared (including performance standards, taxes, and cap-and-trade). Market-based approaches sometimes require a choice between prices and quantities as policy instruments. However, the author discusses how techniques of central bank interest rate management can be adapted in a hybrid climate policy approach to achieve environmental goals while making carbon prices predictable and ensuring well-functioning carbon markets. Key lessons are offered for improving existing and future national and international climate policy architectures.

William C. Whitesell is Director of Policy Research at the Center for Clean Air Policy in Washington, DC. From 1987 to 2006, he served on the staff of the U.S. Federal Reserve Board, where he held management responsibilities for staff work on the formulation and implementation of monetary policy, including market analysis and the monetary regulation of banks. He conducted independent climate economics research from 2006 to 2007.

Dr. Whitesell has also held positions as a financial analyst at the World Bank and as a development finance specialist at the Banque Arabe et Internationale d'Investissement, in addition to proprietary consulting. Earlier he taught economics at New York University and Virginia Tech. He holds an MBA from the Wharton School at the University of Pennsylvania and a Ph.D. in economics from New York University.

Climate Policy Foundations

*Science and Economics with Lessons
from Monetary Regulation*

WILLIAM C. WHITESELL

CAMBRIDGE UNIVERSITY PRESS
Cambridge, New York, Melbourne, Madrid, Cape Town,
Singapore, São Paulo, Delhi, Mexico City

Cambridge University Press
The Edinburgh Building, Cambridge CB2 8RU, UK

Published in the United States of America by Cambridge University Press, New York

www.cambridge.org
Information on this title: www.cambridge.org/9781107002289

First published 2011

A catalogue record for this publication is available from the British Library

Library of Congress Cataloguing in Publication Data
Whitesell, William C.
Climate policy foundations : science and economics with lessons from monetary regulation /
William C. Whitesell.
p.   cm.
Includes bibliographical references and index.
ISBN 978-1-107-00228-9 (hardback)
1. Environmental policy – Economic aspects.   2. Climatic changes – Economic
aspects.   3. Monetary policy – Environmental aspects.   I. Title.
HC79.E5W486   2011
363.738′74–dc22   2010042840

ISBN 978-1-107-00228-9 Hardback
ISBN 978-1-107-61472-7 Paperback

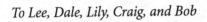

To Lee, Dale, Lily, Craig, and Bob

Contents

Figures and Tables

FIGURES

TABLES

Acknowledgments

I am grateful for comments received from Douglas and Deborah Baker, Heidi Garrett, Donald Wharton, E. Donald Elliott, and anonymous reviewers.

Introduction

This book is intended to offer value to anyone interested in the science and economics of climate change. The text is suitable for use in an interdisciplinary course on climate science and economics. The comprehensive framework presented here could also provide value for scientists, economists, and policy analysts who already have a thorough knowledge of some aspects of climate issues. The work incorporates a survey of the latest journal articles, working papers, and books on climate change issues as of the time of writing. For anyone who has tried to absorb the thousands of pages written by the Nobel-prize winning Intergovernmental Panel on Climate Change, the presentation below will hopefully be seen as mercifully concise yet still informative.

The analysis also reflects a unique perspective of the author. Although I have long been deeply interested in earth sciences, I worked full time on climate issues only in the last several years. For nearly two decades prior to that, I held a day job as an economist at the Federal Reserve Board – an officer responsible for some of the staff work on interest rate management. The history of the Federal Reserve and of central banking around the world holds important lessons for climate policy. Communicating those lessons is one key motive for writing this book.

Since its creation early in the twentieth century, the Federal Reserve has made numerous mistakes in the conduct of monetary policy. A failure to understand the role of the financial sector of the economy contributed to the Great Depression of the 1930s. A misunderstanding of the causes of inflation led to the Great Inflation of the 1970s. In other countries, the framework for money policy was inappropriate because central banks lacking independence tended to generate inflationary extremes. More recently, though not entirely the responsibility of central banks, inadequate regulation of complex new financial instruments and markets helped generate the financial collapse of 2008.

Central banks have adjusted their policies and procedures substantially over the years in response to improved understanding of the economy and of the role of monetary policy. Since the early 1980s, inflation has been reduced to modest levels in most countries around the world. Periods of economic expansion have lasted far longer than was the case in times past. Although lessons regarding the recent financial crisis and economic downturn have yet to be fully digested, the forceful and comprehensive responses of policy makers have averted the worst of the possible outcomes.

Undoubtedly, errors will be made in climate policy as well, especially in the early years of policy formulation and implementation. Unless timely adjustments are made to correct such errors when they become evident, the consequences could be harrowing. On one hand, weak and ineffective policies could mean extreme climate change in the future and great damage to society. On the other hand, poorly designed climate policies could cause an enormous waste of resources and substantial impairment of economic prospects.

Although climate issues are different in many respects from those affecting monetary policy, the similarities are also numerous. Comparable concerns arise regarding the organizing frameworks for climate and monetary policy, including a trade-off between long-range goals and the short-run flexibility needed to avoid economic harm. In monetary policy, the long-run goal is avoiding inflation. In climate policy, the long-run goal is avoiding climate damage. In the short run of a year or two, a central bank's behavior can alter the amplitude of a business cycle for better or worse. An inflexible climate policy can cause unnecessary short-run economic harm, but a well-designed policy can smooth out its effects on the economy over time.

In the face of such trade-offs, the frameworks for monetary and climate policy each need to wrestle with issues regarding the independence and discretionary authority of the implementing agencies, and also the accountability mechanisms. In addition, the conduct of each type of policy involves a balancing of inherent two-sided risks. Many central banks now characterize their conduct of monetary policy as a process of risk management. Probabilities that the policy setting is too easy or too tight must be assessed, and the consequences of an error in either direction must be weighed. To understand the nature and magnitude of the risks, a central bank must learn all it can about the economy. It must also have complete information about the financial sector – the key channel through which monetary policy affects the economy.

Climate policy also is essentially risk management. Just as a central banker studies the economy, a climate policy maker must assess possible future climate outcomes. As a central bank must predict how its policies are transmitted through the financial sector, climate policy must assess its effects on the economic sectors that emit greenhouse gases. An understanding of climate history and of the prospects for emitting sectors, covered in Part One of the book, is essential for making informed decisions regarding the framework and conduct of climate policy.

A risk management approach includes a sense of humility about the state of our knowledge. Economic and climate models have become increasingly sophisticated and as a result, forecasting has improved dramatically. However, we need to remain suspicious about model predictions and sensitive to the underlying assumptions that could dramatically alter the outlook. Like the economy, the climate system is enormously complex and difficult to forecast. Fundamental uncertainties remain about key scientific parameters affecting those projections. We should also expect to be surprised about climate outcomes, just as we have often been surprised about the economy.

Uncertainties about climate science can be exaggerated, however, and uncertainty is no excuse for policy paralysis. The scientific enterprise always involves challenges to conventional understandings, but a policy maker need not give equal weight to all minority points of view that lack the evidence to gain general acceptance. Alternative perspectives do need to be considered, and some important issues remain controversial even within the scientific mainstream. However, the increasing scientific consensus about the risks in the climate outlook should not be taken lightly.

Policy makers need to consider the appropriate emphasis on the objectives of commitment and flexibility in climate policy frameworks. It may be hubris to lock into place the detailed specification of climate policy for decades to come. Risk management cannot be aptly conducted on automatic pilot. In the conduct of monetary policy, central bankers need continuous updates of their knowledge of the economy and the financial sector. In the conduct of climate policy, provision should also be made for policy to adjust to new information about the climate and emitting sectors.

The risks for climate policy seem asymmetric, and this imbalance in risks has important implications for the choice of policy instruments. In both monetary and climate policy, trade-offs exist between the use of quantity and price instruments. Central bankers have wrestled with the issue of whether to try to control the economy using the quantity of money or the level of short-term interest rates (a price measure). An assessment of uncertainties plays a key role in determining the appropriate choice between these two types of policy instruments. The presence of uncertainty alone does not determine the choice. Rather, the result depends on the consequences of uncertainty. A classic paper in monetary theory recommended the use of a quantity instrument (the money supply) if uncertainty about the demand for money was relatively small and uncertainty about the effects of interest rates on the economy was large (Poole, 1970).[1] In modern economies, uncertainty about the demand for money has increased and uncertainty about the effects of interest rates has declined. Financial innovations have created numerous close substitutes for holding deposits, adding to the uncertainty about money demand. Also, deregulation and integration of financial markets have increased the reliability of the interest rate instrument. Largely for these reasons, most central banks now implement monetary policy by setting targets for short-term interest rates rather than the quantity of money.

As discussed in Part Two of the book, climate policy also faces a trade-off between quantity and price instruments. A price instrument could be a carbon tax. A quantity instrument could be a hard limit on the quantity of greenhouse gas (GHG) emissions. A seminal paper on uncertainty in environmental policy found a result resembling that for monetary policy instruments (Weitzman, 1974). In the context of air pollution, this result argues that it is preferable to use a price instrument if the incremental benefit of reducing emissions is about the same across the range of possible emissions (a flat marginal climate damage curve). A price instrument then avoids paying too much when emission reduction costs are greater than expected and it avoids high-cost environmental damage when emission reductions are cheaper than expected. However, if incremental environmental damage rises steeply with each extra unit of emissions (an upward-sloped marginal damage curve), the quantity instrument of an emission limit is preferable.

The presence of climate tipping points is often cited as a rationale for quantity rather than price controls. Indeed, on reaching a tipping point, the environmental damage curve would begin to rise steeply. As discussed in Chapter 1 of this book, Earth's history has demonstrated an extraordinary range of global average temperatures and climate outcomes well before any influence from human activities. A rapid shift to a dramatically different climate than the fairly stable one we have enjoyed over the last 10,000 years would not be harmful to the planet but could impose catastrophic costs on human society. A careful look at the current level of scientific

---

[1]   References are given at the end of the book. Most are peer-reviewed journal articles, but several textbooks and popular books are also mentioned. For convenience, the text mentions only the first name of coauthored papers.

understanding, however, indicates that we do not have a good idea about when a global tipping point may occur.

Nevertheless, the structure of risks around potential climate outcomes is unbalanced in a way that gives an advantage to a quantity instrument over a price instrument. Consider the potential consequences of a climate policy that is wrong in either direction. On one hand, an overly strict policy would impose higher-than-necessary costs on the economy. On observing those high costs, the policy could be reversed before too long, if necessary through legislative action. The economy would likely recover several months after the policy setting was loosened. On the other hand, consider a climate policy that fails to do enough. The evidence that policy action is insufficient may remain ambiguous for some years, because the climate system responds to a new stimulus with considerable delays. Nevertheless, once climate change begins, it develops some momentum on its own. Feedback mechanisms amplify the initial movement. By the time it is certain that policy is too weak, it will be too late to make an effective adjustment; further damage from climate change will be inevitable. The costs to society could then be many times more than the costs of earlier effective action. Thus, the consequences of an insufficient climate policy are more severe than those of a policy error on the other side. A quantity instrument provides greater assurance of controlling the risk of unexpectedly large climate change. A price instrument, by contrast, adds uncertainty about the responses of individuals and businesses to the price signal.

On practical political grounds also, a pure price policy, such as a carbon tax, may be unrealistic. In addition, international agreements on climate policies have focused on a quantity instrument in the form of emission reduction commitments. The international dimension is particularly important in the case of GHGs that mix fairly quickly throughout the world's atmosphere and remain aloft for decades and centuries. Other pollutants that have more localized effects can be addressed adequately with domestic policies, but GHGs cannot be controlled unless all countries with substantial emissions participate in the effort.

Our alternatives, however, are not limited to a stark choice between a carbon tax and an inflexible limit on GHG emissions. A variety of measures can be used to ensure that cumulative emissions of GHG remain contained while the costs of controlling emissions are also kept within some bounds. A cap-and-trade program is a market-based policy approach with differing design options that adjust the emphasis between the predictability of prices and the predictability of quantities. Similar to a carbon tax, cap-and-trade uses a price signal to motivate a broad range of possible emission reduction activities, thereby reducing the cost of achieving environmental goals compared with the more narrowly targeted "command-and-control" approaches.

With cap-and-trade, the overall emissions of economic sectors included in the program are subject to a limit, or cap. The government distributes emission allowances (for free or through auctions) up to the cap level. The allowances (or permits) can be traded among firms, which limits costs relative to a mandate requiring each firm to reduce emissions: Firms that find it expensive to reduce emissions can instead buy an allowance from firms having cheaper emission abatement opportunities. Offset credits (emission reductions achieved in projects outside the cap-and-trade system) can also be used to lower compliance costs within the system.

Unlike a carbon tax, a cap-and-trade program creates new markets for allowances and offsets. A large, new carbon market entails risks of manipulation and excess speculation. Dramatic fluctuations in carbon prices, similar to the booms and busts in energy markets in recent years, would undermine the incentive for investments in emission reduction. Large price swings would cause errors in investment choices, with some firms implementing emission abatement projects that are too expensive whereas others fail to proceed with lower-cost projects that should go forward. Moreover, wide fluctuations in prices could provide cover for manipulative activities or at least raise suspicions that might undermine political support for the program.

A carbon market, created by regulation, need not have prices as volatile as those in an ordinary commodity market. With careful design, opportunities for manipulation and excess speculation can be avoided while incentives for emission reductions are still maintained. One option to achieve that result is a managed price approach that borrows from the procedures that the Federal Reserve and other central banks use to manage interest rates. Central banks announce a target interest rate that guides private trading in a huge overnight loan market. In addition, they use auctions to adjust the supply of money in that market, which helps achieve the target interest rate. Through these procedures, central banks are quite successful at managing interest rates. Trading rarely occurs very far from the target rate, despite the limited government interventions through auctions, the diverse group of market participants, and the enormous volume of private trading (several hundred billion dollars a day in the United States). Because interest rates are kept close to the announced target, there is virtually no opportunity for manipulation of the market and no opening for the speculative bubbles that characterize other financial and commodity markets.

A similar approach could be used to manage prices in a large new carbon market. The government could choose an emission goal several years ahead (e.g., 2020). It could then publish a forecast of gradually rising allowance prices designed to achieve a smooth path of reductions in emissions toward the achievement of the intermediate-term emissions goal. In a given year, the government could announce a hard price target and adjust the supply of allowances in auctions as needed during the year to help achieve that target. At the end of the year, the government could make adjustments in its price forecast as needed to ensure achievement of the intermediate-term emissions goal. Prices would adjust, relative to expectations, from one year to the next, but not because of temporary factors affecting emissions only in a given year, such as fluctuations in the weather. The forecast path for prices would be adjusted only if persistent factors threatened achievement of the intermediate-term emission goal.

Several other design options could be considered for a cap-and-trade program, or for dynamically adjusting carbon taxes, that would also provide some balance between the predictability of prices and the predictability of emissions. Even though cap-and-trade systems have been operational in the United States and Europe for some time now, the experience with different design options in a large, actively traded market is actually rather limited. We do not as yet know what is the best-practice approach for such systems. In those circumstances, it is advisable for legislation to allow mid course corrections to be made in program design. If so, a managed price approach may be an apt choice for the early years of the program because it would allow a new market to develop without the risks of manipulation and excess speculation.

Careful design of a domestic carbon market will not be sufficient to ensure that environmental goals are met; instead, a global effort is needed. Domestic climate policies therefore should have one eye on the international arena. Incentives need to be created for other countries to make substantial efforts, particularly for developing countries struggling to catch up to the living standards of richer nations. Today's advanced economies chose the cheapest path of development, without awareness of the effects on the climate of high emissions of GHG. The world community needs to find a strategy for today's developing countries to raise their living standards as well, but without repeating the errors of high-emission growth. Advanced economies have a responsibility, recognized in a framework treaty ratified by most countries, to assist developing countries in achieving low-carbon growth and adapting to climate change.

International mechanisms were established under the Kyoto Protocol to begin accomplishing these goals. They included enforceable emission reduction commitments by advanced economies and offset projects to be purchased from developing countries. A new international agreement is under negotiation to take effect after the Kyoto Protocol expires in 2012. The Copenhagen Accord of December 2009 brought agreement on a global temperature goal, strengthened reporting from developing countries, and increased financial aid from advanced economies. However, considerable further work is needed to complete the details of the international climate framework for the post-2012 period. Under the Kyoto Protocol and the Copenhagen Accord, individual countries can choose national climate programs from a wide variety of options. Many countries are now considering the implementation of domestic cap-and-trade systems. Given the limited experience to date with such systems, there are advantages of allowing experimentation with alternative designs. Eventually, however, greater harmonization of cap-and-trade programs would allow the systems to be linked, which could result in a unified world price for carbon. A common price signal would provide an incentive for all lower-cost emission abatement projects around the world to be implemented, while higher cost projects are avoided. The global emission reduction goal could then be achieved at the lowest possible cost. International coordination of climate policies is essential to work toward achieving that outcome. Coordination is also likely needed to help spur stronger actions and to address concerns regarding the effects of differing climate policies on the competitiveness of industries in different countries.

Controlling emissions of GHG is not the only possible way to prevent global warming. A variety of geo-engineering options have also been suggested for further investigation, including measures to shield the planet from some solar radiation and methods for enhancing the natural sequestration of GHG. As of now, none of these proposals can be counted on as a panacea. Considerable further research is required to assess the prospects of such schemes and the risks that they could inadvertently cause other types of environmental damage.

Finally, although a variety of adverse scenarios need to be contemplated while studying climate policy, we need not be motivated only by fear. We can allow ourselves to be fascinated by the story of our planet's wild climate history. We can deepen awareness of how human activities affect the climate. With objectivity, we can weigh the economic realities of climate policy options. And we can share a vision of the extraordinary and positive role humans can play in the planet's future. Never before in the nearly 4 billion years of life on Earth has a species arisen with the ability to take conscious control of the climate. Whether we like it or not, we are now the managers of the planet's future.

PART ONE

EARTH'S CLIMATE HISTORY AND OUTLOOK

A study of climate history is an essential foundation for climate policy. Earth's history gives us an appreciation of the wide swings in the types of climate that are possible. It informs us of the forces that have generated those fluctuations and have stabilized the planet's temperature at very different levels for long periods of time. It provides estimates of the temperatures associated with much greater or much less planetary ice cover than we have today. And it offers case studies of episodes of climate change that bear an eerie resemblance to scenarios that could characterize our future.

A sense of the limits of our scientific knowledge is also essential. Uncertainties about the science place extra burdens on the design of policy. We cannot merely implement what "science" tells us to do, because the science itself is evolving and controversial. To make wise policy, we need to assess what is known with confidence and what remains highly speculative. Our uncertainty will condition the degree of flexibility we should build into the framework for policy.

ONE

Salient Events of Climate History

THE FIRST 4 BILLION YEARS

In its long history, Earth has seen extremes of fire and ice that would have made human life impossible. The planet was born in a cauldron of volcanic eruptions and million-megaton impacts from outer space. Any hydrogen or helium in the early atmosphere soon escaped into space. In time, only heavier molecules remained, including nitrogen and the greenhouses gases: water vapor, carbon dioxide, methane, and ammonia. No free oxygen was present.

A gas is called a greenhouse gas (GHG) because it lets sunlight through but absorbs outgoing heat radiation from the surface of the Earth. The absorbed heat energy is reradiated in all directions. Because some of it returns to the surface, the GHG boosts the planet's temperature. If no GHG were present in the atmosphere, the world's current average temperature would be about 0 °F rather than the actual level of 58 °F (14.5 °C).

About half a billion years after its formation as a planet, Earth had cooled enough for rain to fall and the oceans to form. Life emerged soon – in geological terms – thereafter. The Sun was weaker back then, emitting only about 70% of the radiation of today. The Earth would have frozen solid were it not for the high concentrations of GHG in the atmosphere. The Sun was less radiant than today largely because it had less helium. As with any star, nuclear fusion in the core of the Sun converts hydrogen into helium. Because helium is heavier than hydrogen, the density of the Sun gradually increases, boosting the gravitational pull at its core and consequently making it contract and intensifying its radiant output.

Although the planet was warmed by its GHG, no stratospheric ozone layer had formed to provide protection from the Sun's ultraviolet rays. Therefore, although bacteria thrived on the plentiful organic molecules in the ocean, no life existed as yet on the surface. By around 3.5 billion years ago, the organic nutrient supply began to run short. In an environment of increasing evolutionary stress, cyanobacteria emerged, initiating photosynthesis. These bacteria could combine water, carbon dioxide, and sunlight within their cell walls to produce their own source of food – carbohydrates.

Oxygen – a byproduct of photosynthesis – began to be released. At first, oxygen was readily absorbed by iron and other minerals in the ocean. It could also combine with methane in the atmosphere in the presence of ultraviolet light. The natural sequestration of oxygen through such means lasted almost 300 million years. Around 2.5 billion years ago, however, molecules of gaseous oxygen began to accumulate in the ocean and escape into the air. For the older, anaerobic bacteria, free oxygen was toxic. The climate change caused by the development of photosynthesis thus brought on Earth's first major extinction event.

Some bacteria nevertheless thrived in the new environment and developed efficient means of using oxygen to burn energy. They were the first mitochondria, appearing around 2 billion years ago. Mitochondria were soon captured within the cell walls of other creatures. They developed a symbiotic relationship with their hosts, vastly speeding up metabolism in return for a steady supply of nutrients and oxygen. Around the same time, the first cells with a nucleus, the eukaryotes, were born.

Meanwhile, with oxygen (O_2) more plentiful in the atmosphere, an ozone (O_3) layer began to form in the stratosphere. Protected from ultraviolet rays, bacteria soon expanded into new habitats, into sunlight. Eventually, they spread over the land.

Other types of climate change were occurring in Earth's early history because of the birth and death of continents. The evolution of continents reflects forces deep inside the planet. Earth's core is made of iron and nickel; the innermost 1,200 km of it is solid, whereas the next 2,300 km is liquid. The liquid outer core creates a magnetic field as it rotates and mixes. The mantle of the planet lies on top of the core, extending out across almost 2,900 km. The mantle is a solid mixture of silicon, iron, and magnesium under so much pressure that it flows like warm plastic. Only in a few isolated pockets does the mantle become hot enough to liquefy into magma. Finally, nearly 6,400 km from the center of the planet is a thin crust of continents and ocean floor, less than 100 km across (Marshak, 2005).

The Earth's interior heat is in part what is left over from the time of planetary formation and in part a result of the continuing decay of radioactive elements. Modeling studies suggest that the temperature of the inner core may be on the order of 5,500°C, whereas the liquid outer core could average some 4,400°C. Seismic data indicate a temperature at the core/ mantle boundary of 3,700°C (van der Hilst, 2007). On a path up through the mantle, the temperature gradually declines, dropping to approximately 500°C at the point where the crust begins.

The crust is not a single connected skin over the planet, but a series of separate "tectonic" plates. Each plate includes some solid matter from the upper mantle, but they all "float" on softer, lower layers of the mantle. At present, the Pacific Ocean and each of the continents have their own plate (except Europe and Asia, which are combined into one). The continental plates, made largely of granite, are more buoyant than the ocean plates, which are heavier basalts. The plates move in response to several forces: Material from the mantle wells up at mid-ocean ridges, creating new plate material and spreading the seafloor apart. This basaltic lava gets denser as it cools and ages. When meeting with a continental plate, an ocean plate – being heavier – slides underneath (or "subducts"). If the subducting edge of the ocean plate has become heavier than the mantle below, it sinks and helps drag down the rest of the plate. The gravitational force of the moon also tends to tug plates toward the west as the Earth rotates around to the east.

Although continents have survived for more than 4 billion years, all ocean plates eventually return to the mantle. No ocean floor today is more than 170 million years old. If two continental plates collide, however, neither is heavy enough to drop back into the mantle. Instead, the force of the collision raises up mountains. If other continents also join the encounter, a supercontinent can form, combining most of the land mass of the Earth. After many millennia, supercontinents tend to break up as old plates separate and new plates rift apart.

In its early days, when the Earth was very hot, rising plumes of magma kept disrupting the stability of any land masses that tended to form. Geological deposits in the Yilgarn area of Western Australia suggest that lighter minerals emerging from the interior of the Earth may nevertheless have coalesced into a land mass as early as 4.4 billion years ago (or giga years ago, Gya). Stronger evidence from rock formations in Australia, South Africa, and Canada indicates the presence of a major continent around 3.5 Gya (Cheney, 1996). A more conservative view, based on stricter criteria for stability over time, puts the first continent closer to 3 Gya (Rogers, 1996). In any case, the earliest continents evidently split apart fairly quickly by geological standards, because magma plumes continued to open tectonic rifts. However, additional lighter materials kept welling up from the mantle, adding to the size of Earth's early land masses. By around 2.7 Gya, a supercontinent had clearly appeared. Called Kenorland, it held what are now North America, Northern Europe, Africa, and Australia.

The formation and breakup of supercontinents can have an enormous effect on the climate. Almost all the atmosphere's water vapor comes from the ocean. Rainfall also occurs mainly over the ocean and in downwind land areas. By the time the winds have reached the interior of a huge supercontinent, they have lost most of their moisture. The interior of Kenorland therefore was quite dry.

As the supercontinent began to break apart around 2.5 Gya, more rain began to fall on land. When rainwater courses over rock surfaces, a chemical reaction occurs that removes carbon dioxide from the air (as described in more detail later). Carbon dioxide (CO_2) is a key GHG. In addition to the chemical weathering of rocks, cyanobacteria were removing CO_2 from the air at that time and replacing it with oxygen, as noted earlier in the chapter. Atmospheric oxygen helps break down methane, which is an even more powerful GHG than CO_2.

With reduced levels of GHG, the surface of the planet cooled and ice sheets began to spread widely over the land. Telltale signs of the movement of glaciers have been found in Canada and South Africa dating between 2.4 Gya and 2.1 Gya. Glacial deposits are recognizable because of the great diversity of materials they mix together – from huge boulders to fine grains of sand – without any evidence of the sifting and sorting that would occur if the particles had been transported by water or wind. Scientists can date glacial deposits from the radioactive potassium that becomes embedded in igneous rocks, typically basalts, at the time they solidify. Because half of the radioactive potassium decays into argon after 1.3 billion years, current observations of the proportions of the two minerals helps reveal the time elapsed since the rock formed.

The latitude at which basalts were created can also be estimated. These rocks originate from volcanic lava, and when they crystallize, they incorporate a tiny amount of magnetism from the earth's magnetic field. The strength and direction of the magnetism depends on its distance from a magnetic pole when the basalt solidified. Adjustments must be made for changes in Earth's magnetic field over the eons, however, and the latitudes of early glaciation are a subject of controversy (see Schmidt, 2003; Kopp, 2005). If glaciers were present at low latitudes (close to the equator), most of the planet may have been covered with snow and ice, an event that has been called a Snowball Earth.

Two other supercontinents appeared and then broke apart in these ancient times. One, called Columbia, emerged about 2 Gya, and the second,

Rodinia, formed around 1 Gya (Torsvik, 2003). Evidence suggests the possibility of Snowball Earth events between 850 million and 630 million years ago (Mya), toward the end of life of Rodinia. Increases in rainfall on land and removal of CO_2 through the associated chemical weathering may have catalyzed such events. After extensive glaciation had begun, a natural feedback mechanism would have amplified the global cooling. Snow and ice reflect 70% to 90% of incoming sunlight back into space, reducing the Earth's absorption of heat energy. By contrast, the ocean reflects only about 10% and land areas, on average, about 20%. As ice sheets expand, therefore, the increased reflectivity (or albedo) of the Earth cools the planet further. The albedo effects of ice sheets are a major amplifying feedback mechanism for climate change.

Snowball Earth events may have been facilitated by a clustering of the continents around the equator at that time. If oceans occupied the tropics, it would have been more difficult for ice to complete its conquest of the planet. The circulation of water helps moderate the thickness of sea ice and thereby limit its spread, especially across tropical oceans. However, ice sheets forming over land can accumulate to a height large enough to flow under their own weight. Around 850 Mya, land masses apparently occupied most of the tropics. As sea ice began expanding from polar areas, it would have helped cool the planet with its increased reflectivity. Once ice sheets began developing over land, they could more easily accumulate to a height large enough to continue spreading toward the equator.

Aside from estimates of the latitude of glacial deposits, evidence for Snowball Earth events is also available from ocean floor deposits that have since been uplifted onto continents (and therefore preserved). For instance, some types of iron-rich rocks from around 800 Mya could have formed only if most of the ocean's dissolved oxygen had been removed, as might have occurred if the seas had been covered with ice (Kirschvink, 1992). However, other indicators suggest that a portion of the tropics may have remained unfrozen while ice sheets successively expanded and retreated during that period (Condon, 2002; Rieu, 2007). The planet recovered from such Snowball or "Slushball" events because volcanoes continued emitting GHGs. With little or no exposed land available to help remove the CO_2 through chemical weathering, the concentration of GHG eventually rose high enough to melt the ice.

Because sunlight cannot penetrate more than about 100 meters into ice, photosynthesis would have shut down over most of the planet during Snowball Earth events. Nevertheless, evolution continued to advance during these eras. Around 1 Gya, algae emerged as the first multicellular life.

(Cyanobacteria were formerly called blue–green algae, but more recent classification systems restrict the term algae to organisms with cells having a nucleus – eukaryotes.) Despite the environmental stresses of the time, algae and fungi managed to thrive in a variety of biomes and therefore spread throughout the world.

The period of intense glaciation came to an end around 600 Mya, as another supercontinent called Pannotia came into being. A panoply of new soft-bodied life forms then emerged. Similar to jellyfish, they have been called Ediacara, after a place in Australia where their fossils were found. Both Pannotia and the Ediacara came to an end around 540 Mya, the time of the Cambrian explosion of animal life forms. The first creatures with shells and skeletons then appeared, along with many predators, including fish.

In summary, the Earth's first 4 billion years saw two major types of climate. One is called a Greenhouse climate, a time when Earth is warm enough that no permanent ice is present. The other is called an Ice House, a time when ice covers at least one of the planet's poles all year round. The Ice House climates of those times were particularly severe, perhaps including Snowball events. However, they were rare. For most of its first 4 billion years, Earth had an ice-free Greenhouse climate. Over the latest 500 million years, as discussed next, Ice House periods were again evidently infrequent.

GREENHOUSE AND ICE HOUSE CLIMATES

After the catastrophic Snowball or Slushball events, a Greenhouse climate prevailed for almost 200 million years. During this time, one large continent called Gondwana combined most of the lands of what is now the Southern Hemisphere (Scotese, 2002). Around 435 Mya, this continent began to traverse the South Pole and, in the process, developed a cover of ice. The mere presence of a sizable land mass over the pole likely helped an ice sheet develop. The removal of CO_2 from the atmosphere may have also played a role, but in a manner different from the one hypothesized for the earlier supercontinents. In those cases, the *breakup* of a supercontinent may have allowed increased rainfall on land and enhanced chemical weathering. How could the *formation* of a large continent also remove CO_2 from the air?

In chemical weathering, rain and soil moisture combine with atmospheric CO_2 to produce a mild acid, called carbonic acid, which dissolves calcium carbonate and other minerals in silicate rocks. The dissolved materials, which now incorporate the CO_2 from the atmosphere, are eventually washed into the ocean. If the rate of chemical weathering removes CO_2 at about the same pace that volcanoes are emitting it, the atmospheric concentration remains roughly stable. This inorganic carbon cycle can get out of balance when the rates of volcanic releases and chemical weathering diverge.

As noted earlier, the drawdown of atmospheric CO_2 through the weathering of silicate rocks can accelerate with increases in rainfall. It can also speed up when fresh new surfaces of rock become exposed to the air; the carbonic acid in rain and soil waters is then more likely to encounter the calcium and magnesium with which it reacts to sequester the CO_2. New rock surfaces are exposed when mountains are created (orogeny). Evidently, around 435 Mya, the North Atlantic plate began moving under the North American continent, and the frictional forces apparently were sufficient to begin the uplift of the Appalachian Mountains. The fresh silicate rocks exposed by the process likely helped draw down enough CO_2 from the air to put the planet into its brief Ice House at that time (Saltzman, 2005).

The chemical weathering process is also affected by expanding or shrinking ice sheets. When ice expands over land, it shuts down the hydrolysis of rocks. If the carbon cycle was in balance before the ice sheet expanded, the reduction in the global average rate of chemical weathering would allow a buildup of atmospheric CO_2. This would tend to slow the cooling of the planet. Although ice sheet growth slows the removal of CO_2 through chemical weathering, it is a gradual and modest process. The amplifying feedback of increased reflectivity from ice sheets tends to overwhelm it.

Around 435 Mya, any slowing in the rate of chemical weathering because of the expansion of ice sheets was indeed overwhelmed by forces that kept cooling the planet. In particular, the Appalachians were apparently rising near the equator. They could therefore remain largely ice-free and continue removing CO_2 even as ice sheets began expanding from the poles. Moreover, by that time, the ocean had become more effective at sequestering the carbon washed into the sea from the chemical weathering of rocks. In the past, carbon had precipitated to the ocean floor only because of the chemistry of saturated solutions. However, after the evolution of Cambrian-era life forms, carbon could be removed at a faster rate because of biology. Marine creatures began to build shells using the calcium carbonates and other mineral residues from chemical weathering that were brought into the ocean by rivers. When those creatures died, their shells sank and often became sediments that buried their stored carbon in successive layers on the ocean floor.[1]

---

[1] The solubility of carbonate increases when water is colder and under more pressure; at deep enough ocean levels, carbonate is undersaturated, and shells falling from the surface

THE PANGAEA ICE HOUSE

Between about 425 Mya and 325 Mya, the Earth experienced another prolonged Greenhouse period. During that time, Gondwana kept moving through the South Pole toward a rendezvous with scattered northern lands on the other side of the globe. In the "Carboniferous Period" of 360 Mya to 300 Mya, massive amounts of plant material were buried in pervasive swamplands, eventually turning into deposits of coal. Gondwana began growing through the absorption of islands around 325 Mya and eventually formed the global supercontinent that we call Pangaea. The collisions of land masses caused the orogeny of the later Appalachians and the Ural Mountains. Once again, an accelerated pace of chemical weathering may have reduced atmospheric CO_2 concentrations enough to bring on an Ice House period. The cold period lasted around 75 million years until the construction of Pangaea was completed around 250 Mya.

The configuration of Pangaea may have contributed to the persistence of the Ice House. The supercontinent stretched across a North/South direction from one pole to the other. The circulation of the ocean may have therefore been restricted, limiting the usual transfer of heat from the tropics toward the poles. Polar ice could therefore more completely control its own local climate.

After 250 Mya, however, the planet returned to its more typical Greenhouse climate, and the age of dinosaurs began. During the Cretaceous Period between 145 Mya and 65 Mya, the burial of plant matter in pervasive peat swamps again led to the formation of major deposits of coal.[2] Even after the dinosaurs disappeared following the asteroid catastrophe of 65 Mya, the planet remained too warm for permanent ice to form at either pole. But not long thereafter, an unusual episode caused temperatures to reach an extreme level. The event has important implications regarding the potential effects of our emissions of GHG.

---

begin to dissolve. At a deeper level still (the "carbonate compensation depth"), the rate of dissolution begins to exceed the rate at which shells fall; if the ocean floor is below that depth, no shell sediments will survive.

[2]   Formation of coal, petroleum, and natural gas all depend on organic matter being buried before it decays in the presence of oxygen. Coal is created when peat is compressed and heated at depths of 4–10 km underground. Petroleum and natural gas are formed when source rocks, typically derived from algae and plankton sediments, are heated at depths of 3.5–6 km (the "oil window") and 6–9 km ("the gas window"). Petroleum and natural gas deposits were not laid down in limited geological periods, as in the case of coal, but they require trapping with seal rocks to be preserved (Marshak, 2005).

AN EPISODE OF PEAK TEMPERATURE

Paleontologists puzzled for a long time over unusual fossils discovered from a period around 55 Mya. Palm trees and an early version of the alligator were evidently thriving in the Canadian Arctic, less than 10° latitude from the North Pole. How could the planet have been so warm?

Evidence was eventually found in ocean sediments that suggested a surge in atmospheric CO_2 at that time. This interpretation depended on an analysis of the isotopes of carbon. Nearly all carbon atoms have six protons and six neutrons; the sum of these particles found in the nucleus of an atom is shown in a superscript, as in ^{12}C. About one carbon atom in a hundred has seven neutrons, making it ^{13}C, another stable isotope. (The radioactive ^{14}C exists in only trace amounts.)

Around 55 Mya, marine creatures began using much less ^{13}C than usual. What caused the sudden decline in the concentration of ^{13}C? It wasn't a lack of carbon, but rather a sudden burst of ^{12}C. Two sources of carbon high in ^{12}C and low in ^{13}C are present on the ocean floor: underwater volcanoes and blocks of ice and methane. (The latter are often called either "hydrates" because of the presence of water ice or "clathrates" because of a lattice-like structure.) Volcanism and methane hydrates both apparently played a role around 55 Mya. Greenland evidently began separating from the European continent, and as it did, a huge rift opened up on the ocean floor between them. The result was a massive outpouring of lava, a "flood basalt," which released a great volume of methane and CO_2 (Storey, 2007). The heating of the ocean floor also apparently vaporized a vast store of methane hydrates. Scientists have called this event the "great burp." The carbon in methane (CH_4) was fairly quickly converted into CO_2.[3] The CO_2 concentration in the atmosphere, already much higher than today, doubled and then doubled again.

The planet was already in a Greenhouse climate, but it warmed considerably further. Sea surface temperatures evidently rose about 5°C in the tropics and 9°C at high latitudes (Zachos, 2005). Compared with the pace of warming and cooling that had previously occurred with changes in the rate of chemical weathering, this climate change event was rapid: The temperature peak was reached in less than ten millennia.

The after-effects, however, were prolonged. Because of the high concentration of CO_2, the deep ocean became so acidic and anoxic that numerous

---

[3] Reaction of methane (CH_4) with hydroxyl ions ($OH-$) begins a series of reactions that converts the carbon in methane into CO_2.

bottom-dwelling species perished. Shells on the ocean floor dissolved into dark clays. Eventually, shell dissolution slowed enough to be surpassed by new shell production, and carbon once again began to be sequestered on the ocean floor. Extinctions were also prevalent on land at this time. In the aftermath, new species emerged to fill the ecological niches, including modern orders of mammals. The chemical weathering of rocks, intensified by the high concentration of CO_2 in the air, eventually helped return the planet to equilibrium, but it took some 170,000 years (Pagani, 2006). Because of the turnover of species at this time, it is considered a dividing line between the Paleocene and Eocene epochs.

The amount of carbon released into the atmosphere in this "Paleocene-Eocene Thermal Maximum" was evidently about 2,000 billion tons, less than half of the estimated stores of carbon we currently have available in fossil fuels (Zachos, 2008). The pace at which we are emitting carbon into the atmosphere today is considerably faster than the natural releases of 55 Mya. Our recent and prospective GHG emissions are discussed in a later chapter.

OUR ICE HOUSE ARRIVES

Subsequent to the temperature spike of 55 Mya, the planet began a long-term cooling trend. There are competing theories regarding the cause of the climate change, but many scientists believe that plate tectonics were again at work. The Indian subcontinent broke off from southern Africa and began migrating toward the northeast. Eventually, it began pushing into Asia, thereby raising up the Tibetan plateau and the Himalayan Mountains. Even today, India continues moving further into the rest of Asia by a few centimeters each year.

The Himalayan orogeny gradually exposed massive amounts of new rock surfaces to hydrolysis by monsoon rains. As the rate of chemical weathering speeded up, atmospheric CO_2 levels began to fall. By approximately 35 Mya, seasonal ice on Antarctica began to last all year long. Earth's long Greenhouse period, which began around 250 Mya, finally came to an end. The cold gradually deepened until, somewhat after 7 Mya, Greenland also developed a permanent ice cover.

In trying to estimate the amount of CO_2 removed from the air since 55 Mya, scientists have been forced to work through several steps of logic. First, the concentration of CO_2 in the air is closely correlated with its concentration in the upper ocean.[4] Second, the CO_2 in ocean water can be estimated

---

[4] Henry's law states that the concentration of a dissolved gas in solution is proportional to the partial pressure of that gas above the solution if temperature is held constant.

from the pH of the water, because water becomes more acidic when CO_2 is added.[5] Finally, a signal of the ocean's pH can be found in the isotopes of boron present in trace amounts in marine shells. Stable boron isotopes come with either five or six neutrons, and the lighter, five-neutron variety is more prevalent in shells when water has a low pH.[6]

Using such methods, the atmospheric concentration of CO_2 was estimated to be an astoundingly high level of about 3,200 parts per million (ppm) between 60 Mya and 52 Mya (Pearson, 2000). In the subsequent ten million years, after India began pushing into Asia, CO_2 dropped to an average of around 1,000 ppm. By around 34 Mya, the CO_2 level had dropped to about 760 ppm, and Antarctica began forming its ice sheet (Pearson, 2009). By around 20 Mya, the CO_2 concentration had fallen to about 400 ppm. Average temperatures continued to drop, and an ice sheet formed on Greenland. Since about 10 Mya, the CO_2 concentration has averaged only approximately 250 ppm, with no evidence until recently of concentrations above 350 ppm (Tripati, 2009). The CO_2 concentration in 2009 had risen to about 387 ppm.

Apart from the creation of the Himalayas and the Tibetan plateau, other reasons have been proposed for the development of our Ice House. Theoretically, CO_2 levels could have declined because of lower output from volcanoes and mid-ocean ridge vents. However, a major, persistent change in volcanism seems implausible, and the rate of seafloor spreading evidently remained fairly stable during the time when our Ice House got underway (Ruddiman, 2001).

A case can also be made that changes in the configuration of continents caused or contributed to the development of ice sheets. For instance, Australia separated from Antarctica around 35 Mya, and South America broke away around 20 Mya. A circular Southern Ocean was thereby created that isolated Antarctica, put it into a deep freeze, and probably promoted its ice cover. In addition, an ocean passage used to exist between Panama and South America. When it closed around 4 Mya, warm tropical water turned northward, creating the Gulf Stream. The resulting increases in moisture in the atmosphere may have boosted snowfall and helped build ice sheets on Greenland and Northern Europe. The enormous drop in atmospheric CO_2 as the planet entered our Ice House would not be explained by these changes

---

[5] pH stands for potential of Hydrogen and equals the log (to the base ten) of the reciprocal of the moles of dissolved hydrogen ions (H+) per liter of solution. A decline in pH by one means ten times more hydrogen ions are present in solution, implying greater acidity. Pure water has a pH of 7, which is neutral, as the free hydrogen ions are then balanced by hydroxyl ions (OH–).

[6] About 80% of naturally occurring boron is ^{11}B and 20% is ^{10}B.

in ocean circulation. However, at least part of the drop in atmospheric CO_2 has occurred as a feedback effect from global cooling: The ocean absorbs CO_2 from the air as it cools because CO_2, like other gases, is more soluble in water of lower temperatures.

Other sources of data have been used to estimate the decline in temperature as the world entered its current Ice House. Scattered fossils on land can give qualitative indicators of broad temperature changes. More precise estimates can be obtained when a continuous record of fossils is available at the same site. Such records exist in sediments deposited on the ocean floor and at lake bottoms, where they receive protection from storms, erosion, and other disruptions. Ocean sediments provide the longest continuous climate archives, but even these cover only a limited time span because all ocean plates eventually sink into the mantle, as mentioned above.

Ocean sediments do provide indicators for the Greenhouse climate that existed before 35 Mya. The buried shells of marine creatures can be analyzed to uncover signals of the water temperature at the time the shells were formed. The relative shares of two stable isotopes of oxygen are a key measure. Oxygen atoms have eight protons and, almost always, eight neutrons. However, one in 400 oxygen atoms has ten neutrons instead of eight, making it an ^{18}O isotope instead of the usual ^{16}O. Marine creatures preferentially take in the lighter isotope, but they more readily accept ^{18}O as water gets colder. Experiments show a precise relationship between water temperature and the ratio of oxygen isotopes built into marine shells: Other things being equal, the share of the heavy isotope goes up by one-tenth of a percentage point with a temperature drop of 4.2 °C.

Based on evidence from such marine shells, the deep ocean is colder now than at any other time over the 70 million years for which such evidence has been gathered. The marine shells indicate a temperature peak around 55 Mya, corresponding to the global thermal maximum. At that time, the ratio of light to heavy oxygen was 0.4 percentage point higher than today. Aside from temperature, the oxygen isotope ratio is also affected by the shares of the isotopes present in the water. Those shares have not always been today's average of one ^{18}O for every 400 ^{16}O. The main factor that changes the isotope proportions is the evaporation of ocean water, its transport toward the poles, and its storage on ice sheets. Water molecules with the lighter oxygen isotope more easily make that journey. After deducting the estimated effect of today's ice sheets, the isotope evidence indicates that the deep ocean of 55 Mya was about 16 °C compared with only around 1.5 °C today. By around 40 Mya, just before an ice sheet began developing on Antarctica, the deep ocean temperature had dropped to an estimated 9.4°C (Ruddiman, 2001).

It would likely take many millennia to warm the deep ocean by 8°C and bring its temperature back to the level prevailing before Antarctica had any ice. Ocean sediments cannot reveal rapidly changing conditions because creatures burrow into the seafloor and mix remains that have been deposited over a thousand years or more. More fundamentally, alterations in surface temperatures take many centuries to affect the deep ocean. Heat is transferred through the ocean mainly by the movement and mixing of water, because thermal diffusion takes much longer. The upper one hundred meters of ocean waters are well-mixed by winds and can respond within a few years to changes in atmospheric conditions. However, the deep ocean responds mainly through the descent of surface waters toward the bottom of the ocean, which occurs at places where the surface water becomes denser than the water below it. Density increases when water becomes colder and saltier. Thus, surface water can sink after it has been chilled by moving closer to the poles, and especially after becoming saltier either through evaporation or freezing at the surface (as either phase change leaves salts behind in the liquid water). About a thousand years is needed for enough surface waters to sink to achieve one complete replacement of the water in the deep ocean at present (Hartmann, 1994). To raise the temperature of the deep ocean by as much as 8°C, it would probably take considerably longer, in part because it is harder for warm water to sink.

To achieve that result, however, the average global temperature would not have to rise as much as 8°C. Most of the ocean's deep water is created close to the poles, where frigid air can cool it. The temperature of deep water therefore depends on surface air conditions at high latitudes. Because of large changes in local albedo effects as polar ice expands and shrinks, those regions warm and cool by more than the Earth's average temperature. For an 8°C warming at high latitudes, therefore, the global average temperature might need to rise only around 5–6°C (Hartmann, 1994).

To summarize, for both the Earth's first 4 billion years and the most recent half a billion years, where better data is available, the evidence suggests that the planet has usually had a Greenhouse climate with no permanent ice cover at either pole. Since 500 Mya, permanent ice sheets were present at the South Pole for only three periods, accounting for a total of about 130 million years, or about one-fourth of the time. The North Pole glaciated less frequently over that period because it usually lacked a continental land mass and was therefore warmed by circulating ocean waters. Our current

Ice House period is not the most common global climate regime. It has been associated with a substantial reduction in the CO_2 concentration in the atmosphere since the earlier era before 35 Mya.

ICE HOUSE TEMPERATURES

As noted earlier in the chapter, the oxygen isotopes in shells found in ocean sediments indicate that the planet's average temperature was about 5–6°C warmer before Antarctica got its permanent ice cover around 35 Mya. As the planet cooled, the alligators and the palm trees became confined to the tropics and new, cold-adapted spruce and larch trees emerged in the Arctic Circle. Eventually, in the far north, those trees also gave way to the scrub grass of steppe lands, to tundra and permafrost, and then to ice.

Although ice has covered wide areas of northern continents at various times in the last several million years, the first date at which ice sheets began moving into North America and northern Europe and Asia is not discernable from glacial deposits. Because the ice has melted and reformed numerous times, the evidence of previous glacial episodes has been erased. However, when icebergs "calve" off the edge of an ice sheet into the ocean, they carry their embedded debris with them out to sea. When the icebergs melt, they drop onto the ocean floor an unsorted jumble of rocks and fine particles of all types, which is their characteristic footprint. Ice-rafted debris of this nature began to appear sporadically in northern oceans after 7 Mya, suggesting the development of an ice sheet on Greenland. Continental size ice sheets covering northern areas in both the Western and Eastern Hemispheres evidently began to form around 2.75 Mya (Ruddiman, 2001).

How much had the planet cooled by the time Greenland got its ice? The oxygen isotope ratios in marine shells cannot give a pure reading because they were affected by the greater storage of ^{16}O in the ice sheet on Antarctica. Fortunately, however, the shells contain another thermometer-like instrument aside from the oxygen isotopes. In building their exoskeletons, marine creatures can use either magnesium or calcium, and they prefer magnesium at higher temperatures. Experiments indicate that the ratio of magnesium (Mg) to calcium (Ca) provides a good estimate of the water temperature at the time the shell was made. As in the case of oxygen isotopes, however, the relative concentrations of Mg and Ca in the water also affect the result. Nevertheless, unlike oxygen isotopes, the Mg and Ca concentrations do not change much over time and, in particular, are not affected by the development of ice sheets.

One study of Mg/Ca ratios indicated, as expected, a close agreement with the oxygen isotope record between 70 Mya and 40 Mya (Lear, 2000). Like the oxygen record, the Mg/Ca ratio signaled a deep ocean temperature of approximately 10°C around 40 Mya. Thereafter, the Mg/Ca temperature signal diverged from the oxygen record, roughly to the extent predictable with other estimates for the advance of the Antarctic ice sheet. The average deep ocean temperature had dropped to around 4°C between 10 Mya and 7 Mya, just before glaciers began spreading over Greenland. Data from this study also indicated a further drop in the ocean temperature since 3 Mya, when ice sheets often extended widely over the Northern Hemisphere. As noted above, the current average temperature of the deep ocean is about 1.5°C. This study suggests that an increase in the average temperature of the deep ocean of only about 2.5°C would bring it to a level last seen when Greenland had no ice. To produce that much warming of the deep ocean, a warming of slightly less than that amount would be needed on average over the surface of the globe. However, as discussed earlier, the warming at the surface would probably need to be maintained for several millennia before the deep ocean completed its adjustment.

ICE AGE FLUCTUATIONS

To avoid confusion, we need to distinguish between an Ice House and an "Ice Age." As noted above, an Ice House is a time when Earth has at least one perennial ice sheet, in contrast to a Greenhouse period when even the two poles are ice-free, at least in summer. Our current Ice House began when Antarctica developed permanent ice cover around 35 Mya. An Ice Age refers to a shorter interval when ice sheets covered much of North America and northern Eurasia. For most of the last 2.75 million years, we have been in an Ice Age. Between 2.75 Mya and 1 Mya, northern ice sheets tended to expand gradually for twenty to twenty-five millennia, then retreat for nearly as long a period. Since about 1 Mya, however, the swings in the climate have been larger and less symmetrical. Northern glaciation has been more prolonged, persisting for around 100 millennia or so. By contrast, the intervals between these Ice Ages, called "interglacials," have been less frequent and more abrupt, lasting only about 10 millennia. The most recent interglacials occurred around 420, 330, 220, and 125 thousand years ago (kya). Our own interglacial began about 11 kya.

As noted earlier, ancient glacial deposits do not provide a good record of the waxing and waning of ice over time because they are overrun time and again by subsequent Ice Ages. Scientists have instead pieced together the fluctuations in climate over the last few million years from other sources such as the isotope ratios in marine shells mentioned above. In the case of temperature differences between Ice Ages and interglacials, however, the shells constructed by creatures in the deep ocean are not of much help. The resolution of such records into millennial-level time intervals is impaired because of delays in the response of the deep ocean to changes in the surface climate. Some scientists have tried to obtain better estimates from the shells of plankton living closer to the surface of the ocean. Because the region of the top one hundred meters of the ocean is well-mixed by winds, it responds to atmospheric temperature changes within only a few years. However, even in the case of shells formed by creatures living in the surface ocean, the mixing of their sediments on the ocean floor limits the resolution of the records to about a millennium-average basis.

Estimates of the temperature of the surface of the Pacific Ocean have been made from several sites using the sediments of plankton shells. One study used the Mg/Ca ratio of those shells to estimate temperatures over the last 1.3 million years (Medina-Elizalde, 2005). Sea surface temperatures in the Western Pacific, averaged over many years, are thought to be highly correlated with global average temperatures rather than regional conditions because they are far removed from the influence of growing and shrinking ice sheets and of upwelling from the deep ocean. The swings in ocean temperatures, especially in the tropics, are likely to be less pronounced than the global average temperature, however. The records indicate that these surface ocean temperatures varied over a range of about 3 °C between extreme glacial conditions and interglacial periods like today.

Another study found that the Pacific surface ocean warmed by 3 °C between the time of the last maximum glaciation, about 20 kya, and the most recent reading that could be obtained with the sediment record, dating to about 1 kya (Lea, 2000). Evidently, at least through about a millennium ago, the temperature change over our current interglacial period has been fairly typical. Interestingly, the sediments indicated that the temperature of the surface ocean peaked around 6 kya. Between then and 1 kya, the ocean surface had cooled about 1 °C. The authors of the study cautioned, however, that the cooling since 6 kya was an uncertain result, as 1 °C was about the limit of temperature changes that could be reliably deciphered using the Mg/Ca methodology.

To obtain a more precise resolution of temperature changes than is possible with ocean sediments, scientists have teased out estimates from the ice piled up on Greenland and Antarctica. Unfortunately, the earliest ice deposited there millions of years ago is no longer available to be sampled. As new snow falls and freezes, year after year, the ice sheets grow in altitude. They now reach more than 3 km high on both Greenland and Antarctica. The weight of all that ice creates massive pressures on the oldest ice at the bottom. Indeed, the mountainous weight of ice even depresses the crust of the earth, squashing it into the softer mantle below. From the elevated central domes, glaciers are driven down and out over the land, eventually causing icebergs to calve off into the sea. The oldest ice that has survived on Antarctica dates to around 800 kya. Greenland has more snowfall than Antarctica; as a result, its glaciers build quicker and move faster. Greenland's ice generally dates to only around 100 kya, although some has been found older than 200 kya.

Ice cores provide indicators of ancient polar temperatures but not measures of the global average temperature. Like marine shells, ice also holds a mixture of the two stable oxygen isotopes, ^{18}O and ^{16}O. Snowfall takes down *more* of the heavy isotope from the atmosphere when it is *warmer*, the opposite of marine creatures building shells. However, this temperature signal depends importantly on the isotope shares of the water vapor source, which change when more ^{16}O is stored in ice sheets, as noted earlier in the chapter. A less noisy temperature signal can be obtained from hydrogen isotopes in the ice. Most hydrogen atoms in water molecules have a solitary proton in the nucleus, but one in 6,000 also has a neutron. This heavy hydrogen isotope, called deuterium, is more prevalent in snowfall at higher temperatures (an increase of 1 °C increases the deuterium share by about 0.9 percentage points).

Using these isotope signals, polar areas experienced wide estimated temperature swings of 12 °C or more between Ice Ages and interglacials (Petit, 1999). Whereas tropical sea surfaces changed only about 3 °C across these periods, the global average temperature, on which there are no direct readings, probably moved about 5–6 °C. What could have caused such swings in temperatures and the movement of ice sheets over the Northern Hemisphere that accompanied them? A variety of hypotheses have been proposed over the years; two leading contenders are solar radiation and changes in Earth's orbit.

SOLAR RADIATION

Since the middle of the nineteenth century, controversies have raged about the role of the Sun in causing changes in weather and climate (Weart, 2003), with sunspots as the leading indicator in the debate. Astronomers have kept fairly complete records of sunspot activity since the invention of telescopes more than four centuries ago. However, precise measurements of solar radiation, undertaken by satellite since 1978, show only small changes in solar radiation – about 0.1% – between the maximum and minimum of recent sunspot cycles.[7] Although sunspots are cooler regions of the Sun, they appear at times when the Sun is generally more active and emitting more radiation overall.

To investigate solar radiation before the era of telescopes, some scientists have estimated the strength of the Sun from its effect on the number of cosmic rays hitting the Earth. When solar activity is intense, the Sun and solar wind provide a stronger magnetic shield to deflect away cosmic rays coming into the inner solar system. High-energy cosmic rays leave visible traces on our planet. On striking molecules in the upper atmosphere, they produce radioactive isotopes of carbon (^{14}C) and beryllium (^{10}Be). These isotopes mix readily throughout the atmosphere and some even become embedded in glacial ice. The ^{14}C, which is quickly incorporated into carbon dioxide molecules in the air, is also built into plant tissue during photosynthesis and therefore shows up in tree rings. The relative concentration of ^{14}C in the atmosphere reflects both its production through new cosmic rays and also the growth of vegetation, as plants preferentially absorb lighter carbon isotopes. In estimating the strength of past solar radiation from the record of ^{14}C and ^{10}Be concentrations in ancient atmospheres, adjustments also have to be made for the strength of the Earth's magnetic shield, which plays a prominent role in deflecting cosmic rays away from the planet.

Aside from its use in estimating the level of solar activity, the cosmic ray effect could add to the climate impact of solar radiation. The ion particles created by cosmic rays may act as seeds for cloud formation. Clouds play a dual role in the climate, cooling the planet by reflecting the Sun's radiation but also contributing to greenhouse warming. The clouds formed by cosmic rays are thought likely to have a net cooling effect. Therefore, lower solar radiation would reduce Earth's temperature directly and perhaps indirectly as well through increased cloud cover caused by cosmic rays. In a more extreme suggestion, Shaviv and Veizer (2003) argue that the movement of the solar system through the Milky Way galaxy alters the flux of cosmic rays itself, but this effect remains speculative. Moreover, evidence

---

[7] On average, the Earth receives 342 Watts/m² of solar radiation, implying about 0.3 W/m² less radiation when there are no sunspots. The IPCC (2007) estimates that our GHG emissions since the industrial revolution, net of the effects of other human activities, have increased the effective radiation Earth receives by about 1.6 W/m² – more than five times the temporary sunspot effects.

for cosmic ray effects on cloud formation is rather sketchy (IPCC, 2007). A recent paper argues that cosmic rays are ineffective stimulants for cloud formation because the ions produced from cosmic rays accumulate too little water vapor to form droplets during their short lifetimes in the atmosphere (Pierce, 2009).

With isotope analyses extending the estimates of solar activity to much earlier times, researchers took renewed interest in examining the Sun's effect on the climate, and some hoped to learn new insights on the fluctuations of the Ice Age. Enthusiasm for the possibilities was heightened when a few Sun-like stars were seen to emit radiation that varied over a range of more than 0.5%, some five times the range observed in our star's recent sunspot cycles. However, as has so often been the case for ideas linking the Sun to the climate, the excitement proved to be short-lived. A larger sample of stars and more careful identification of those similar to our Sun showed that radiation did not vary more than the 0.1% observed in our recent sunspot cycles, implying therefore only minor potential effects on climate (Foukal, 2004).

EARTH'S ORBITAL CYCLES

Variations in the *total amount* of solar radiation are now seen as having only a minimal effect on long-term climate change. However, changes in the *distribution* of that radiation over the surface of the Earth are thought to be a key driver of Ice Age fluctuations. The distribution of radiation is altered by variations in the tilt of the Earth and the shape of its orbit. These orbital factors have no effect on the total solar radiation received by the planet during a year, but they do affect seasonality and the share of radiation received by the Northern and Southern Hemispheres.

The theory of orbital effects on climate was developed by Milutin Milankovitch in the 1930s, following earlier work by John Croll in the 1870s. Milankovitch added the insight that ice growth is promoted when seasonal temperature swings are restrained, because less ice is melted when summers are relatively cool. To a lesser extent, glacial expansion also may be fostered by relatively warm winters that increase the rates of evaporation of ocean water and snowfall on land.

The easiest orbital effect to understand is a change in the tilt of the Earth. If the North and South Pole were straight up and down relative to the Sun, there would be no seasons. In those circumstances, when snow fell and froze into ice, it would just remain in place. Glaciers would cover a large area of Earth, but change little over the course of the year. In contrast, the more the planet's north-to-south polar axis tilts down toward the Sun, the more radiation is received by the poles and other high latitudes in the summer, and the more snow and ice will melt. Actually, the Earth's tilt (or *obliquity*) varies between 22.1 degrees and 24.6 degrees over a period of 41,000 years.[8] At present, the tilt is 23.5 degrees and decreasing toward its minimum.

The other orbital effect is a combination of two factors: a stretching of the orbit away from a perfect circle and the timing within the annual calendar of the closest approach of the Earth to the Sun (the perihelion). If the perihelion occurs in one hemisphere's summer, ice sheets there are subject to greater summer melting. The perihelion is currently in January and therefore helps melt ice in the Southern Hemisphere but not in the north. It turns out, however, that only the Northern Hemisphere matters for effects on ice sheet growth. The main reason is that the Northern Hemisphere has twice as much continental land mass as the South. Moreover, a large portion of northern lands are at latitudes susceptible to the periodic expansion of ice sheets. The timing of the perihelion moves around our annual calendar in cycles of 21,000 to 23,000 years; these movements are called the *precession of the equinoxes*.

If Earth's orbit were a perfect circle, there would be no precession of the equinoxes; the distance from the Sun would be the same in every season. Because the planet's orbit has gradually become more circular over the last several tens of millennia, the precession effect has weakened. Although the eccentricity (noncircularity) of the orbit can imply changes in distance from the Sun as large as 9% or more, currently Earth's distance from the Sun varies only about 3% over the year. The eccentricity, which adjusts in slow cycles of 100,000 years and longer, will gradually diminish until reaching a minimum about 27,000 years from now.

The variations in the planet's orbit over past epochs can be mapped out with great precision. The resulting solar radiation effects match fairly well with the estimated timing of changes in size of the ice sheets and in average temperatures, after allowing for a lag in the response of the climate system. In particular, the cycles of about 40,000 years in length that were observed in ice sheet movements between 2.75 Mya and 1 Mya correspond fairly well with cycles in the tilt of the Earth.

However, it is more difficult to explain a shift that occurred in the periodicity of the Ice Ages since 1 Mya. Over the last million years, interglacials

---

[8] Earth's unusually large moon helps keep the planet's tilt relatively stable compared with other planets in the solar system. The tilt of Mars, for instance, may vary from near zero to as high as 80% (Jakosky, 2005).

have come only about once every 100,000 years rather than once every 40,000 years as before. A leading hypothesis for the shift begins by noting that the Earth on average has become colder over this time, perhaps because of the increasing removal of atmospheric CO_2 with the Himalayan orogeny. In a generally colder climate, the ice sheets on North America and Eurasia may grow to a larger size and thickness than was the case before 1 Mya. As a result, they may be able to survive some of smaller swings in northern summer radiation that used to melt them. It may take a particularly strong warming from the combination of tilt and precession effects to remove continental ice sheets of the size that the planet has been producing over the last one million years (Ruddiman, 2001).

ALBEDO AND GHG FEEDBACKS

Early opponents of the Milankovitch theory argued, rightly, that solar radiation changes attributable to orbital factors are too small to send ice sheets as far south as Nebraska and Paris and then melt them back to a refuge on Greenland and the Arctic Ocean. However, orbital effects persist for thousands of years and generate feedback loops that amplify their impact. Feedbacks that could account for the full response of the climate system are the change in the albedo of the planet with the expansion or melting of ice sheets, as discussed above, and the responses of GHG.

The key GHG feedbacks involve CO_2 and water vapor. A considerable amount of carbon is dissolved in the ocean, but the ability of water to hold CO_2 depends on its temperature. When the ocean warms, it releases CO_2, thereby boosting greenhouse effects. The air also holds more water vapor when its temperature rises. Like CO_2, water vapor plays a greenhouse role by allowing sunlight through while absorbing heat radiation rising up from the Earth. In the case of water vapor, however, that warming effect can be partly offset by increases in cloud cover that boost the planet's albedo. Nevertheless, the net effect of CO_2 and water vapor responses is a strong amplification of any initial warming or cooling of the planet. Other, smaller greenhouse feedbacks may also occur, such as an altered rate of release of methane when wetlands and permafrost areas are affected.

As for timing, water vapor responds almost immediately to an altered air temperature. The CO_2 feedback depends on the transmission of an atmospheric temperature change into the upper level of the ocean, which can take a few decades. Ice sheets respond very slowly to a swing in summer radiation in the Northern Hemisphere and to the atmospheric temperature changes brought on by GHG feedbacks. Albedo and GHG feedbacks can thus mutually reinforce each other for several thousand years before the climate system settles down and completes its response to a movement in the orbital factors.

Why weren't orbital effects important in causing climate change earlier in Earth's history? For one thing, the bulk of the world's land must be either north or south of the equator for the precession of the equinoxes to play a role. But even with a favorable configuration of continents, the planet's climate system has to be fairly close to a threshold level for small differences in radiation to trigger major amplifying feedbacks. In particular, continental ice sheets need to be poised to expand or contract. That state of climate fragility did not develop until atmospheric CO_2 fell to a low enough level to bring the planet into an Ice House period. When CO_2 was 1,000 ppm, the greenhouse effects were strong enough to keep the planet ice-free despite any perturbations in Earth's orbit. Over the last several million years, however, with the CO_2 level averaging only around 250 ppm, Antarctica and Greenland have had permanent ice sheets and the climate system has been poised for orbital effects to trigger expansions and contractions of ice sheets over North America and Eurasia.

Largely because of feedback effects, the CO_2 concentration hasn't been steady over our Ice Ages, as indicated by the particles of air trapped in polar ice. The CO_2 observed in ice cores is a good indicator of its average atmospheric concentration because the gas mixes fairly quickly throughout the atmosphere. Also, it takes several centuries for a change in CO_2 concentration to subside, aside from the usual fluxes across the seasons of the year. The same cannot be said for water vapor, which remains in the air for only about nine days on average and has widely varying local concentrations.

Air bubbles may enter ice with the original snowfall that created it. Air can also continue to penetrate congealing snow up to a depth of 50 meters or more before the ice hardens enough to seal it off. Each layer of an ice core therefore includes air trapped over a range of different times. The range is more limited in Greenland, where glaciers build and seal off more rapidly. Aside from uncertainties about timing, researchers must take into account another possible bias in the CO_2 readings from ice cores. Along with the air bubbles, atmospheric dust also gets embedded in ice. The dust often contains calcium carbonate, which decomposes over time, releasing CO_2 and therefore distorting the estimates of the composition of ancient atmospheres. Dust is more of a problem in Greenland than in the more isolated Antarctica (Ruddiman, 2001).

The relatively dust-free readings from ice cores in Antarctica show that, excluding the last century, atmospheric concentrations of CO_2 have varied between 180 and 300 ppm over the last 650,000 years. The highest CO_2 levels are found in interglacial periods, as expected. As noted earlier, the ice also holds hydrogen isotopes that can be used to estimate ancient temperatures in polar areas. A comparative analysis shows that temperatures have changed first in the swings of climate during recent Ice Ages; CO_2 levels followed with a lag of up to a few thousand years (Petit, 1999; Siegenthaler, 2005b). This pattern reinforces the idea that CO_2 has not been an initiator of the temperature movements that made ice sheets grow and contract, but rather another amplifying feedback along with the ice-albedo feedback. The prime mover of the ice ages seems to have been orbital factors.

A TYPICAL ICE AGE CYCLE

Consider what might have been a typical fluctuation in Ice Age climate: The tilt of the Earth reaches a maximum on one of its 41,000-year cycles just as the 23,000-year precession cycle puts the planet's closest approach to the Sun in northern summer. With the combination of a strong tilt of the pole toward the Sun and an early July perihelion, solar radiation in the summer at 65-degree latitude north is 25% above its previous minimum. Ice sheets on North America, Europe, and Asia begin to melt. As sea ice melts and as land ice begins to give way to expanding tundra, more sunlight is absorbed. The planet's albedo falls, and the initial regional warming in the north begins to spread around the world. The rise in temperature is amplified with little delay by an increase in water vapor. The warmth spreads from the atmosphere to the upper ocean within a few years. With the rising temperature, the ocean surface releases some of its CO_2 into the air. In addition, CO_2 and methane are vented from the soils and permafrost as they warm, raising GHG levels further. With mutually reinforcing feedbacks, the planet continues to warm and northern ice sheets continue to shrink over several thousand years. When ice sheets have largely disappeared from North America and northern Eurasia, the climate enters a fairly stable interglacial period that lasts approximately ten millennia. Toward the end of that interval, the precession cycle has put Earth's closest approach to the Sun in northern winters. With the reduction in northern summer radiation, the continental ice sheets gradually begin building again. Their growth phase lasts much longer than the time it took for them to melt. With some ebb and flow, the ice sheets don't reach a new maximum until 100 millennia have gone by.

This description reflects a leading hypothesis of the causes of Ice Age climate cycles, but the issue is not fully settled for all scientists. Some researchers have pointed to strong increases in summer radiation in the Southern Hemisphere, rather than in the north, as a possible initiator of interglacial periods (Timmermann, 2008). They point to evidence suggesting that the melting of sea ice in the Southern Ocean leads to a release of CO_2 from upwelling waters. The greenhouse effects of those CO_2 emissions then warm the rest of the planet enough to bring on interglacial periods.

A lesson from business cycle research may be relevant here. Despite the efforts of our best macroeconomists over many decades, no single "smoking gun" variable has been found that causes economic recessions to begin. The economy is too complicated to be determined by a single causative factor; each business expansion seems to have some unique features that prove crucially important to its demise (Gordon, 1986). The same complexity may be involved in climate cycles. Northern summer radiation may often be the critical factor that causes Ice Ages to begin and end. However, other forces may be needed to bring the climate close to a turning point so that those changes in solar radiation (with amplifying feedbacks), or other causative factors, can push the climate into an Ice Age or interglacial period. The forces that bring the climate close to a tipping point may themselves vary from one Ice Age cycle to another.

TWO

Human and Climate Interactions

The last interglacial prior to our current period occurred around 120,000 years ago. At that time, natural forces brought about a much higher sea level than today. Distinguishing the role of natural forces from human influences on the climate is a critical and controversial topic, particularly when considering the rapid rise in the global average temperature in the last century or so. The implications are profound for climate forecasts and the need for climate policy responses. If natural forces are likely to halt or even reverse the current warming trend within a few decades, only limited investments would be needed to counter the prospective effects of climate change. But if the recent pace of warming is likely to be sustained or even accelerate in the future, a more urgent and substantial policy response is required.

CLIMATE AND HUMAN EVOLUTION

Around 160 Mya, while circling the Sun in the inner portion of the region between Mars and Jupiter, an asteroid 65 km wide struck another of 160 km in diameter. Fragments from the collision, known as the Baptistina family of asteroids, continued orbiting the Sun, but on new, less stable trajectories. Many of the pieces gradually found their way into the inner solar system, doubling the usual rate of impact by large objects. One mountain-sized chunk may have hit the moon around 108 Mya, blasting out the 80-km-wide Tycho Crater. An even larger fragment, about six miles wide, may have been responsible for the asteroid strike in Chicxulub, Mexico, which gouged out a crater 180 km in diameter around 65 Mya. It is unclear as yet, however, whether that impact reflects the chemistry of a Baptistina asteroid (Majaess, 2008).

Alvarez (1980) hypothesized that the Chicxulub impact was the cause of the extinctions of dinosaurs and many other species around that time. However, other asteroid impacts may have contributed to the extinctions (Mullen, 2004). In addition, climate stresses over a longer period of time may also have played a role, including a massive flow of lava from an area in

Western India known as the Deccan Traps. The flood basalts of the Deccan Traps spread over about 1.5 million square kilometers, roughly half the current size of India (Keller, 2008). Large asteroid impacts may have intensified the ongoing volcanic releases.

The asteroid impacts and volcanic emissions would have thrown a huge cloud of dust and sulfur particles into the atmosphere. Persisting cloud cover would have blocked sunlight, shutting down photosynthesis and causing an unrelenting "volcanic winter" for several years. With acid rains also poisoning the ground, vegetation would have disappeared, contributing to the extinctions. In addition, there is evidence of a drop in sea level at that time, which would have also contributed to the environmental stresses causing extinctions (Archibald, 2004).

While most of larger fauna perished, small, shrew-like mammals survived. By 60 Mya, many species of mammals were flourishing and the earliest primates appeared. Apes did not split off from monkeys until about 25 Mya. In the next 20 million years, the lineage to humans successively diverged from gibbons, orangutans, gorillas, and then chimpanzees.

The local African environments where much of the primate evolution occurred were powerfully affected by global climate forces. The gradual drop in temperatures as the Ice House took hold after 35 Mya, and especially after Greenland picked up an ice sheet around 7 Mya, likely changed wind patterns and helped cool and dry African tropical forests, converting many to open grasslands. And after 2.7 Mya, the highly variable climates of the Ice Ages left their imprints on the ecosystems of our ancestors.

The climate of Africa, as well as South Asia, depends heavily on the strength of monsoons – persistent seasonal winds between the ocean and the land. In the summertime, land areas heat up more than the ocean, and as hot air over the land rises, breezes come in from the ocean, bringing moisture. Monsoon winds then reverse direction in the winter, pushing dry air from the interior of the continent out toward the ocean. When orbital factors increase northern summer radiation, the difference between land and sea temperatures increases, and the moisture-laden summer winds are strengthened (Kutzbach, 1997). In addition, in a generally warmer climate, evaporation from the ocean increases and the monsoons deliver more moisture. Monsoon winds, along with broader atmospheric circulation patterns, can also be affected by the waxing and waning of ice sheets (Weldeab, 2007).

Over the last one million years, Ice Age climate shifts have become more severe, increasing the variability of African ecosystems and intensifying natural selection pressures. Archaic species of homo sapiens were evolving over this time. Our own species evidently appeared on the scene between

250 and 200 kya, an interval when the climate was highly variable but not pushed to extremes. Between 240 and 194 kya, three brief periods of warming occurred, each separated by around 20,000 years, the length of the precession cycle. The locations of fossil coral suggest that the sea level over this period remained about thirty feet or so below current levels. Coral provide an estimate of sea level because they grow only at particular, relatively shallow depths in the ocean. These sea level estimates, along with oxygen isotope records, indicate that ice sheets melted somewhat less than during our current interglacial period (Siddal, 2006). Polar ice core records indicate that temperatures and CO_2 concentrations temporarily spiked around 238 kya and again, at lower levels, around 218 and 202 kya (Fischer, 1999). Thereafter, ice sheets held sway again for around seventy millennia.

It was a long wait for our young species, but when the next interglacial period arrived, it was a balmy one. Northern summer radiation peaked at an unusually high level around 130 kya and remained high for about 3,000 years. Solar radiation received at the Arctic Circle, for example, was about 4% above the maximum of our own interglacial period, and the temperatures over Greenland likely averaged nearly 3.5°C above today's levels (Otto-Bliesner et al., 2006).

The general level of the ocean around 125 kya was about five meters above its level today, as indicated by coral growth in tectonically stable areas (Intergovernmental Panel on Climate Change [IPCC], 2007). However, the global average temperature was evidently not much higher than what it is today. In consequence, little of that additional ocean height can be attributed to the thermal expansion of water. Instead, the polar ice sheets must have melted more. Fossil records indicate that plants were thriving along Greenland's coastal areas and in southern regions. Definitive data are not available, but modeling studies suggest a substantial thinning of ice sheets in central and northern Greenland. The rising seas from the melting of ice on Greenland likely helped dissolve ice shelves off the coasts of Antarctica as well, speeding the flow of southern glaciers into the sea despite southern air temperatures that were not much different from today (Overpeck, 2006). Following a long interglacial period of around fifteen millennia, northern ice sheets once again began to build after 115 kya. They continued growing, with some ebb and flow, for nearly 100,000 years.

Around 71 kya, our species witnessed a climate catastrophe of apocalyptic proportions. A volcano at what is now Lake Toba, Indonesia, erupted with a force 67,000 times more powerful than the atomic bomb that was dropped on Hiroshima. The eruption ejected enough material into the air to cause a six-year volcanic winter, followed by the coldest millennium in more than a million years – summertime temperatures in Europe and Asia were as much as 12 °C lower than they are today. Apparently, the human species was almost wiped out. The tiny range of variation in the human genome, relative to what would be expected for a species with our number of generations, indicates a population bottleneck. Only a few thousand breeding couples evidently survived (Ambrose, 1998).

Homo sapiens recovered from that threat of extinction and began to thrive, despite the continuing Ice Age conditions. We expanded beyond our home in Africa, bringing advances in stone technology with us. We learned how to cope well with glacial climates in Europe and left lasting artwork in caves. We proved more competitive in those environments than our sister species, the Neanderthals, who finally died out in their last refuge in Spain around 30 kya while the climate moved toward maximal glacial cover. Around 21 kya, the Earth was closest to the Sun in northern winters, and ice sheets had grown to their greatest extent; they stretched from the North Pole all the way to Long Island and to the English Channel. Thereafter, the Ice Age finally began to loosen its grip.

THE AGRICULTURAL REVOLUTION

The Earth's tilt gradually increased and the perihelion moved along the calendar. With both orbital factors combining to boost northern summer radiation, glaciers began to melt. In time, massive lakes formed on top of the ice on North America. Around 13 kya, as suggested by iridium deposits, a modest-sized asteroid may have grazed North America, providing a burst of heat.[1] In any case, at about that time, a vast amount of glacial meltwater broke through an ice dam and poured into the North Atlantic. For reasons discussed further in this chapter, it was enough to shut down the Gulf Stream.

The strength of circulation in the Atlantic Ocean depends on the sinking of surface water into the deep ocean in areas near Greenland and Iceland. Downwelling occurs when surface water is denser than the water below it. The deep ocean is under great pressure, but that doesn't alter its density much because water resists physical compression. Density increases mainly when water becomes colder and more salty. As the warm Gulf Stream moves north, evaporation increases its salinity and the colder air sharply lowers its

---

[1]   Kennett (2009). The asteroid may have been only around twenty meters in diameter, similar to the one that vaporized over the Tunguska forest in Siberia in 1908. That event nevertheless devastated an area of about 2,000 square kilometers.

temperature. Eventually, the surface waters become heavy enough to sink. The volume of deep water created in the North Atlantic is immense, equal at present to one hundred Amazon Rivers or all the rain falling on the Earth (Broecker, 1997). The warmth brought to Northern Europe by the ocean conveyor belt normally amounts to about 25% of the heat provided by the Sun.

The huge lake of glacial melt-water that drained out of North America around 13 kya shocked the North Atlantic system (Alley, 2000). Being largely salt-free, the glacial melt-waters dramatically reduced the density of the surface ocean. Downwelling came to a sudden halt. The sudden failure of water to sink created a backup all along the North Atlantic conveyor belt. The Gulf Stream itself shut down and, in consequence, Northern Europe plunged back into glacial conditions for the next 1,500 years. Evidence for this event first emerged when fossil pollen from the tundra-loving Dryas plant was found in locations characteristic of an older glacial period. The episode has therefore been called the "Younger Dryas."

Despite the 1,500-year cooling of the North Atlantic, orbital factors and global feedback loops continued to warm the planet on average. The ocean conveyor belt was recovered by around 11.5 kya. Shortly thereafter, Earth's tilt reached a maximum and, at the same time, the planet was closest to the Sun in July; the result was a strong enough peak of northern summer radiation to bring on a full interglacial.[2] Northern continents finally became ice-free, and the planet experienced a millennium of peak warmth around 7 kya. Relative to the glacial maximum at 21 kya, the global average temperature had risen by about 5 °C. Roughly half of the warming is attributable to a 10% lower planetary albedo and half to greenhouse gas (GHG) feedbacks (Ruddiman, 2006).

After 11 kya, Earth's tilt began decreasing from its peak level. It will reach a minimum in about 10,000 years from now. The perihelion has also moved around the calendar since 11 kya; it reached the December solstice in about 1250 CE and now falls in January. Both orbital factors have therefore promoted an expansion of northern ice sheets in recent centuries. Indeed, we have already completed the typical interglacial period of about 10,000 years.

In some interglacials, a shift in the perihelion to northern winters was not enough of a change to initiate another Ice Age. For instance, in the interglacial period of around 430 kya, when orbital factors returned to a setting that promoted ice cover after a typical warm interval of about ten millennia, ice

---

[2] At 65 degrees north, for instance, solar radiation around 11 kya was 50 Watts/m^2 greater than today (Berger, 1978).

sheets failed to get a strong enough hold in Canada and northern Europe. The perihelion cycle continued through another complete round before a full return to Ice Age conditions. The interglacial thus lasted 30,000 years rather than the usual 10,000. Could natural forces also give us an extra-long interglacial period? Could northern continents remain ice-free through the current low point of northern summer radiation and allow us another 20,000 years of interglacial warmth before a new Ice Age begins?

In our interglacial, the biosphere has added a new component that is helping extend the period of warmth: human beings. When did we start influencing the climate? William Ruddiman (2006) and other scientists believe it was thousands of years ago, based on an analysis of atmospheric concentrations of CO_2 and methane since 11 kya. Ice core evidence indicates that CO_2 hit a peak (of 267 ppm) near that time of maximum northern summer radiation. When ice sheets thereafter receded rapidly, northern forests expanded, drawing CO_2 out of the air (Broecker, 2006). The CO_2 concentration should have continued to fall because of natural feedbacks. The lagged effect of the turn in orbital factors would have lowered the planet's temperature, and a cooler ocean would have absorbed more CO_2 from the air. By one calculation, these natural feedbacks would have caused the CO_2 concentration to decline gradually, and its level should have reached about 242 ppm today. However, the downtrend in CO_2 concentrations was halted around 8 kya. A possible cause was the initiation and spread of slash-and-burn agriculture, which began removing forest cover around that time and continues to do so even today. Whatever the cause, the CO_2 concentration bottomed out around eight millennia ago at 260 ppm and then gradually rose till reaching a plateau of around 280 ppm by the middle of the last millennium.

A similar story can be told from the methane record. The maximum of northern summer radiation between 12 and 11 kya probably brought the monsoons of Africa and South Asia to a peak of intensity. The related expansion of wetlands evidently caused a spike in atmospheric methane at that time (Petrenko, 2009). Thereafter, as the monsoons weakened, many natural wetlands probably dried out. Because substantial amounts of methane are released into the air from natural wetlands, the contraction of wetlands would have lowered the concentration of methane in the atmosphere. Ice core data do show a decline in methane levels from around 725 parts per billion (ppb) to 575 ppb between 11 and 5 kya. Thereafter, however, the downtrend halts, despite the fact that monsoons have continued to diminish, particularly in Africa. These natural forces would have reduced the methane concentration to an estimated 450 ppb today (Ruddiman, 2006). Instead, by the late eighteenth century, atmospheric methane had climbed back to the 11 kya peak of 725 ppb. Ruddiman hypothesizes that the unexpected reversal of methane trends was caused when humans began irrigating rice fields in Asia around 5 kya. The wetlands created through cultivation then more than made up for the decline in natural sources.

The combination of methane releases through irrigated rice farming and CO_2 emissions from deforestation may have had a profound effect on climate developments. Indeed, this early anthropogenic interference in the climate may have prevented our interglacial period from coming to its natural demise. By now, the cycling of orbital factors should have already initiated a spread of glaciers over northeast Canada. The GHG released from millennia of deforestation and rice farming may have therefore prevented the beginning of another Ice Age (Ruddiman, 2006).

However, other scientists believe that human influences on climate were not significant before the industrial revolution. For instance, the additions of CO_2 to the air after 8 kya may have come not from deforestation but from the ocean. Despite a slight cooling of the planet after 6 kya, the ocean may not have drawn down CO_2 from the air through the temperature-related feedback mechanism discussed earlier. Instead, the ocean's carbon cycle may have still been recovering from the CO_2 lost when northern forests expanded with the melting of ice. With the ocean's loss of CO_2 at that time, the rate of creation and dissolution of marine shells would have adjusted in a way that, after several thousand years, would return ocean chemistry to an equilibrium state. The extra CO_2 produced in the ocean through this recovery process would have been shared with the atmosphere as well (Broecker, 2006).

The controversy over early anthropogenic influences on the climate remains unresolved. The ocean carbon-cycle recovery process evidently did not cause noticeable increases in atmospheric CO_2 at the inception of some other Ice Ages. However, in those cases, its effects may have been masked by stronger swings in solar radiation. Deforestation and the ocean CO_2 recovery process may well have both contributed to the rise in preindustrial GHG. Additional unresolved questions arise regarding a possible anthropogenic role in climate developments at the end of the medieval period, as discussed below.

MEDIEVAL WARMTH AND THE LITTLE ICE AGE

Ice core data suggest a modest global cooling after 4000 BC. For the period since about 1000 CE, additional sources of data are available to estimate temperatures in the Northern Hemisphere, including tree rings, lake deposits, ground boreholes, and debris left by mountain glaciers, along with historical record keeping (IPCC, 2007; Kaufman, 2009). These sources tend to support the idea that a longer-term cooling trend, at least in the Northern Hemisphere, was interrupted by a "Medieval Warm Period" between about 800 and 1300. It was warm enough during that interval for Vikings to begin raising crops and livestock on Greenland. Thereafter, the cooling resumed with a vengeance. It became so frigid in Europe at times between 1350 and 1850 that the period has been dubbed the Little Ice Age. Evidence for both the Medieval Warm interval and the subsequent centuries of deep cold has come mainly from Europe; it remains unclear whether these climate developments were limited to the North Atlantic region.

Some scientists believe that global temperature swings were involved and anthropogenic activities were again at work. It has been suggested that variations in human population and the associated land devoted to agriculture could have altered atmospheric CO_2 enough to cause these worldwide climate changes. Ruddiman (2006) identifies a decrease in epidemics and pandemics between 750 and 1350, implying a rapid growth in population. As a result, forests would have been cut and burned at an increasing pace to clear land for crops and pastures. The emissions into the atmosphere of the CO_2 stored in forests could have caused the Medieval Warm Period.

According to Ruddiman's hypothesis, the population boom began to be reversed when the Mongols laid waste to vast areas during the 1200s. Around 1350, bubonic plague returned to Europe, killing perhaps 40% of the population. Within a few decades, forests began to recapture abandoned farmlands and pasture. New growth of trees pulled CO_2 out of the air, helping cool the planet. Not long thereafter, as temperatures plummeted, the Vikings had to abandon their settlements on the southern coast of Greenland. The Little Ice Age was prolonged through the sixteenth century in part because smallpox and other diseases from Europe killed up to 90% of Native Americans. Farmlands in the Western Hemisphere were then abandoned, allowing forests to expand again and extract more CO_2 from the air.

An alternative theory for global temperature movements over this period focuses on the role of the Sun. As indicated by the general level of sunspots over many eleven-year cycles, solar activity evidently reached a plateau between 1100 and 1250 (Jirikowic, 1994). Thereafter, solar output dropped to very low levels over several intervals during the Little Ice Age and may therefore have been responsible for at least part of the temperature drop during that period.[3]

---

[3]   The intervals have been named for astronomers who helped identify them: Oort (1010–1050), Wolf (1280–1340), Sporer (1425–1575), Maunder (1645–1715), and Dalton (1790–1820).

Other scientists favor the idea that the Medieval Warm Period and Little Ice Age were regional developments caused by changing patterns of ocean circulation. A strengthening of the Gulf Stream may have helped produce the three warm centuries for the North Atlantic region, but the warming itself in that case may have set in motion feedbacks that eventually brought it to a halt. As northern glaciers melted, fresh water drained into the ocean, reducing the density of surface waters. Eventually, the North Atlantic conveyor belt slowed. The Gulf Stream did not stop in its tracks as at the onset of the Younger Dryas period, but it may have weakened enough to more than reverse the medieval warming of Europe. It may have brought the Little Ice Age to that continent (Cronin, 2003).

A case can also be made that the Little Ice Age was nothing more than a return to a trend of natural forces after a transitory interruption during the Medieval Warm Period. As noted above, after a period of peak warmth around 7,000 years ago, orbital factors have been moving in a direction associated with a long-term cooling trend. By the year 1250, just before the onset of the five-century-long cold period, Earth's perihelion had moved to the December solstice, and northern summer radiation was therefore at a minimum. The lagged response of the climate system to that orbital effect might have helped bring on the Little Ice Age.

The continuing controversies regarding the causes of the Medieval Warm Period and the Little Ice Age should give pause to those considering forecasts of the climate over the coming century or two. The enormous complexity of the climate system suggests that we view potential outcomes as working hypotheses of varying probability rather than as certainties on which to base unwavering convictions.

Whatever the causes of the Little Ice Age, it came to an end around 1850. If orbital factors had been slowly pushing the planet toward the inception of a new, full Ice Age, they were soon overwhelmed by shorter-term forces that began to warm the Earth. The global cooling trend underway for some six millennia has been dramatically overturned in the last century and a half.

INDUSTRIAL AGE TEMPERATURE READINGS

By the late 1800s, air and water measurement facilities became widespread enough for direct estimates of Earth's average surface temperature to be constructed. The National Aeronautics and Space Administration's (NASA) Goddard Institute, for instance, computes a monthly average temperature by combining meteorological data from satellites, buoys and ships at sea, and more than 6,000 land-based weather stations. A virtual grid of 8,000 points is placed over the globe, and the monthly average temperature of each grid point is estimated using data from stations up to 1,200 kilometers away, with weights depending on distance. The global temperature estimate is then the average over all the grid points.

These estimates indicate that the planet's annual average temperature has gone up 0.8 °C between 1880 and 2009 (or from 56.8 °F to 58.2 °F), as shown in Figure 2.1. Could a statistician dismiss this result as random noise? A typical change in the annual average temperature, the "standard deviation," amounts to only 0.1 °C. Using that measure alone, the probability would be less than 25% of a temperature rise of 0.8 °C or more since 1880 in a world that was not on a genuine warming trend.

Over longer spans of time, how sizable is the recent rise in temperature? The 0.8 °C rise in the global average temperature since 1880 more than reversed the slight cooling of about 0.2 °C that was estimated to have occurred between the years 1000 and 1900. A plot of the estimated temperatures for the last millennium is fairly flat for nine centuries, before rising sharply since 1900, resembling the shape of a hockey stick (Mann, 1998, 1999). This chart engendered considerable controversy, and the temperature estimates from prior to the 1880s are now seen as reflecting evidence for the Northern Hemisphere, but not necessarily the global average (IPCC, 2007). Since the year 2000, our average temperature has edged above the earlier peak for our interglacial period, reached around 7,000

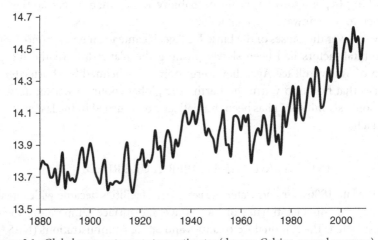

Figure 2.1. Global average temperature estimates (degrees Celsius, annual averages). *Source*: NASA Goddard Institute for Space Studies.

years ago. The estimate for 7 kya represents an average of 1,000 years, long enough to imply substantial climate impacts around the globe. Because of the gradual responses of the climate system, however, a similar high temperature reading for a single decade would have little lasting climate effects if it were reversed in a subsequent decade.

If recent global average temperatures were sustained for an entire millennium, how would they compare with even more ancient records from ice cores and ocean sediments? One study noted that the average temperature between 1870 and 1900 was observed in millennium-average data eighteen times over the past 1.3 million years (Hansen, 2006). The mean temperature of 2001–5 had been reached only five times in the ancient records, most recently around 420 kya; it was within 1 °C of the highest millennium-average temperature over the entire period. Indeed, we may now be within a few degrees Celsius of temperatures last seen in a prolonged manner only in the times before Greenland had any ice. A further rise of 5–6 °C could put us at levels experienced for long periods only back when Antarctica was also ice-free. Of course, the peak temperature reached in a decade or two is not of crucial importance to the climate, which adjusts only slowly to temperature fluctuations. Predicting the duration of the current warming trend requires an investigation of its causes.

CAUSES OF THE RECENT TEMPERATURE RISE

Urban Heat Islands

Urban areas tend to be heat islands for a variety of reasons. Tall buildings are more efficient than landscape at capturing solar radiation and retaining heat; they also interrupt the flow of wind that could carry heat away by convection. Moreover, concrete and asphalt eliminate the cooling that occurs when water evaporates from the soil. For such reasons, along with vehicle and industrial exhausts, cities are warmer than surrounding suburban and rural areas. A representative share of urban temperature readings should be included in the global average, but cities are only a tiny portion of the land area of the Earth. Nevertheless, they are the locations of most of the world's weather stations. A global temperature estimate would be biased upward if it assumed that urban temperatures applied to wider geographical areas. Moreover, the degree of urbanization and the intensity of heat island effects have grown over time. The warming indicated by urban weather stations therefore might merely reflect the growth of cities and not genuine climate change.

Estimates of the magnitude of heat island effects differ across studies. The IPCC (2007) reviewed the extant research and concluded that such biases have had "a negligible influence" on long-term temperature trends. The IPCC estimated the global average contribution of heat island effects to be less than 0.006°C per decade over land and zero over the oceans, implying a net effect of only 0.002°C per decade across the planet. The small size of the urban biases is attributable to the location of many weather stations in cool parklands rather than in congested areas of cities. The IPCC noted that some studies finding larger effects had evidently included other factors that were not the result of urbanization, such as changes in atmospheric circulation and the natural tendency of land areas to warm by more than the surfaces of lakes and oceans.

Scientists attempt to remove heat island effects when estimating broad temperature trends. At the Goddard Institute, for instance, the readings of each urban weather station are adjusted so that its long-term trend matches that of the neighboring rural stations (Hansen, 1999, 2001). Urban stations that cannot be adjusted are dropped. For the United States, these modifications removed about 0.15°C from the indicated warming over the last century. It could perhaps be argued that such adjustments are not large enough. However, the opposite could also be true.

Solar Activity

As noted earlier in the chapter, direct measurements since 1978 indicate moderate changes in solar radiation over sunspot cycles, about 0.1%. This would amount to a range of radiation received by Earth of 0.3 Watts per square meter (W/m^2) around the average of 342 W/m^2. Recent research has led to downward revisions in estimates of how much solar activity varies over longer periods of time (Foukal, 2004). For instance, in its 2007 report, the IPCC estimated that solar radiation had increased by only 0.12 W/m^2 between 1750 and 2005. That was less than half the increase that the IPCC estimated for the same period in 2001. Most of the rise in solar activity occurred between 1900 and 1940, so little of the global temperature increase since 1970 is now attributable to changes in the behavior of the Sun.

Measurements of temperature changes in different parts of the atmosphere support the idea that solar activity has played a minimal role of late. An increase in solar radiation would increase the temperature of both the stratosphere and the lower atmosphere (troposphere). However, whereas the troposphere and the surface of the Earth have warmed in recent decades, the stratosphere has actually cooled. This pattern of temperature response is not consistent with an increase in solar radiation. The stratosphere may have cooled in part because chlorofluorocarbons (CFCs) released by human activities have destroyed some of its ozone. The stratosphere would also tend to cool owing to the capture of outgoing heat radiation by GHGs in the troposphere.

Natural Oscillations?

Complex dynamics of the climate system have played a key role in many regional climate developments over the last century and have also perhaps contributed to the warming. For instance, a variety of "oscillations" in atmospheric circulation and ocean currents are being actively researched but are not yet well understood.

The most well-known oscillation is the El Niño warming of the Eastern Pacific, which has wide-ranging effects on regional climate patterns around the world. In normal times, trade winds push warm water from the surface of the tropical Pacific toward the west. In its place, bottom waters well up along the Pacific coastline of South America, providing a nutrient-rich ecosystem for thriving fisheries. When the differences in air pressure between the Eastern and Western Pacific diminish in what is called the negative phase of the Southern Oscillation, the trade winds weaken. Warm water sloshes back into the Eastern Pacific, and an El Niño occurs. With warm water spread over a wider surface of the ocean, global average temperatures are boosted a bit. Rainfall increases all along the Pacific coast of the Americas, but droughts are experienced in Southeast Asia, Australia, and the Amazon. In North America, the polar jet stream shifts northward.

An El Niño event is typically followed within a few years by a strong reversal of these conditions, called La Niña. The effects on the long-term trend of the global average temperature are thus offsetting. Longer-term cycles in atmospheric and ocean conditions may also contribute to El Niño/La Niña fluctuations. For instance, recurring patterns of warming across broader areas of the North and South Pacific have been observed over twenty-to-thirty-year periods and are called the Pacific Decadal Oscillations.

The North Atlantic also has an important oscillatory pattern. Seasonal weather extremes in Europe depend on the strength of westerly winds that are sucked into the continent through the rotation of two enormous atmospheric gears. One is a low-pressure system located near Iceland. Air is drawn toward the low-pressure center of that system. As the air moves in, it is pulled toward the right by the Coriolis force that sends it in a huge counterclockwise circle. The other gear is a high-pressure system over the

Azores. Air is pushed away from the high-pressure center of that system. As the air moves out, it is also pulled to the right, which sends it in a clockwise circle. Between the clockwise gear in the south and the counterclockwise gear in the north, winds are pulled strongly across the Atlantic and into Europe. When these two gears slow down (in what is called the North Atlantic Oscillation), Europe loses the moderating effect of westerly ocean breezes and gets hit with baking summers and freezing winters.[4]

We are still far from having achieved a full understanding of the dynamics of the climate system. Some investigators hypothesize the existence of oscillatory patterns of various types that could last many decades or centuries. However, supporting data for longer-term cycles, other than those associated with orbital effects, are generally lacking.

Industrial Era Greenhouse Gas

While human activities generate a number of GHGs, CO_2 stands out among the rest in its importance for recent and projected climate effects. Data from air bubbles in ice cores indicate that the atmospheric concentration of CO_2 remained close to 280 ppm for most of the last millennium, rising a bit during the Medieval Warm Period and edging lower thereafter in the Little Ice Age (Siegenthaler, 2005a, 2005b). This level was near the top of the 180-to-300-ppm range for CO_2 concentrations since 810 kya (Jouzel, 2007), but it was often reached during interglacial periods. The ice core record also indicates that CO_2 began rising in the eighteenth century and then accelerated as coal burning surged with the spread of the industrial revolution. Atmospheric CO_2 broke out of its millennium-average range for the last 810,000 years by the early 1900s.

As noted earlier, ice cores do not provide precise timings for their atmospheric samples because of the mixing of air of different vintages. Over the last half century, however, direct measurements of atmospheric CO_2 have been undertaken at a variety of sites. They all show a similar pattern of change (Keeling, 2005). Air samples taken from the Mauna Loa Observatory in Hawaii provide the longest continuous record, dating from 1958. Mauna Loa has the advantage of a remote location, largely unaffected by seasonal

---

[4] The Coriolis effect moves air to the right in the Northern Hemisphere because of the Earth's rotation speed and center of gravity. Air moving north from the equator seems to turn to the right because it inherits the faster eastward rotational speed of the equator. Air moving due east along any northern latitude seems to turn to the right because the gravity of the Earth pulls it in a "great circle" around the center of the planet rather than letting it continue around in a smaller circle at that same latitude.

plant growth or industrial emissions. Vegetation causes strong swings in CO_2 concentrations, pulling it from the air as photosynthesis picks up in the summer and returning it as plant matter decomposes in the winter. To purge any remaining seasonality from the data, readings for the same month can be compared across the years.

The Mauna Loa record indicates that the atmospheric concentration of CO_2 had reached 315 ppm by late 1958, well above the recorded peaks for other interglacial periods. The rise evidently reflected the increased burning of coal and oil in the twentieth century, as well as further deforestation as populations surged. By 2009, the CO_2 level had jumped to about 387 ppm, almost 25% higher than a half-century ago (see Figure 2.2). Moreover, the CO_2 concentration has been rising at a faster annual rate of about 2 ppm over the last decade, compared with about 1.25 ppm in the previous four.

The IPCC estimates that a doubling of atmospheric CO_2 would cause a 3°C increase in the global average temperature. This calibration would imply that the 24% rise in CO_2 between 1958 and 2009 should boost the global average temperature by about 0.7°C. The actual temperature increase over those years (as measured by the Goddard Institute) was only 0.4°C. These data may seem to suggest that if the CO_2 increase caused the warming, other factors must have offset part of it.

However, the picture is more complicated. Because of lags in feedback loops, the surge in CO_2 in recent decades should not have fully worked its way through the climate system. In addition, a mere correlation between CO_2 and temperature doesn't prove that CO_2 caused the temperature to rise. As noted earlier, longer-term climate records show that CO_2 tended

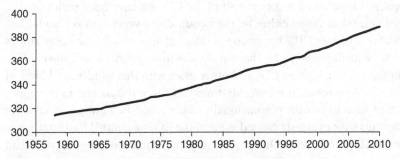

Figure 2.2. Atmospheric CO_2 concentrations (parts per million).

Note: The CO_2 concentration ranged from around 180 to 300 ppm over the prior 810,000 years (Siegenthaler, 2005b and Jouzel, 2007)

Source: NOAA (seasonally adjusted monthly data from Mauna Loa)

to follow temperature changes as an important natural feedback mechanism. In particular, as temperatures rose, the ocean released some of its CO_2 into the air. Was the CO_2 increase in this case also a consequence of global warming rather than its cause?

It is not possible to check the feedback story directly by measuring changes in the CO_2 concentration in the ocean. Although CO_2 mixes fairly quickly throughout the atmosphere, its concentration varies widely across the ocean and at different depths. Moreover, the processing of carbon in the ocean is complex; disturbances can set off reaction sequences there that don't settle down to a new equilibrium for thousands of years. The ocean holds roughly sixty-five times more carbon than the atmosphere (Ruddiman, 2001), but the year-to-year fluctuations in the CO_2 present in the ocean are not known.

It is possible, however, to obtain measures of the emissions of CO_2 from human activities into the atmosphere and compare those emissions with the data on atmospheric concentrations. Production records on the burning of fossil fuels by the energy industry go back to the late eighteenth century. Using such sources, along with geological survey data on the process emissions from cement production, the U.S. Department of Energy constructs estimates of the global emissions of CO_2 (Marland, 2007), as shown in Figure 2.3. Between 1960 and 2006, the cumulative emissions amount to about 910 billion metric tons (gigatons, or Gt) of CO_2. The Mauna Loa data show an increase in CO_2 concentration in the air of 69 ppm between December 1959 and December 2006, equivalent to 540 Gt – only about 60% of the emissions from the production and use of energy and from the production of cement.[5]

Other data sources have tended to corroborate the finding that the atmosphere has retained just over half of the CO_2 we have been emitting. The rest was taken down either by the oceans or by vegetation on land. How does that happen? The upper one hundred meters or so of the ocean comes into frequent contact with the atmosphere through winds and storms. The air freely exchanges its CO_2 and other gases with this wind-mixed layer of the sea. As a result, the concentrations of CO_2 in the air and in the upper ocean tend to remain proportional to each other. In addition, circulating currents have evidently carried some of the CO_2 we emitted into intermediate levels of the ocean. One key investigation combined the data on ocean

---

[5] Based on a total mass of the atmosphere of 5,148,000 Gt (Trenberth, 2005), and average molecular weight of 29 compared with the molecular weight of CO_2 of 44, one ppm of CO_2 would weigh $44*5.148/29 = 7.8$ Gt.

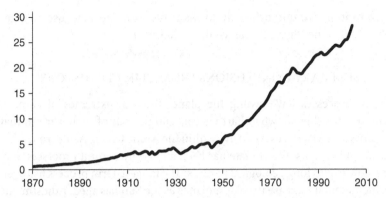

Figure 2.3. World CO_2 emissions from fossil fuels (billions of tons, annual data).
Source: U.S. Dept. of Energy, Carbon Dioxide Information Analysis Center (includes process emissions from cement production).

water samples taken on more than 116 scientific cruises between 1972 and 1999 in order to locate anthropogenic CO_2 in the ocean (Sabine, 2004). A human fingerprint was evident wherever CFCs were found, because CFCs remain inert in sea water and have no natural sources. In estimating the ocean's uptake of anthropogenic CO_2, adjustments had to be made for the CO_2 removed by ocean biology. The researchers found that the ocean had absorbed more than one-fourth of the anthropogenic emissions of CO_2 between 1980 and 1999. Anthropogenic CO_2 was found in ocean waters up to depths of more than two miles. The implication was that terrestrial plants had also taken down a little more than one-fourth of the CO_2 emissions.

What about the CO_2 feedback effect? A warming ocean is expected to release CO_2; indeed, this amplifying mechanism helped melt continental ice sheets in the past. In recent years, however, this feedback effect has been overwhelmed by the diffusion process that works to equilibrate CO_2 concentrations in the air and the sea. The amount of warming that has occurred so far would have reduced the ocean's takedown of CO_2 by only a small amount (Keeling, 2005).

Other GHGs have also evidently contributed to the current warming trend. The IPCC (2007) estimated that CO_2 was responsible for a little more than one-half of the overall greenhouse warming caused by anthropogenic emissions since 1750. However, the human footprint seems clear. According to the IPCC, "Warming of the climate system is unequivocal ... Most of the observed increase in globally averaged temperatures since the mid-20th century is *very likely* [greater than 90% probability] due to the observed increase in greenhouse gas ... Increases in carbon dioxide concentration are due primarily to fossil fuel use and land-use change" (IPCC 2007, The Physical Science Basis: 2, 5, 10.).

SUMMARY CONCLUSIONS FROM CLIMATE HISTORY

Natural processes have swung the planet through extremes of climate, including possible Snowball Earth events and periods of such warmth that alligators and palm trees could live within the Arctic Circle. Aside from a few catastrophic events, the climate has been altered by natural processes only very slowly over long geological periods. The longest-term process has been the incremental increase in solar radiance as the Sun has aged. Adjustments in the configuration of continents, the related mountain building, and the resulting changes in the rate of chemical weathering have also affected the climate only over millions of years.

More often than not, Earth has had a Greenhouse climate, with no permanent ice cover anywhere on the planet. Our own Ice House climate began when Antarctica first developed a permanent ice sheet around 35 Mya. Greenland did not develop a permanent ice cover until around 7 Mya. Earth's average temperature was apparently only about 2°C higher than today just before Greenland got permanent ice and perhaps 6°C higher than today immediately prior to formation of the Antarctic ice sheet. These estimates do not imply, however, that a merely temporary warming of the planet to such levels would cause loss of those ice sheets.

Our Ice House period may have been initiated by an increased rate of chemical weathering caused by the uplift of the Tibetan plateau and Himalayan mountains, which helped lower CO_2 concentrations in the atmosphere from thousands of parts per million to an average of around 250 ppm during the last several million years. With lowered CO_2 levels, the climate became more sensitive to other factors, particularly changes in the Earth's orbit around the Sun. Over the last 2.75 million years, ice sheets have more often than not covered parts of North America and Northern Eurasia. When Earth tilted toward the Sun more than usual and simultaneously, the perihelion of its orbit occurred in June or July, the resulting increase in solar radiation in northern summers was strong enough to initiate a melting of the continental ice sheets. Over the last million years, interglacial periods have lasted only about ten millennia before ice cover returned to northern continents for intervals of one hundred millennia or so.

Our own interglacial period began around eleven millennia ago. Natural forces might have initiated another Ice Age by now were it not for human activities. With the agricultural revolution, the clearing of forests, and the development of rice farming may have prevented CO_2 and methane levels from falling. With the industrial revolution, the burning of fossil fuels has pushed CO_2 levels above any observed over the last 800,000 years. Temperature levels have risen about 0.8 °C since preindustrial times, and the increase in GHG appears to be the main cause.

Whereas most natural processes affect the global climate very slowly, asteroid strikes, volcanic releases, and pulses of glacial melt-water can have dramatic and immediate effects. One or more asteroids, along with heightened volcanism, evidently helped cause extinction of the dinosaurs and many other species around 65 Mya. Flood basalts from a rifting of the ocean floor between Greenland and the European mainland apparently released enough methane and CO_2 around 55 Mya to warm the planet around 7 °C or so, again causing numerous extinctions. The increase in atmospheric carbon in that case was less than what we have available in fossil fuel resources today. It was released over a period of about ten millennia, a snail's pace compared with our current rate of emissions. Finally, around 13,000 years ago, a pulse of fresh glacial melt-water from North America evidently reduced the density of ocean waters enough to shut down the North Atlantic conveyor belt and return Europe to a deep freeze for an interval of about 1,500 years.

Climate history also highlights the importance of amplifying feedback effects. The changes in solar radiation attributable to orbital factors are far too small on their own to cause continental ice sheets to grow and shrink. However, as ice melts, more solar radiation is absorbed rather than reflected away from the planet. Moreover, a warming ocean is less able to hold its stores of CO_2. Finally, a warming atmosphere can hold more water vapor. Such feedbacks can amplify a fairly small initial impetus of climate change and push the global system to a profoundly different equilibrium.

We need not look very far back in Earth's history to find an equilibrium period that would have profound implications if it occurred today. The last interglacial period of around 125,000 years ago witnessed sea levels that were about five meters higher than at present. That high stand lasted several thousand years. It was caused by natural forces alone – greater melting evidently caused by more intense radiation in northern summers. The global average temperature of the time was apparently not much higher than today.

Finally, the climate is an enormously complex system, and our understanding of it is still woefully limited. Although we may take guidance from paleo-climate records that bear some similarity to our current situation, scientists often disagree over the precise causes of major climate changes in the past. Almost every data series has a considerable range of uncertainty surrounding it. Often, direct measurements of past climate developments are unavailable and proxy indicators may be subject to errors of interpretation. Extrapolating developments based on linear trends raises further issues, because interacting effects may vary and nonlinear shifts may emerge at points that are not yet clear.

THREE

Greenhouse Gases

As noted above, the weight of evidence suggests that the current warming trend has been caused by anthropogenic emissions of greenhouse gases (GHGs). If we are going to try to manage future GHG emissions, we need to understand these gases and the human activities that are causing their buildup in the atmosphere. Those are the subjects of this chapter and the next.

THE MAIN GASES

A GHG is transparent to sunlight, similar to a physical greenhouse made of glass. However, a GHG does not physically block the rising warm air. Rather, it absorbs outgoing infrared radiation emitted from the warmed surface of the planet. The gas then reradiates its absorbed thermal energy in all directions, some of which goes back to the surface of the Earth. Each GHG differs in its ability to absorb various parts of the spectrum of infrared radiation.

GHGs represent only a small share of the atmosphere, which is mainly composed of nitrogen (78%), oxygen (almost 21%), and argon (almost 1%). The three main GHGs released by human activities are carbon dioxide (CO_2), methane (CH_4), and nitrous oxide (N_2O). Other GHGs include several compounds of fluorine (the "F-gases") and ground-level ozone. In addition, chlorofluorocarbons (CFCs) play a greenhouse role and also damage the ozone layer of the stratosphere. Some anthropogenic emissions provide cooling effects. For instance, coal-burning industries release considerable CO_2, but they also emit particles of sulfur dioxide (SO_2). SO_2 is harmful to breathe, but it also reflects sunlight and helps seed clouds, thereby providing some planetary cooling. Eventually, SO_2 falls from the atmosphere as acid rain, causing potentially severe local health effects.

Carbon dioxide accounted for about 0.0386% of the atmosphere by volume in 2008, which means the same as 386 parts per million (ppm). The estimated concentration in the year 1750 (which is taken as the preindustrial benchmark) was only 280 ppm. As noted earlier, CO_2 is released from volcanoes and mid-ocean rift vents; it is also generated when organic carbon burns or decays in the presence of oxygen. In addition, when energy is produced (through "respiration") in both plant and animal cells, CO_2 is released.

About 97% of the CO_2 released into the atmosphere each year is from natural sources, whereas only 3% comes from human activities. However, the creation of CO_2 by natural sources is largely self-reversing over daily and seasonal cycles. In photosynthesis, plants combine sunlight with water and atmospheric CO_2 to produce glucose and oxygen. In daylight, therefore, plants, on net, remove CO_2 from the air. At night, plants continue to use their stored glucose energy in respiration, releasing some CO_2 back into the air. The takedown of CO_2 by vegetation also has a seasonal pattern. In the spring and summer, vast amounts of carbon are drawn from the air to fuel new growth of plants. In the late fall and winter, as plant material decays, CO_2 is released. Because of the greater land area in the Northern Hemisphere, global average CO_2 levels are lowest during the northern harvest period of September and October.

CO_2 is stored for longer than seasonal periods when roots and dead plants are buried in soils and when perennial plants add biomass on net. But soil bacteria also emit CO_2 with their metabolism, and they become more active when the soil is worked.

The ocean draws down and releases almost as much CO_2 each year as terrestrial plants and soils. Unlike the daily and seasonal patterns of the terrestrial carbon cycle, the ocean tends to be both a source and sink for CO_2 at the same time, but in different places. Ocean water cools as it moves out of the tropics toward higher latitudes. Because colder water can hold more CO_2, ocean currents moving toward the North or South Pole tend to remove CO_2 from the air. But CO_2 is released into the air from currents that move toward tropics and also from areas where deep, CO_2-rich waters rise to the surface. Ocean vegetation also takes up a small amount of CO_2 from the air.

Anthropogenic emissions of CO_2 are not part of a two-way seasonal or circulatory cycle. Humans release especially large amounts of CO_2 when they warm their homes in the winter, but they do not pull CO_2 back out of the air in the summer. The burning of fossil fuels releases CO_2 that was originally absorbed by vegetation, not last spring, but up to 350 Mya. Our emissions thus shift the level of atmospheric CO_2 from seasonal oscillations around a natural equilibrium level and put it on a rising trend.

The typical molecule of CO_2 remains aloft in the atmosphere for only about four years before being absorbed by plants or the ocean. However, that average duration merely reflects the large flux of the seasonal and circulatory cycles. The molecules of CO_2 emitted in a single year would actually experience a wide range of residence times in the atmosphere. IPCC reports from 2001 and earlier gave the misleading impression that anthropogenic emissions of CO_2 would be removed from the atmosphere in less than 200 years. The latest report corrects that mistaken implication, stating that "about 50% of an increase in atmospheric CO_2 [from anthropogenic emissions] will be removed within 30 years, a further 30% will be removed within a few centuries and the remaining 20% may remain in the atmosphere for many thousands of years" (IPCC 2007, The Physical Science Basis: 514).

Methane (CH_4) is formed when organic matter decays through bacterial activity in the absence of oxygen. A pure form of natural gas, methane is found deep underground, often associated with deposits of petroleum, and closer to the surface in permafrost areas. A vast amount of frozen blocks of methane and water (methane hydrates) are buried in sediments on the ocean floor.

The atmospheric concentration of methane rose from an estimated 715 parts per billion (ppb) in 1750 to a level of 1,774 ppb in 2005 (IPCC, 2007). More than one-third of the methane released into the atmosphere each year comes from rice farming and natural wetlands. Livestock release another one-fifth of the total, and the energy industry emits another one-fifth. The remainder, in about equal shares, comes from landfills, waste treatment, biomass burning, and additional natural sources (Houweling, 1999). Although methane is a tiny fraction of the atmosphere, it is very effective in absorbing infrared radiation. When methane burns, its carbon converts into CO_2. Chemical reactions initiated by hydroxyl ($OH-$) ions, which are present in the atmosphere and the ocean, also eventually transform the carbon in methane into CO_2. A methane molecule that enters the atmosphere generally survives a little less than ten years before being converted to CO_2 through such reactions.

Nitrous oxide (N_2O) is used as an anesthetic in dentistry and other surgery. It is known as "laughing gas," but its greenhouse effects are no laughing matter, because it is hundreds of times more powerful than CO_2. Nitrous oxide concentration in the atmosphere rose from an estimated preindustrial value of 270 ppb to 319 ppb in 2005 (IPCC, 2007). Bacteria in soils and oceans emit an estimated 15,000 metric tons of N_2O per year. Cultivation of the soil stimulates microbial activity, enhancing the production of nitrous oxide, especially when nitrogenous fertilizers are applied. The gas is also generated by livestock and by the burning of fossil fuels and biomass (wood, charcoal, and agricultural and municipal waste). Anthropogenic emissions of N_2O are estimated to be about 2,000 tons/year. The gas is distinct from the poisonous nitrogen oxide pollutants (NO and NO_2) released by power plants and in automobile exhaust.

Other GHGs, mainly **compounds of fluorine**, are released in small quantities by anthropogenic activities. They include hydrofluorocarbons (HFCs) and perfluorocarbons (PFCs) that are used as refrigerants and propellants (in fire extinguishers and other aerosols). These compounds have replaced chlorofluorocarbons (CFCs), like freon, that damage the ozone layer of the stratosphere. CFCs have been banned under the terms of the Montreal Protocol that went into effect in 1989. However, the HFCs and PFCs that have replaced them, if released into the air, have long-lived greenhouse effects thousands of times more powerful than CO_2. Therefore, the relatively low-cost measures available to control the emissions of these gases can deliver a big payoff in reducing global warming. The same is true of sulfur hexafluoride (SF_6), which is the most potent GHG yet evaluated. It is used in electrical applications as an insulator or dielectric (a substance that holds an electric field without passing a current). Efforts to reduce leakages of SF_6 into the air from these applications have proved successful, as shown by a voluntary program among U.S. utilities that reduced emissions from 17% to 9% between 1999 and 2002 (Blackman and Kantamaneni, 2003). Sulfur hexafluoride was also a replacement chemical, used instead of the toxic polychlorinated biphenyls (PCBs), which damage the skin and the liver. No natural processes emit HFCs, PFCs, or SF_6. Each of these gases, along with CO_2, methane, and nitrous oxide, come under the terms of the Kyoto Protocol, as discussed in Part Two of the book.

Ozone (O_3) also absorbs infrared emissions from the surface of the Earth, but unlike other GHGs, it also absorbs radiation from the Sun. In the stratosphere, ozone blocks enough of the Sun's ultraviolet radiation to cool the planet as well as to protect life. However, when ozone accumulates as smog near ground level, it is not only harmful to breathe but also provides substantial net greenhouse warming. Ozone is produced from chemical reactions involving emissions of nitrogen oxides, carbon monoxide, and hydrocarbons, which were especially prevalent in vehicle exhausts before the use of catalytic converters. Even today, they continue to be emitted from vehicles, though at lower rates.

WATER VAPOR AND CLOUDS

An estimated 1.4 billion cubic kilometers of water is present on or near the surface of the Earth. The oceans hold 97% of the total, whereas 2% is stored in ice sheets and 0.7% in groundwater. Trace percentages only remain for lakes and rivers, the atmosphere, and the biosphere. Each year, about 0.5 million cubic kilometers of water evaporates, mostly from the ocean, of course, and an equal amount falls in various forms of precipitation. Evaporation absorbs heat energy, whereas the condensation of vapor into liquid water releases heat. Evaporation in the tropics and precipitation of the resulting water vapor at higher latitudes is a major channel for the transfer of heat on the planet.

Water vapor averages about 0.25% of the atmosphere by volume (Trenberth, 2005) – about six times the concentration of CO_2. Unlike other GHGs, water vapor molecules remain aloft for only a short time; on average, they fall as precipitation about nine days after becoming airborne. As a result, the concentration of water vapor varies substantially across regions. Water vapor is not directly released in significant volume by human activities.

Warmer air can hold substantially more water vapor, roughly 7% more for an increase of 1°C.[1] Relative humidity, which is the quantity of water vapor divided by the capacity of that air to hold vapor, has remained fairly constant as global temperatures have risen over recent decades. The greenhouse effects of water vapor feedbacks may have provided nearly half the swings in global temperature during the Ice Ages. Recent satellite data indicate that the average water vapor concentration of the atmosphere may have risen by about 2% over the last ten to fifteen years (Soden, 2005). Observations over the last couple decades indicate that average rates of evaporation and precipitation may have risen about as fast as the water-carrying capacity of air, although models predict a slower pickup over the long term (Previdi, 2008).

Aside from its presence in the atmosphere in vapor form, water is also suspended in the air as droplets of liquid water and tiny ice crystals, which we observe as clouds. However, less than 1% of the H_2O in the atmosphere is in liquid or ice form. On average, clouds cover about half the surface of the Earth. They double the planet's average albedo, from 15% to 30%.

---

[1] The "Clausius-Clapeyron" relationship indicates that under typical conditions on Earth, a rise in air temperature of about 3°C would allow an increase of about 20% in the concentration of water vapor (the saturation vapor pressure) above a liquid surface (Hartmann, 1994).

The condensation of water vapor into droplets or ice crystals depends on relative humidity, which is the amount of vapor in the air relative to the ability of the air to hold water as vapor, given its temperature and pressure. Because relative humidity remains fairly constant as the planet's average temperature changes, it is unclear how cloud cover would respond to global warming. Moreover, the greenhouse effects of clouds are ambiguous. Low clouds (cumulus or stratus) are good reflectors of sunlight and do not absorb much infrared radiation; they, therefore, provide a net cooling effect. Thin cirrus clouds are more transparent to sunlight and more effective at capturing outgoing heat radiation; they provide net warming. Although all clouds taken together lower the temperature at the surface of the Earth, it is unclear whether incremental increases in cloud cover would cool or warm the planet.

RADIATIVE FORCING MEASURES

Scientists have devised several methods for comparing GHGs and their potential effects on global average temperature. One procedure is to estimate the amount of radiation that the gas delivers to Earth's surface, a measure called radiative forcing.

The Sun is the primary source of the radiative forcing. It provides an average of 342 Watts per square meter (W/m^2) to the planet, but 30% of that radiation is reflected away before it can warm the surface. After accounting for albedo effects, therefore, solar radiation provides 240 W/m^2 of radiative forcing on average. If that were our only source of heat, the temperature at Earth's surface would be about −18°C (0°F). As noted earlier, however, GHG boosts the radiation received at the surface by enough to give us a comfortable global average temperature of 14.4°C (58°F).

The radiative forcing of a GHG includes only the direct change it causes in the radiation received at the surface of the Earth, ignoring climate feedbacks from temperature responses. In current conditions, climate models typically indicate a global temperature response of about 0.75°C for each W/m^2 of radiative forcing, no matter which GHG is involved (IPCC, 2007).

The radiative forcing concept can at times be confusing. For instance, the word "forcing" sometimes refers to prime movers of climate changes, as distinguished from mere feedback effects. However, as noted earlier, increases in the atmospheric concentrations of GHGs can be caused either by feedback effects (such as the warming of the ocean and the melting of permafrost) or by sources not associated with climate feedbacks, such as volcanic releases and coal burning. Nevertheless, the word "forcing" is typically used in either case.

Another potential confusion involves the distinction between radiative efficiency and radiative forcing. Radiative efficiency is the instantaneous change in surface radiation from a one-unit increase in the atmospheric concentration of a GHG, given prevailing conditions. Radiative efficiency varies depending on the amount of the gas already in the air and the presence of other gases that can substitute for it. For instance, one more ppm of CO_2 is less effective at finding and capturing outgoing heat radiation if there is already a lot of CO_2 in the air doing the same job. For current conditions, the radiative efficiencies of methane and nitrous oxide are about 24 and 200 times that of CO_2, respectively.[2]

Radiative forcing, by contrast, typically measures anthropogenic effects relative to the atmospheric concentrations of GHGs estimated for the designated preindustrial year of 1750. Computing radiative forcing over long time periods requires models that take account of changing concentrations and the evolution of radiative efficiencies. The cumulative anthropogenic forcings from 1750 through 2005 have been estimated to be 1.66 W/m² for CO_2, 0.48 W/m² for methane, and 0.16 W/m² for nitrous oxide (IPCC, 2007). Other GHGs, including ozone-depleting substances but excluding water vapor, contributed an additional 0.35 W/m² in 2005. Ground-level ozone also added about 0.35 W/m² of greenhouse forcing. Human activities also boosted the planet's albedo through the production of aerosols and the cutting of forests, reducing radiation received at the surface by an estimated 1.4 W/m². The net anthropogenic effect in 2005 from all these sources was estimated to be 1.6 W/m² of warming, about the same as the forcing by CO_2 alone. This would imply an anthropogenic boost to the global average temperature of at least 0.8°C – the entire measured warming since the late 1800s. Indeed, the Sun is now estimated to have contributed only 0.12 W/m² of additional radiative forcing since 1750.

Other confusions can arise in trying to calculate the total greenhouse role of a particular gas. The bands of the radiation spectrum that different gases can absorb overlap to some extent. For that reason, the overall greenhouse effect of a particular gas can be calculated by giving it credit either for *any* outgoing radiation it *could trap* or only for the radiation it absorbs that *no other gas could have captured*. For instance, by one estimate, if water vapor were the only GHG in the atmosphere, it could provide 85% of the current greenhouse effect. However, if water vapor were removed entirely from the atmosphere, other GHGs would pick up part of its role, and Earth

---

[2] To be more precise, a 1 ppm increase in concentration would produce an estimated surface radiation change of 0.0155 W/m² for CO_2, 0.37 W/m² for methane, and 3.1 W/m² for nitrous oxide (IPCC, 2001, table 6.7).

would still have 34% of its greenhouse warming. Thus, water vapor could be thought to account for something between 66% and 85% of the total greenhouse effect. For CO_2, the same calculations indicate a contribution to greenhouse effects of between 9% and 26% (Schmidt, 2006).

CO_2 EQUIVALENT

Another area of potential confusion involves attempts to combine all GHGs in a measure known as the equivalent amount of CO_2 (CO_2e). In constructing this measure, key GHGs are converted into the amount of CO_2 that would provide the same radiative forcing over a given time period. Conversion factors for different gases are called Global Warming Potentials, and they differ depending on time interval. For instance, methane has an atmospheric lifetime of only about ten years, so its average radiative forcing decreases substantially if longer time periods are used. An interval of one hundred years is often used in constructing CO_2e. Water vapor and ozone-depleting substances are not generally included in CO_2e measures, nor are the cooling effects of aerosols.

Radiative efficiencies are measured for a unit increase in the concentration of a gas by *volume*. In computing Global Warming Potentials, equal *weights* of gases are compared. Methane has a low molecular weight of 16, compared with 44 for CO_2, so an equal weight of each gas implies a much larger volume of methane. Averaged over a hundred years, a kilogram of methane nevertheless provides about twenty-three times the radiative forcing of a kilogram of CO_2, similar to the difference in radiative efficiency. Nitrous oxide, with a molecular weight of 40 and an average lifetime of 115 years, has a one-hundred-year Global Warming Potential of about 296 times CO_2 (IPCC, 2007). To add to the complexity, the methods used to construct CO_2e sometimes differ across studies. For instance, Stern (2006) used radiative efficiencies rather than Global Warming Potentials.

Additional confusion may arise because CO_2 and non-CO_2 gases are treated differently in the construction of CO_2e. The standard measure includes the overall concentration of CO_2 in the atmosphere but only the difference between preindustrial and current concentrations for non-CO_2 gases (IPCC, 2001).[3] The CO_2 concentration as of 2005 was 380 ppm.

---

[3] In particular, the exponential of the sum of the changes since 1750 in the radiative forcings of Kyoto Protocol GHGs is multiplied by the 1750 concentration of CO_2 alone. The European Environment Agency gives a summary presentation at: http://themes.eea. europa.eu/IMS/ISpecs/ISpecification20041007131717/guide_summary_plus_public

Adding the incremental increase in non-CO_2 gases since 1750, the level of CO_2e was estimated to be about 455 ppm for that year (IPCC, 2007, WG3). As noted earlier, however, after taking into account the albedo effects of aerosols and land use changes, as well as the greenhouse effects of ozone and ozone-depleting substances, which are not included in CO_2e, the net radiative forcing by humans is currently about equivalent to the change in CO_2 alone in the atmosphere.

FOUR

Emitting Economic Sectors

An understanding of the economic activities responsible for emissions of greenhouse gas (GHG) is essential for assessing the potential for emission mitigation and the likely costs of such policies. Emitting activities are pervasive throughout the economy, involving nearly all types of production and use of energy, as well as agriculture, industrial processing, and waste management, as discussed further in this chapter.

OVERVIEW OF THE ENERGY SECTOR

In 2005, total anthropogenic emissions of GHGs were estimated at about 44 Gt of CO_2e (CAIT, 2010). GHG is emitted with energy use, other industrial processes, deforestation, agriculture, and waste management. Approximately 55% of total emissions were from the production and use of energy. When energy is derived from nuclear, hydroelectric, or other renewable resources, no substantial GHG is emitted. Combustion of fossil fuels, however, produces about 80% of the world's energy. (Unless otherwise specified, data in this chapter are from IPCC, 2007, WG3.)

Energy use can be attributed to three broad sectors of final demand: buildings, industry, and transportation. In 2004, about 40% of the world's energy was employed for the lighting, space heating, water heating, and cooking in residential and commercial buildings (including the energy consumed in creating the electric power used). Another one-third of the world's energy was used by industry, including iron and steel, other metals, chemicals and fertilizers, petroleum refineries, cement, lime, glass and ceramics, and pulp and paper. The remaining one-fourth of the energy use was for the transportation sector – mainly combustion of fuels by road vehicles, trains, airplanes, and boats.

In transforming fossil fuel energy into more usable forms, more than one-third of the available energy is lost, mainly as waste heat. Electricity production is particularly inefficient, with two-thirds of the energy consumed never making it to a power grid. Additional heat is lost in the final stage of energy use. Automobile engines generally deliver less than half of the energy of combustion to the power train. Light bulbs are extremely inefficient: 98% of the energy consumed by a standard bulb is lost as heat. Compact fluorescent bulbs produce less waste heat and can therefore provide equivalent lighting using only about one-fifth of the electricity.

Table 4.1 provides a breakdown of the fossil fuels and other sources of the world's energy, along with the end uses. The first row of the table shows the amount of energy extracted from various fuels and other sources, measured in exa-joules (EJ), which is a billion billion joules.[1] One watt is a joule per second, so 1 EJ is equivalent to 278 billion kilowatt hours (kWh). Out of the global 2004 energy use of about 470 EJ, petroleum accounted for 35%, coal approximately for one-fourth, and natural gas for one-fifth. Roughly 80% of our energy consumption came from these three fossil fuels, and the

Table 4.1. *Energy sources and end-use sectors (2004)*

	Oil	Coal	N. Gas	Biomass	Nuclear	Hydro	Other renewables
Energy Used (EJ)	165	116.5	95.3	49.5	29.9	10.1	2.4
CO_2 Release (GT)	10.2	10.6	5.3	n.a.	0	n.a.	0
End Uses (% shares):							
Losses	21	56	36	9	70	0	0
Buildings	14	16	32	75	17	57	63
Industry	18	27	30	15	13	43	38
Transport	48	1	2	1	0	0	0
Total	100	100	100	100	100	100	100
Electricity (% of total fuel use):							
Losses	5	47	27	4	70	0	0
Buildings	1	12	7	1	17	57	50
Industry	1	9	5	1	13	43	38
Total	7	68	38	6	100	100	88

Note: In 2004, estimated total energy use was 470 EJ, GHG emissions were 49 Gt of CO_2e, and electricity supply was 17.4 PWh.
Source: Adapted from IPCC (2007), WG III, Figure 4.4

[1] In the metric system, if you multiple a unit by 1,000, it gets a new prefix. Going up in sequence, the prefixes are: kilo, mega, giga, tera, peta, exa, zetta. Also, 1.055 EJ is equivalent to a quadrillion Btu.

CO_2 emitted from their combustion was about half of overall anthropogenic GHG emissions (in CO_2 equivalents [see Chapter 3]) in 2004. Total CO_2 emissions from petroleum and coal were each about twice those from natural gas.

A little more than 10% of the world's energy supply in 2004 came from biomass (mainly wood, along with some fuels from crops and waste materials). Although CO_2 is emitted from the combustion of biomass, the same materials would release CO_2 (or worse, methane) through natural processes as well. Therefore, biomass combustion is not considered a net anthropogenic source of GHG. Nuclear reactors (just 6% of total energy consumption) of course emit no GHG, but they lose a high proportion of their energy (70%) as waste heat. Hydroelectric plants represent only 2% of global energy sources. Hydro power might seem emission-free, but extensive shallow reservoirs created by some dams can release methane; for this reason, large hydro projects with significant water storage are not eligible for offsets under the Kyoto Protocol. Other renewable energy sources, including wind, solar, and geothermal projects, provided only approximately 0.5% of the total supply of energy in 2004.

The bottom portion of the table shows the percentage of the total energy from each source that was used for the production of electricity. As indicated in the last row, nuclear and hydroelectric energy are employed entirely for electricity generation, but the electric power industry accounts for only about two-thirds of the world's consumption of coal. Although power plants using fossil fuels, biomass, and uranium lose nearly 70% of their energy production in the form of waste heat, no such heat losses occur with hydroelectric and other renewable sources. Of course, only a small share of the energy in the movement of water and wind and in solar radiation is converted into electricity, but that energy would be lost even if humans weren't trying to capture it. Because renewables do not waste energy, their shares of electricity supplied are larger than their shares of energy used in the production of power. A homeowner's electricity use is often measured in kilowatt hours. In 2004, the world's total electricity output was about 17.4 petawatt hours (PWh), where one PWh equals a trillion kWh. The portions supplied were about 40% for coal, 20% for natural gas, 16% each for nuclear and hydroelectric, 6% for petroleum, and 2% for other renewables.

Compared with the alternatives, fossil fuels are a cheap and convenient source of energy if the costs of associated greenhouse effects are ignored. Will we run out of fossil fuels before they cause excessive global warming? In investigating that question, a distinction needs to be made between the proven *reserves* and the total potential *resource* of a fuel. To be classified as a proven reserve, the amount of the fuel must be known, the method of recovery needs to be identified and linked to currently available technology, and the recovery costs must be evaluated and found to be economic. Potential resources are much larger than reserves. However, resource estimates are uncertain because new discoveries may still occur and many identified resources have not yet been carefully assessed. Some observed resources may remain too costly to develop for many decades, whereas others may never be exploited because of environmental concerns. However, as the supplies of traditional fuel sources dwindle and new extraction methods are developed, unconventional resources are likely to become a major agenda item for social policy. Estimates of the total potential resources of the main fossil fuels are summarized in Table 4.2 and discussed further in the chapter.

PETROLEUM

The main products of oil refineries are gasoline, diesel, and jet fuel. Outside the transportation industry, petroleum is also the source of fuel oil, which is used primarily to heat residential and commercial buildings. Some fuel oil is burned to run steam turbines for the generation of a small portion of total

Table 4.2. *Estimates of total fossil fuel resources*

	Share of 2005 energy supply %	Total resource (EJ)	Years' supply (at 2005 rate)	Potential CO_2 (Gt)
Conventional Sources				
Petroleum	33	10,000	63	763
Coal	25	> 100,000	> 833	9,200
Gas	21	13,500	135	707
Subtotal	79	123,500	n.a.	10,670
Unconventional Sources				
Petroleum	< 1	35,000	n.a.	High
Coal	0	32,000	n.a.	2,900
Gas	0	> 76,000	n.a.	High
Subtotal	< 1	> 143,000	n.a.	?
Estimated Total	~ 80	266,500	n.a.	?

Note: Unless later removed by natural processes or human sequestration activities, each extra 7.8 Gt of CO_2 would raise the atmospheric concentration of the gas by 1 ppm.
Source: Adapted from IPCC (2007), WG III, Table 4.2.

electricity supplies. Combustion of petroleum products releases mainly CO_2, but also some methane and nitrous oxide. Venting or flaring of methane at oil wells accounts for about 0.3 Gt of CO_2e per year. A small portion of refinery output is feedstock for making petrochemical products (including plastics, fibers, lubricants, detergents, and adhesives); these products store carbon rather than emitting it as CO_2.

Observers widely suspect that, for strategic purposes, national governments sometimes deliberately misreport their proven reserves of crude oil. For instance, OPEC countries have at times abruptly raised their proven reserve figures to get a larger production quota from the cartel. That said, estimated proven reserves of conventional oil as of the end of 2007 were over 1.2 trillion barrels (BP, 2008), equivalent to around 8,000 EJ of energy. New discoveries of oil have been lower than the volumes extracted over the last two decades or so. However, improved technology has enabled commercial exploitation of additional deposits in existing fields and, as a result, proven reserves have edged higher over time. Including probable and possible reserves in the future, estimates of the total remaining resources of conventional oil vary over a wide range. The IPCC (2007) reports a very conservative figure of 10,000 EJ (1.6 trillion barrels), as noted in Table 4.2, but some estimates are as much as 70% larger. At the 2007 rate of use, it would take fifty-three years to run through the IPCC's estimate of total oil resources. However, the IPCC notes that conventional oil could actually be gone in 30 to 40 years, given the number of new vehicles that China, India, and other rapidly developing countries may be putting on the road.

Unconventional sources of petroleum include oil sands and oil shale. As indicated in Table 4.2, these resources are roughly three times the remaining conventional oil deposits. Oil sands (also called tar sands or heavy oil) are a mixture of heavy crude along with clay, sand, and water. They are currently being strip-mined in Canada. The extraction requires removing forests and peat bogs and then transporting the extracted oil sand to processing plants with conveyor belts or trucks. Hot water is added to the sands and the mixture is agitated, allowing the separation of bitumen (heavy oil). Because the recovered bitumen is too viscous to flow through pipelines, it must be diluted with lighter fuels. Before it can be processed in a refinery, it also needs to be heated to break its exceptionally long hydrocarbon chains. About one-fourth of the bitumen remains embedded in the residual sands, which are typically deposited in "tailing ponds" along with other impurities and toxins.

However, most of the oil sands in Canada, as well as the large deposits that have been identified in Venezuela, are buried too deep for such surface mining operations. In these cases, extraction typically involves steam injection; a much smaller portion of the oil is then recovered (less than 10%).

Natural gas is used extensively in the mining and processing of oil sands. It is the fuel employed to boil water and then heat the bitumen during upgrading. The energy requirements to produce a barrel of synthetic oil from oil sands, and the related CO_2 emissions, are three-to-four times higher than those involved in producing oil by conventional means.

Oil shale is found in many places around the world. Small-scale mining operations have been undertaken in Estonia, Israel, Germany, and China. Oil shale is sedimentary rock containing a solid, organic-rich substance called kerogen. The organic materials in kerogen do not dissolve with the addition of hot water or other solvents, but if enough heat is applied, kerogen will release gases that can be distilled into bitumen. The bitumen is then processed and upgraded to produce synthetic oil. Because of the difficulties and the high temperatures required for extraction, it takes about five times more energy (and CO_2 emissions) to produce a barrel of oil from shale than from conventional sources. Recently, abundant sources of natural gas have been found in shale.

COAL

As indicated in Table 4.1, coal is burned mainly to generate electricity. Lower- and middle-grade coals (lignite and bituminous) are employed for that purpose. Bituminous coal can also be heated in the absence of oxygen to remove moisture and volatile components in order to produce coke, which is the main fuel used to smelt iron in blast furnaces. High-grade (anthracite) coals, which have the fewest impurities, are used mainly for home heating.

In standard power plants, coal is pulverized to the consistency of powder and then blown into a furnace. Water circulating in pipes along the sides of the furnace is converted to steam at around 370°C and a pressure of about 220 bar. This is just below the "critical point" for water (the minimum temperature and pressure at which a fluid's gas and liquid phases are indistinguishable). The steam then runs through a turbine to produce electricity. Whereas these standard plants can convert only up to approximately 38% of the energy content of coal into electricity, plants designed for "supercritical" temperature and pressure combinations of around 600°C and 280 bar can achieve efficiencies higher than 40%.

Coal can also be heated to high enough temperatures to release a mixture of carbon monoxide and hydrogen, a synthetic gas fuel. Biomass materials can be gasified similarly. The resulting "syngas" can then be injected with air, ignited, and run through a gas turbine to generate electricity. Exhausts from the gas turbine are hot enough to boil water. The resulting steam can also be sent through a turbine to generate another round of electricity. Simultaneously running both gas and steam turbines is called a "combined cycle." Although gasification requires additional energy input, operating a combined cycle improves efficiency. Integrated Gasification Combined Cycle (IGCC) plants also facilitate separation and removal of sulfur, mercury, and potentially CO_2. Because of the high investment and operating costs, very few IGCC demonstration plants have been put into operation as of yet.

Energy efficiencies of 85% and higher can be achieved in coal power plants that are able to use what would otherwise be waste heat to warm buildings. These "combined heat and power," or cogeneration plants, are operating in local areas of some cities, in hospitals, prisons, and some industrial establishments. The heat must be used nearby to avoid substantial transmission losses and insulation costs. Combined heat-and-power plants account for less than 10% of total electricity production.

Unlike oil, the world has abundant resources of coal. Proven reserves of coal have a total energy content of 22,000 EJ, enough to last 180 years at the 2005 rate of consumption. Many other coal deposits have been identified, but their technological and economic potential have not yet been fully assessed because there is no imminent need to use them. As shown in Table 4.2, total coal resources are thought to exceed 100,000 EJ that, if burned, would release up to 13,000 Gt of CO_2. This is far more than the roughly 3,000 Gt of CO_2 now in the atmosphere. The U.S. has about one-fourth of the world's total resources of coal, followed by Russia (17%) and China (13%).

As indicated in Table 4.2, global energy consumption through the combustion of coal was about 30% less than that from oil in 2005. However, because coal has, on average, nearly one-third more carbon per unit of energy than petroleum, total CO_2 emissions from coal were slightly higher than those from oil. Carbon capture and storage (CCS) is widely viewed as the key technological development that will allow the use of the world's coal resources without causing severe damage from climate change. Considerable research is underway to try to find ways to reduce the heavy energy requirements of capturing and compressing CO_2 in order to facilitate its transportation and storage. At present, CO_2 is being removed from flue gases using chemical solvents (e.g., monoethanolamine), but new materials are being investigated that could potentially reduce the energy costs of separating the CO_2 from the solvent material (Howell, 2009). In comparison with scrubbing CO_2 from flue gases at pulverizing coal plants, capture is easier at the higher CO_2 concentrations and temperatures at gasification plants. However, even with IGCC operations, the likely procedure will be to absorb CO_2 from a mixture of gases, then separate the CO_2 from the absorbing material through further heating, which will take more energy.

Issues related to potential leakage from storage sites are also under investigation. Some CO_2 is now being injected into oil wells and natural gas fields to try to boost recovery rates. Underground storage sites could also include spent coal mines and salt domes. The geological trapping mechanisms must be secure enough to prevent the escape of CO_2 for many, many years, because a sudden release – with an earthquake, for instance – could be asphyxiating. Because of such risks, the acceptability of CO_2 storage sites and pipelines to local populations may also limit the use of the technology. Storage in the ocean has the disadvantages of increasing acidification of the ocean and possible eventual release of CO_2 back into the atmosphere. Burying CO2 deep under the ocean floor may prove costly and could disturb methane deposits there. Because of the storage problem, biological removal of CO_2 might eventually prove preferable. It may be possible to pass flue gases through algae or bacterial solutions to produce biodiesel fuels, for instance, with the residues used as animal feed. While the CO_2 would not thereby be permanently stored, its reuse could avoid emissions from the combustion of other fossil fuels.

Liquid fuels can be produced directly from coal using chemical processes or indirectly after gasification. Coal-to-liquids plants may be one way that the world copes with the diminishing supply of oil. If the production of liquid fuels from coal takes off, however, carbon capture and storage will be necessary to avoid a major ratcheting up of CO_2 emissions; the large energy requirements for coal-to-liquids operations would otherwise greatly increase CO_2 emissions relative to those associated with the recovery and processing of oil. Even with CO_2 capture at coal-to-liquids plants, however, the combustion of resulting fuel in the transportation sector would continue to release CO_2.

NATURAL GAS

Natural gas has the lowest carbon content of the fossil fuels, approximately 25% less than oil and 40% less than coal per unit of energy.[2] The reason is

---

[2] The carbon content of fuels, per unit of energy, averages: 15.3 kg per billion joules (GJ) for natural gas, 20 kg/GJ for oil, and 26 kg/GJ for coal (WRI, 2006 and IPCC, 1997). By weight, carbon content averages 85% for crude oil and 74.6% for coal, using standard quality "ton equivalents," which hold 42 GJ of energy per metric ton of oil (6.841 barrels) and 29.3 GJ per ton of coal. Carbon is 75% of methane by weight.

the relatively high ratio of hydrogen to carbon in methane (CH_4), the purest form of natural gas. In addition, natural gas operations are more efficient, in part because gas can be burned at more elevated temperatures than coal or fuel oil (1,000°C or higher). Combined-cycle operations are therefore standard, because the exhaust from a gas turbine is generally hot enough to boil water for a second steam turbine. Efficiencies approaching 60% can thereby be achieved.

Because of the lower carbon content, natural gas was responsible for only half of the global CO_2 emissions of coal in 2004, despite accounting for more than 80% of the energy used in burning coal, as indicated on Table 4.1. Many observers believe that a substantial increase in the share of electricity generated by natural gas and a reduction in coal's share will be needed to reduce emissions until improved CCS technology is available to make coal more environmentally friendly. Both coal mining and the extraction and processing of natural gas also result in some emissions of methane. In the case of natural gas, approximately 1% of its methane content generally escapes into the atmosphere.

Proven reserves of natural gas are reported to be around 6,800 EJ, but total resources from conventional drilling sites are estimated at 13,500 EJ, which would last about 120 years at the 2007 rate of use (BP, 2008). Most of the identified resources are in the Middle East and Eastern Europe. Natural gas is also abundant in shale formations in many locations around the world. Recent advances in hydraulic fracturing of shale and in horizontal drilling have made extraction of natural gas from these formations more attractive economically.

Unless a natural gas source is connected directly to a major gas pipeline, transportation becomes a problem. It would take over 600 tankers of methane, in uncompressed gaseous form, to carry as much energy as one tanker of liquid petroleum. For that reason, natural gas is generally liquefied before transporting from regions far from pipelines. Liquefaction requires removing impurities and then cooling to less than −160°C (when at atmospheric pressures). To avoid evaporation, the liquefied natural gas (LNG) must be transported in cryogenic containers. The energy supplied to liquefy and transport LNG can raise the GHG emissions from natural gas use to 70% or more of those from coal. LNG accounts for less than 10% of the current global supply of natural gas, but its share is growing rapidly.

LNG needs to be distinguished from liquefied petroleum gas (LPG), which is composed of propane, butane, and similar refinery byproducts. At ambient temperatures, LPG remains liquid under only moderate pressure (20 bar or less), and therefore can be stored safely in ordinary steel containers. The share of LPG in total production of natural gas is holding fairly steady at approximately 10%.

In the LNG process, gas is converted to a liquid only temporarily for the purpose of transportation. An alternative "gas-to-liquids" process turns natural gas into a product that is intended to be used as liquid fuel. However, conversion of methane to a liquid requires high temperatures and is difficult to control using current technology. Synthetic gases can also be converted to liquids in a manner similar to the coal-to-liquids process mentioned earlier. Exhausts from oil refineries include hydrogen and carbon monoxide, which can be converted into liquid diesel fuel through the Fischer-Tropsch process that involves catalyzed chemical reactions at high temperatures and pressures. The process was named after the German scientists who invented it in the 1920s. Diesel fuel thus produced has a low level of sulfur and other pollutants. Although only a small amount of gas-to-liquids production has occurred to date, many new projects are under development in major oil-exporting countries.

The methane embedded in coal seams is one type of unconventional natural gas resource. The total energy content of such coal-bed methane may exceed 8,000 EJ. In most of the world's coal mines, however, methane escapes freely into the air. Sudden methane releases are a major source of coal mine accidents. Estimated global emissions of coal-bed methane were one-fourth of a Gt of CO_2e in 2000. In some mines, however, methane is already being captured. Environmental problems can nevertheless ensue, because water must be pumped out of the mines before methane capture, and a variety of toxins may be present in the water.

The largest potential natural gas resource is methane buried under permafrost and in ocean sediments. As mentioned earlier, at very cold temperatures and high pressures, methane combines with water to form lattice-like structures that clump into blocks of material called clathrates or hydrates. The total amount of methane hydrates in ocean sediments is unknown, but estimates of the potential energy content range from around 60,000 EJ to 800,000 EJ. If technology were developed to exploit all these sources, the potential CO_2 release would be from 3,000 to 42,000 Gt, enough to raise the atmospheric concentration 100% to 1,400% above current levels.

BIOMASS

As is evident from Table 4.1, biomass accounted for a little more than 10% of total energy supply in 2004. Wood and wood products were 87% of the total estimated use of biomass energy, with animal dung, straw, fuel crops, and municipal waste processing each taking roughly equal shares of the rest. Modern facilities are producing increasing volumes of solid, liquid, and gaseous bio-fuels, including pellets, wood chips, ethanol, diesel, and gases from landfills and other municipal wastes. Prior to processing, bio-mass is more costly to transport than fossil fuels per unit of embedded energy. Efficient use of these resources, therefore, requires local combustion or transformation into another energy-carrying form. From ancient times, biomass in the form of wood and animal dung has been used for heating homes and cooking. Modern applications include co-firing with coal in the production of electricity. Biomass is now also an energy source for some pulp mills and food-processing plants.

The most highly publicized growth area for biomass is its role as a fuel for transportation. With substantial government support in the form of incentives and protective tariffs, ethanol production has been expanding rapidly using sugar cane in Brazil and corn in the United States. Ethanol is used directly in internal combustion engines in Brazil, whereas it is blended with petroleum-based gasoline in the United States. The overall CO_2 savings from ethanol combustion are reduced after taking account of the GHG released during cultivation of the source crop, transportation of the output, and production of the liquid fuel. The CO_2 emissions from combustion of the biomass itself, however, would likely have occurred in any case through natural organic decay. Indeed, combustion could even imply less release of methane and thus lower CO_2e emissions than might have otherwise occurred. Finally, although substantial amounts of CO_2 are released when trees are cut for firewood, these emissions are generally tallied under defor-estation rather than the energy sector.

NUCLEAR POWER

Nuclear power represented about 6% of energy use and 16% of electricity production in 2004. Nuclear plants were built at a rapid clip after the surge in oil prices in the early 1970s, but in the last couple of decades, construc-tion of new plants has generally tailed off except in China. Reduced com-petitiveness and concerns about safety following the accidents at the Three Mile Island in 1979 and Chernobyl in 1986 contributed to the slowdown. However, a number of new projects with improved safety features and effi-ciency are now being developed, partly in response to the rising prices of fossil fuels. Nevertheless, the disposal of nuclear wastes remains an unsolved environmental issue. In some countries, storage sites have been found for lower-level wastes. However, in the absence of agreements on long-term repositories, high-level nuclear wastes continue to be held on site at the power plants that generated them. Reprocessing spent fuel would reduce long-term storage requirements but increase the production of weapons-grade plutonium, heightening concerns about the possible proliferation of nuclear weapons.

Known resources of uranium are likely to be ample for hundreds of years, especially given likely improvements in reactor efficiencies. Uranium mining, as well as the construction and decommissioning of nuclear power plants, are responsible for a small amount of GHG emissions. However, these ancillary GHG emissions, when spread over the life cycle of a nuclear power plant, are generally thought to be as low as those associated with wind power.[3]

HYDROELECTRIC

Because hydroelectric systems do not waste any energy by producing heat, hydro power was able to match the share of global electricity supplied by nuclear plants in 2004 (16%) despite having a much smaller share of total energy use (only 2%). Unlike most other renewable resources, hydro systems provide a continuous power source for base load requirements. They are also flexible, because the flow of water through the turbines can be adjusted to ratchet up production for peak demands, particularly if the system includes a supplementary storage reservoir.

Plants now under construction would boost global hydroelectric capacity by about 25%, whereas other potential sites and efficiency improvements in existing systems could more than double the current power output. However, construction of large-scale hydroelectric systems may be held back in some cases because of local opposition, particularly when people would be forced to move from their homes and when farming, fisheries, and ecosystems would be impaired. Moreover, as the better sites are taken, new facilities will be more costly to construct, produce less output, and require longer transmission lines to reach the power grid.

Smaller scale, so-called run-of-the-river hydro systems that include no dam or reservoir could also be installed at many sites. Some applications involve remote locations lacking other sources of electricity. In other cases, however, run-of-the-river systems may be employed as a supplementary power source. For instance, turbines have already been placed in the East

---

[3] Lifecycle emissions from wind turbines have been estimated to be between 13 and 156 g of CO_2e per kWh, depending on location (Liberman, 2003).

River next to Manhattan Island on an experimental basis. Systems located near a river mouth can take advantage of the velocity boost provided by tidal forces, and some "tidal-stream" systems may even be designed to flip direction for flood and ebb tides. In some locations, narrow estuaries and strong tides allow construction of barrages that operate in a manner similar to river dams. However, the intraday power output then varies with the tides, and environmental issues can arise because of fish mortality and the blockage of sediment flow to the sea.

Experiments to generate electricity from waves have also been conducted. Substantial challenges are involved in constructing systems that can withstand storms and salt water corrosion and also capture power efficiently from ocean sources that fluctuate in strength and direction.

Although some GHG is emitted in producing and transporting materials for the construction of dams, the amounts are insignificant when taking account of the fact that such projects have a potential useful life of up to a hundred years or more. However, increased ongoing emissions of methane can occur if dams create shallow reservoirs over extended areas, especially at tropical latitudes. Creation of deep reservoirs, however, may put existing wetlands under enough water to reduce natural methane emissions. The GHG emissions of hydro power therefore need to be evaluated on a project-by-project basis.

OTHER RENEWABLE ENERGY SOURCES

Even though wind, solar, and geothermal sources of energy have been growing rapidly, they still, combined, accounted for only about 0.5% of total energy supply in 2004. The cost and usefulness of these energy sources depend substantially on location. For large-scale applications, winds must be strong and steady, sunlight must be plentiful, or geological hot spots must be available. Because the best sites are typically not close to consumers, the usefulness of these renewables as wholesale power sources also depends on the adequacy of the transmission grid.

Modern wind turbines incorporate design features that minimize bird mortality, including slow-turning rotors and towers contoured to avoid providing perches. Efficiency has also improved to the point that, in the best locations, wind is competitive with fossil fuel power. Construction of taller towers has been a key technological advance, as the wind is stronger at higher altitudes. However, wind will remain an intermittent source of energy requiring supplementation by more flexible generation sources unless further technological advances allow inexpensive power storage.

Moreover, advantageous sites for locating wind resources, including off-shore facilities, will require construction of new transmission lines. The expansion of wind facilities may also be constrained because of capacity limits on equipment production in the near term and because of resistance from local communities.

Solar power remains more expensive than wind, but intense research is underway to develop improved solar technologies. In solar thermal applications, water is heated by the Sun for direct use as hot water or for space heating or electricity generation through steam turbines. In wholesale power projects, a variety of mirror designs are used to concentrate the Sun's heat; the efficiency of conversion of solar energy into power on the grid in such operations can now exceed 20%. A second type of application is the conversion of solar radiation into electricity through photovoltaics, which remains a less efficient and more expensive proposition, at least for industrial-scale projects. Nevertheless, photovoltaics may be the least-cost option for generating electricity in smaller-scale projects in remote areas. As in the case of wind, solar power is subject to interruptions, requiring flexible backup power sources or energy storage facilities to maintain continuity of supply during extended periods of cloudiness. Nevertheless, if sufficient transmission facilities could be constructed, the solar energy available in the world's deserts is many times the world's current power consumption. The only question is cost. Major investments in current technology would entail the risk that a much more efficient method might become available soon.

Geothermal resources have been used for centuries as a means of heating homes and have been employed since early in the twentieth century as a means of generating electricity. At the best sites, high pressures keep underground water in a liquid state despite temperatures far above the usual boiling point. When the water is pumped to the surface, it flashes into steam as the pressure falls. After passing through a turbine, the hot water exhaust can be returned underground. A small amount of sulfur, CO_2, and other pollutants are typically released in the process. At sites where the water is not hot enough to flash into steam, a "binary" process can be used: The hot water is sent through a heat exchanger to vaporize another fluid with a lower boiling point, which then drives the turbine. Although geothermal sources currently represent a tiny fraction of total energy supply, they have enormous worldwide potential. The resource limit of a particular geothermal reservoir generally depends on the availability of underground water. At many locations, geothermal energy could last for centuries, especially with deeper drilling or additional water injection.

LIMITATIONS OF THE TRANSMISSION GRID

As noted earlier, the energy that can be derived from renewable resources depends substantially on location. Why not place such resources at the best sites all around the world and then transmit the energy wherever it is needed? Given the success of the Internet, why not create a similar web for electricity supplies? Solar collectors in the Sahara desert could light all the homes of Europe. Wind farms in North Dakota could run air-conditioning units in Atlanta and heat pumps in Washington, DC. Geothermal sources in Arizona could power Boston's plug-in hybrid cars.

Intruding on this sweet dream is a wake-up call from the transmission grid. Power is lost as it is transmitted, thereby increasing the cost of electricity supplied from remote sites. The losses occur mainly because wires heat up when they carry electricity, and also because the air around electric cables becomes slightly ionized and releases a little charge into the ground. Losses are more substantial when the grid traffic is heavy. In the United States, transmission and distribution losses increased from about 5% in 1970 to 9.5% in 2001, largely because of increased congestion (DOE, 2006).

Aside from an expansion of the grid's capacity, a number of innovations could reduce grid losses in the future. For instance, over long distances, direct current (DC) transmission is more efficient because it is less subject to grounding losses than the usual AC lines. However, some of the benefit would be lost when the DC power is converted to AC prior to distribution to consumers. AC is needed in the distribution network because it better facilitates the transformation of voltages to the lower levels needed by consumers. In the longer run, improved materials (including superconductors) may be developed for transmission lines. Upgrades may also include the implementation of "smart grids" that provide greater connection opportunities for distributed power sources.

AGRICULTURE AND FORESTRY

Earth has a total surface area of 510 million square kilometers, of which more than 70% is ocean. More than one-quarter of the land areas are forested, nearly that much is grassland, and about 10% is devoted to crops. Ice sheets cover about 11% of the land, and the remainder is largely desert with a sprinkling of mountains.

Human activities, driven by population pressures, have been altering land cover substantially. In recent years, about 60,000 km^2 of forests and 70,000 km^2 of other lands have been converted to agriculture annually. The

IPCC (2007) estimates that deforestation, other land-use changes, and agriculture account for about 31% of anthropogenic emissions of GHG. Data uncertainties are considerable, however.

The clearing of forests to prepare new land for cultivation is a major source of CO_2 emissions. However, land-use estimates are typically based on infrequent sample surveys that cover only limited areas in most countries. Satellite data, where available, can record broad changes in land cover but cannot fully account for the degradation of land and loss of biomass from fires, disease, pests, and erosion. Anthropogenic emissions attributable to removal of fuel wood and to logging operations are also difficult to tally. On one hand, the cutting of trees does not necessarily imply that their carbon ends up in the atmosphere. If timber is used for home construction and furniture, the carbon continues to be sequestered. Moreover, natural regrowth of forests and deliberate tree planting take CO_2 out of the air. On the other hand, logging activities typically leave considerable organic matter behind on the forest floor, which emits GHG as it decays. The IPCC estimated that greater recovery of residues from logging and timber processing could boost biomass energy supplies by an estimated 14 EJ per year or more.

Improved forest management could help preserve the biosphere's largest natural store of carbon. More than 3% of forests are still damaged each year by fire, disease, and insects. Despite some successes in controlling wildfires, one study estimated that they caused nearly 8 Gt of CO_2 emissions in the 1997–1998 El Niño year (Werf, 2004). Fire suppression alone is not enough, however, as tree stands also need to be thinned to avoid a buildup of dangerously heavy fuel loads. Sustainable development of forest resources can have other important benefits, including erosion control, preservation of wetlands, and conservation of biodiversity.

In cultivating crops and raising livestock, methane and nitrous oxide are the main emissions, accounting for more than 10% of total GHG emissions. The uncertainty range is wide, however. Nitrous oxide is released by bacteria in the soil, but human activities boost these natural releases. Tilling the soil stimulates bacterial growth, and the application of nitrogenous fertilizers enhances the microbial release of N_2O. Emissions from cultivated soil account for more than 60% of anthropogenic emissions of nitrous oxide (the rest is largely from fuel combustion). Methane is produced during wetland rice cultivation and when cattle and other ruminants digest fodder. Also, both nitrous oxide and methane are released from manure. Over half of anthropogenic methane emissions are from agricultural activities, and the rest is from the production and use of fossil fuels.

Agricultural emissions are expected to rise with population growth and with a shift to increased consumption of protein, especially from animal sources, in developing countries. As of early in this decade, the average consumption of protein per person in developing countries was only one-fifth of that in advanced economies, and the per capita consumption of meat and milk was about one-tenth. The gap has been closing, however.

Continuing improvements in crop yields will be needed to help provide for the world's increased demands for food and animal protein without substantial further conversion of forests to cropland. Demands on land resources will also intensify with the development and expansion of biofuels.

INDUSTRIAL PROCESS EMISSIONS

Industrial companies use energy for processing minerals as well as for electricity and space heating. Chemical reactions involved in transforming ores and creating alloys also give rise to GHG emissions. For instance, oxygen must be removed from many mineral ores to convert them to a useful form (such as aluminum, iron, lead, and zinc). The procedure typically involves smelting with coking coal. In this process, the carbon in the coke combines with oxygen from the ore, creating CO_2. For aluminum, a carbon anode removes the oxygen. Also, early steps in the manufacture of cement and glass involve removing CO_2 from limestone and trona ore, respectively. In addition, CO_2 is released when natural gas and steam react with nitrogen from the air to produce ammonia. Ammonia and nitric acid are key ingredients for fertilizers and explosives, and the manufacture of nitric acid releases nitrous oxide. N_2O is also emitted when producing adipic acid, a base material for nylon and other synthetic fibers. In addition, PFCs are released in manufacturing aluminum and semiconductors, whereas HFCs are produced for refrigeration and air-conditioning systems. Sulfur hexafluoride is released in making magnesium and in electrical switchgear. Overall, industrial processes outside the energy sector account for about 12% of total CO_2e emissions.

A variety of means can be used to limit industrial GHG emissions, aside from obvious recycling of materials and greater efficiencies in the use of energy. For instance, oxygen can in some cases be removed from ores without smelting with coking coal. Iron, for instance, can be produced through "direct reduction" using natural gas, which substantially reduces CO_2 emissions. In addition, catalytic or thermal methods can be used to destroy the N_2O released in nitric and adipic acid production. Capture and thermal destruction of HFC emissions is an inexpensive add-on for a refrigerant plant. Research is underway on new processing methods, as well as carbon capture and storage, which have the potential for major reductions in future industrial GHG emissions.

WASTE PROCESSING

Waste processing accounts for about one-fourth of total methane emissions and a small share of nitrous oxide releases, although these estimates are based on sparse data. Methane is released in roughly equal amounts from organic materials left in landfills (including paper, food, and yard wastes) and from the processing of sewage. Sewage also emits N_2O. In sum, waste processing represents about 3% of total CO_2e emissions.

Intensive management of wastes, including modern sewage treatment plants as well as mechanical and biological processing of garbage (sorting, recycling, shredding, crushing, composting, combustion, etc.) can substantially reduce GHG emissions. Since the 1970s, projects have been implemented to capture landfill methane, either for flaring or for combustion as an energy source. In some cases, methane capture may not be attractive to power companies because of the small scale of operations and uneven volumes of fuel flow. In such projects, the recovery of methane may cumulate to only about 20% of the lifetime emissions of a landfill. Delays in implementing methane capture contribute to the low recovery rates. It typically takes a couple of years before enough methane is released from a landfill to make capture cost-effective. Earlier implementation of projects, however, as well as careful monitoring and installation of secondary recovery facilities where needed, would reduce "fugitive" emissions.

FIVE

Forecasts of GHG Emissions and Global Temperatures

The planet's temperature has been rising over the last century in large part, evidently, because of anthropogenic emissions of greenhouse gas (GHG). The prospects for future emissions depend on a host of variables, including population growth, economic development, technological advances, and the efforts and policies that will be undertaken to mitigate climate change. The consequences for the atmospheric concentrations of GHG and the global average temperatures depend on the responses of various natural mechanisms, including both amplifying and restraining feedbacks. Potential tipping points in the climate system are a major concern. It is difficult to assess the likely outlook for emissions and temperature change. Weighing the uncertainties surrounding possible outcomes is an even more daunting task, but an essential one.

BUSINESS-AS-USUAL TRENDS

Anthropogenic emissions of GHGs may have affected Earth's climate as early as the invention of agriculture; in any case, they are surely a key to future climate change. A number of forecasters expect that under business-as-usual (BAU) assumptions, meaning no new mitigation policies, emissions will likely continue to grow for some time at rates similar to those observed over recent decades once the current economic recession has passed. The IPCC's measure of anthropogenic emissions of carbon dioxide (CO_2)-equivalent GHG, which leaves out ozone, ozone-depleting substances, and aerosols, grew an average 1.5% per year between 1970 and 2004. Stern (2006) projected a continuation of that trend growth through 2050 under BAU policies. Three teams of researchers for the U.S. government's inter-agency Climate Change Science Program projected that global BAU emissions of CO_2 would grow 1% to 2% per year through 2050 (Clarke, 2006).[1]

[1] The research was based on three Integrated Assessment Models: one developed by the Massachusetts Institute of Technology, another a joint product of Stanford University and

The IPCC (2007) reported on a wide range of scenarios, with annual CO_2e emission growth rates ranging from 0.7% to 2.2% through 2030.

A key component of these forecasts is the expectation that the production and use of energy, which represents nearly two-thirds of GHG emissions, will continue to expand rapidly. Since 2007, BAU forecasts have been lowered only modestly because of higher energy costs, the worldwide economic slowdown, and some climate mitigation policies that have already been implemented. For example, in 2009, the U.S. Energy Information Agency lowered its forecast for annual growth of the world's energy-related CO_2 emissions through 2030 from 1.7% to 1.4% (EIA, 2009). The International Energy Agency reduced its forecast growth rate of a similar measure through 2030 from 1.6% to 1.5% (IEA, 2009). These forecasts thus remain very close to the historical growth rate. Global energy demands have been increasing at a 1.5% annual clip despite an average 1% per year decline in energy intensity (energy per unit of economic output). The drop in energy intensity reflects efficiency improvements and a shift in consumption toward services rather than goods – trends that are likely to continue over the long run. In the near future, however, rapid development in China, India, and other emerging economies will likely put upward pressure on global average energy intensity.

An estimate of the energy use required to support economic activity is only one of the factors needed to project GHG emissions. Another key factor is the carbon content of energy. The average carbon intensity of energy trended slightly lower (by an average of 0.2% per year) between 1970 and 2000. Since then, however, carbon intensity has backed up a little mainly because of increased construction of coal-burning power plants. With oil and natural gas becoming scarcer and more expensive in the years ahead, the carbon intensity of energy will depend heavily on whether the world turns increasingly to coal and unconventional sources of oil and gas or instead to nuclear power and renewable energy sources.

Forecasters generally expect that emissions growth will slow later in this century, even under BAU policies. The IPCC reports a few BAU scenarios that even show outright declines in emissions between 2030 and 2100. Two of the three BAU model simulations used by the U.S. Climate Change Science Program predict a moderating trend over the second half of the century, but emissions still grow by 1% per year or more.

What could explain a slowing of BAU emissions growth over the longer term? Not a shortage of fossil fuels. Before the end of the century,

the Electric Power Research Institute, and the third a joint creation of the University of Maryland and Pacific Northwest National Laboratory.

conventional sources of petroleum will probably be exhausted and natural gas resources will diminish, but coal and nontraditional sources of oil and gas will remain abundant. Moreover, the processing of nonconventional energy resources, absent carbon capture and storage, would release considerably more CO_2 per unit of usable energy than traditional sources.

Thus, emissions growth will not decline because of resource shortages or a shift, under BAU policies, to low-emission fuels or technologies. Slower emission growth over the second half of this century is instead projected because of an expected moderation in the growth rates of population and personal incomes.

A rising population boosts GHG emissions because of heightened demands on the materials and energy needed for buildings and transportation. It also increases the need for food that must be met through better yields, more intensive animal husbandry, or expansion of agricultural lands largely through deforestation. Waste production also rises with population. The world's population grew at an average annual rate of 1.6% between 1970 and 2004, but the United Nations forecasts a halving of that growth rate over the first half this century and a further tailing off thereafter (UN, 2006). The projected deceleration depends importantly on greater adoption of family planning practices in developing countries. Only a little moderation in global population growth has occurred as yet, judging by the estimated 1.4% per year pace of expansion over the first seven years of this century.

A slowing in growth of personal incomes later in this century could also restrain the rate of BAU emissions. The world's economy expanded about 3.7% per year between 1970 and 2004. Growth has been at nearly double digit rates in the two developing giants, China and India (IMF, 2008). As individuals emerge from poverty, they tend to shift their diet toward animal protein, the production of which requires higher GHG emissions than vegetarian fare. As wealth expands further, people build bigger homes, buy cars, and travel more frequently and over greater distances, ramping up their energy use and emissions.

It may take a couple of years before the world emerges from the current economic recession. Thereafter, however, the global economy seems likely to continue growing rapidly as developing countries continue to catch up to advanced economies. To the extent that the world's economies eventually converge, trend growth would likely settle down to around the rate of population expansion plus perhaps 1.5% to 2% per year, representing the long-term pace of productivity improvements in a mature economy (Edge, 2004).

Slower longer-term expansion in population and per capita incomes should moderate the rates of growth of energy use and food production.

In addition, deforestation may reach some natural limits. The IPCC, for instance, predicts that BAU emissions from deforestation will eventually diminish as choice sites for conversion to agriculture become scarcer. In addition, forest conservation efforts may be undertaken for reasons other than climate change (erosion control, ecosystem preservation, tourism, etc.).

Suppose then that global GHG emissions were to continue rising at a 1.5% annual rate through 2030 and drop to a pace of just below 1% per year thereafter. From a base of 44 Gt of CO_2e in 2005, that would put emissions at about 64 Gt of CO_2e in 2030 and nearly 130 Gt in 2100. This forecast is similar to one of the higher IPCC scenarios. Its emission growth rate is toward the lower end of the BAU energy sector forecasts in the U.S. Climate Change Science Program studies.

To construct an outlook for the climate, a GHG emissions forecast needs to be translated into a forecast of GHG concentrations. The responses of environmental feedback mechanisms are crucial for determining that outcome.

THE RESPONSE OF THE CARBON CYCLE

Carbon is continuously exchanged between the atmosphere, the ocean, and the land areas of the Earth. Flows from one storage region to another have regular daily, seasonal, and geographic patterns, as well as multiyear trends. In the atmosphere, nearly all carbon is held in the form of CO_2. For stable greenhouse effects, the atmospheric concentration must remain unchanged on average over the years. The concentration remains steady as long as the ongoing emissions and removals are equal. A partially filled bathtub with an open faucet and drain is often used as an analogy. The atmospheric concentration of carbon did remain fairly stable for many years prior to the industrial revolution. In periods when the planet's average temperature is little changed, the removal of CO_2 through the chemical weathering of rocks may be balanced on average over the years by occasional releases of CO_2 from volcanoes and a little net outgassing from the ocean.

When a volcano erupts, enough CO_2 can be ejected into the air to throw the carbon cycle temporarily out of equilibrium. Anthropogenic emissions have a similar effect, although they continue to be released year after year, more like a flood-basalt than a simple volcano. The rate of chemical weathering responds only a little to changes in the atmospheric concentration of CO_2: The extra CO_2 does increase the production of carbonic acid in rain and soil waters a bit and thereby slightly speeds up the dissolution of silicate rocks. However, a vigorous response to CO_2 occurs through the air-sea gas exchange and the growth trends of terrestrial vegetation.

In recent decades, good data have been collected on both the atmospheric concentration and emissions of CO_2 from fossil fuel burning and cement production, as discussed above. Comparison of the two data sources indicates that the atmosphere has retained only about half the CO_2 we have emitted from these sources. Thus, the ocean and land vegetation, on net, must have removed the rest. However, the amount of CO_2 taken down by the ocean and by land vegetation in any particular year does not depend on the anthropogenic emissions for that year. The rate of takedown is not a function of the *flow* of new emissions, but rather of the *stock* of CO2 in the air. At recent CO_2 concentrations of around 370 to 387 ppm, natural processes have been removing about 15 to 20 Gt of CO_2 per year. As the CO_2 concentration rises, the natural removal rate will increase, but it is unclear how much.

To be more specific, the rate of CO_2 takedown by the ocean reflects a gas law discovered by the German scientist, Adolf Fick: the speed of diffusion from one medium to another depends on the difference in concentrations of the gas in the two mediums. Thus, the takedown of CO_2 by the ocean depends on the concentrations of CO_2 in the air and in the surface ocean. If the gap between the concentrations widens because of continued anthropogenic emissions in excess of natural removals, the rate of removal by the ocean will increase. When the concentration gap diminishes because CO_2 is building up faster in the surface ocean than in the atmosphere, the ocean's rate of removal will slow. At present, the ocean is estimated to be extracting some 8 to 11 Gt of CO_2 from the air per year (Clarke, 2006).

When will the ocean's takedown come to a halt? Another gas law, discovered by the English chemist, William Henry, states that, at a given temperature, the amount of gas held by a liquid will be proportional to the partial pressure of that gas in the air above the liquid. (Partial pressure is the pressure that a gas would exert at that temperature if it were the only thing occupying the space.) Henry's law thus suggests that the ocean will eventually absorb enough CO_2 to reestablish a balance between the concentrations of the gas in the air and in the surface ocean.

However, chemical reactions substantially enhance the capacity of the ocean to absorb CO_2. Most of the CO_2 that dissolves in water combines with H_2O and carbonate ions ($CO_3=$) to produce bicarbonate (HCO_3-). Indeed, the upper ocean holds about 90% of its inorganic carbon in the form of bicarbonate. Conversion of CO_2 to bicarbonate reduces the concentration of dissolved CO_2 in the ocean and therefore allows more CO_2 to be taken down from the air through diffusion. However, the supply of carbonate ions that fuels this chemical reaction is limited. Moreover, marine creatures also need the carbonate ions to form their shells.

As noted above, temperature changes also alter the ocean's capacity to absorb CO_2. Other things being equal, water holds about 4% less CO_2 for each 1 °C rise in temperature (Weiss, 1982). There is some evidence of a warming trend in ocean waters to depths of 700 meters in some places (Barnett, 2005). However, because of lags in the warming of the ocean, temperature changes have not been substantial enough as yet to provide much offset to CO_2 absorption. Nevertheless, this feedback is an important factor conditioning longer-term forecasts. One modeling study estimated that for a surge in atmospheric CO_2 up to 700 ppm over a 70-year period, the ocean's cumulative CO_2 withdrawal would be reduced by about 10% because of the temperature feedback (Friedlingstein, 2001).

In addition, with increased global average temperatures, the density of surface waters may diminish in key downwelling areas, such as the North Atlantic. Consequently, the overturning circulation of the ocean may slow. That could lead to a buildup of CO_2 in the surface ocean and a reduction in the pace of removal from the air. But if less ocean water sinks, less must also come up somewhere else. If upwelling slows from intermediate levels of the ocean, net CO_2 takedown by the ocean would likely fall. But if upwelling slows from the deepest levels of the ocean, the net effect is less clear. When deep water that is cold and CO_2-rich rises to the surface, it releases CO_2 as it warms. The concentration of the gas in the atmosphere remains less than that of the deep ocean. For instance, considerable CO_2 is still being released in the Eastern Pacific, except when El Niño events tend to shut down the upwelling (Feely, 1999). As the atmospheric concentration of CO_2 continues to rise, less gas will be released from areas of ocean upwelling. One study estimated that outgassing from the Southern Ocean would cease once the atmospheric concentration of CO_2 reached 640 ppm (Le Quere, 2008).

The situation is complicated further because biological activity in the ocean is affected by CO_2 levels and changes in overturning circulation. As discussed earlier, when marine creatures die, their shells and skeletons sink. If they drop all the way to the ocean floor, their carbon may be buried and thereby sequestered. This is called the biological carbon pump. Its vigor is affected by the availability of nutrients and carbonate ions, and by acidity. Additional CO_2 slows the pump by reducing the carbonate concentration and increasing acidity, which impairs shell formation and increases dissolution of shells before they can be buried. The rate of upwelling is also important for the biological pump because it brings nutrients from the deep ocean into more biologically productive surface waters. Indeed, upwelling areas are the locations of the world's best ocean fisheries. Aside from impairing the biological pump, therefore, a slowing of the overturning circulation of the ocean could cause more immediate economic harm to human livelihoods by reducing the catch of the sea.

Because of all the uncertainties, estimates and projections of CO_2 takedown by the ocean vary greatly across studies. Models can be compared, between each other and over time, in their estimates of the ocean's CO_2 removal relative to the concentration gap between the air and the sea. The extra CO_2 in the atmosphere, relative to preindustrial times, is a proxy for the concentration gap, at least until the ocean's CO_2 concentration builds up. The three studies undertaken for the U.S. Climate Change Science Program estimated that the ocean absorbed between 6.1 and 9.8 Gt of CO_2 in 2000 (Clarke, 2006). That was 0.9% to 1.4% of the extra 194 Gt of CO_2 in the air that year, relative to preindustrial times. With different BAU scenarios for future emissions, the three models projected a decline in the ratio of ocean drawdown to extra CO_2 in the air to a range of 0.4% to 1.2% by the year 2100. Increased ocean temperature and slower overturning circulation could account for such declines.

Assessing the takedown of atmospheric CO_2 by plant growth is even more complicated. For global estimates, therefore, it is generally found as a residual, equal to anthropogenic emissions of CO_2 less its observed increase in the air and its estimated increase in the ocean. As noted earlier, the results suggest nearly as much natural withdrawal of CO_2 by land areas as by the ocean.

Aquatic vegetation plays a minimal role in the ocean's direct drawdown of CO_2 from the air. The natural response of terrestrial plants, however, can be a substantial CO_2 sink, because higher atmospheric CO_2 concentrations stimulate photosynthesis and speed growth. The response of terrestrial vegetation also depends on the stock of CO_2 in the air, not on the flow of new emissions. A boost to plant growth from higher CO_2 levels has been demonstrated in both greenhouse and free-air experiments. Studies of forests are especially important, because they account for about 80% of the inter annual drawdown of CO_2 by plants. The concentration of CO_2 in the air around a stand of trees can be adjusted through a controlled release of the gas upwind in what are called Free-Air CO_2 Enrichment (FACE) studies. The results indicate that, with other factors kept unchanged, a rise in CO_2 from 380 to 550 ppm would induce an increase of about 25% in the carbon uptake of trees at midlatitudes (Norby, 2005).

Satellite observations indicate that plant growth has increased across most regions of the Earth in recent decades. Aside from the direct effects of "CO_2 fertilization," higher plant growth may be attributable to changes in temperature, rainfall, cloud cover, and soil nutrients. For instance, growing seasons at midlatitudes have lengthened owing to warmer average temperatures. Also, monsoon rains have strengthened somewhat in Africa, Asia, and Australia. Finally, cloud cover has diminished in the tropics, thereby allowing more sunlight for photosynthesis (Nebani, 2003).

Climate-related changes in such environmental factors could have important effects on the future terrestrial drawdown of CO_2. Withdrawals of CO_2 could increase because of the spread of forests into warming tundra areas. However, most climate feedbacks seem likely to slow the pace of CO_2 removal from the air. For example, when temperatures rise above 35°C (95°F), photosynthesis slows and pollination begins to fail for key food crops such as corn and rice (Brown, 2008). One study estimated that, if atmospheric CO_2 rose to 700 ppm over 70 years, the associated temperature and rainfall changes could reduce the cumulative removal of CO_2 by vegetation that would otherwise occur by nearly one-fourth (Friedlingstein, 2001). Other studies have predicted that natural terrestrial sources could begin to release CO_2 on net, rather than removing it (Cox, 2000; Friedlingstein, 2006).

The terrestrial drawdown of CO_2 depends on more than the growth of plants. Scientists use the phrase "Net Primary Production" for the removal of carbon in photosynthesis, net of its release as plants burn energy (in respiration). However, a variety of other factors need to be considered before arriving at the bottom line on natural carbon sequestration. For instance, soils play a key role. They hold about one-third more carbon than vegetation in tropical forests and about four times more at higher latitudes. As noted above, the carbon held in soils is released with the metabolism of bacteria residing there. Microbial activity is stimulated when a field is plowed and intensifies with higher CO_2 concentrations. One experimental study found that a rise in CO_2 to 580 ppm would boost bacterial respiration enough to cut carbon sequestration in the fine roots of trees by about 40% (Heath, 2005). The net takedown of carbon by vegetation, after accounting for soil bacteria effects, is called Net Ecosystem Production. Finally, forest fires are becoming more prevalent and intense in some regions with increasing temperatures and aridity. The net conversion of carbon into organic form, after taking account of fires and harvests, is called Net Biome Production.

Methane is the only GHG other than CO_2 that enters into the carbon cycle. As mentioned earlier, atmospheric methane (CH_4) converts into CO_2

in about ten years on average, catalyzed by the presence of hydroxyl ions (OH−). Other types of pollutants can reduce the availability of these ions and delay the conversion of methane, indirectly enhancing greenhouse effects because of the higher radiative efficiency of methane than CO_2. Methane is also a concern because of possible dangerous feedback thresholds that are as yet unknown. For instance, permafrost peat bogs in Siberia hold an estimated 70 Gt of methane, compared with only about 5 Gt currently present in the atmosphere. Also, as mentioned above, a vast amount of methane is stored in hydrates on the sea floor. If global warming caused any significant release of these stores of methane, greenhouse effects could jump dramatically.

Other key GHGs do not involve carbon and thus are not removed by the natural carbon cycle. While HFCs are broken down chemically in the atmosphere within a few decades, nitrous oxide, PFCs, and sulfur hexafluoride remain aloft for much longer periods. Although these gases are emitted in much lower quantities than the anthropogenic releases of CO_2 and methane, their persistence and enormous radiative efficiencies make them important targets for emission abatement.

TIPPING POINTS IN AMPLIFYING FEEDBACKS

Will the pace or level of warming push the climate system to a natural trigger point at which amplifying feedbacks shift abruptly into a higher gear? Although speculation about this subject is rampant, little is actually known. Recent surveys indicated that the top concern of scientists was a possible shift to a faster rate of ice loss in the Arctic and Greenland (Lenton, 2008; Kriegler, 2009). Instability of the West Antarctic ice sheet ranked next. With enough melting at the periphery of the major ice sheets, enhanced by albedo feedbacks, the flow of ice into the sea could accelerate to such an extent that the climate system would become committed to a substantial rise in sea level, even if GHG concentrations were subsequently reduced.

The surveyed scientists also indicated that they were worried about the risk of irreversible decline of the Amazon and boreal forests. Persistent El Niño conditions could be associated with a weakening of easterly winds that bring rainfall to the Amazon. Increased fires and continued deforestation could contribute to the decline of the rainforest. Because a great deal of the Amazon's water is recycled by vegetation, a threshold might be reached from which the water cycle would be unable to recover. Rapid warming could also cause a dieback of northern forests because of increased disease, pests, and fires. Some scientists argue that the amplifying feedbacks of fires have been underestimated in previous analyses (Bowman, 2009). Loss of forests would not only release GHG but could also cause irreversible effects on ecosystems.

The possibility of reaching temperature thresholds at which methane is released in substantial amounts from northern permafrost areas is also a concern. Uncertainties have yet to be resolved in this area. However, the scientists surveyed for these studies judged it likely that the warming of permafrost will proceed in a fairly linear fashion rather than reaching any tipping point. Also, the ocean is not likely to warm enough to unleash the methane hydrates buried in sediments there. It would probably take a major undersea volcanic event to cause a catastrophic outgassing of those methane deposits.

WILL THE NORTH ATLANTIC CONVEYOR BELT SHUT DOWN?

Patterns of ocean circulation could also have dangerous tipping points. The most notable of these is not an amplifying feedback process, however. As noted earlier, a complete shutdown of the North Atlantic conveyor belt around 13 kya returned Europe to Ice Age conditions for about 1,500 years. Also, around 8.2 kya, a major deceleration of the Gulf Stream was responsible for another episode of regional cooling, though briefer and less severe (Kleiven, 2008). Each of these events was evidently caused by a massive surge of glacial melt water from North America, which freshened the North Atlantic, reducing its density enough to slow or stop deep water formation – the gear that drives the ocean conveyor belt. Could it happen again? Could ocean circulation slow enough in this century or the next to cause a sudden reversal of climate trends in Europe, returning it to extreme cold?

A considerable volume of fresh water would be needed to break the speed of the North Atlantic current, which transports as much water as all the rain that falls on the planet, equal to about a hundred Amazon Rivers, as noted earlier. To produce that surge of water, the Greenland ice sheet and Arctic sea ice would need to release fresh water in a fairly sudden surge, not gradually over several centuries. Unlike in the previous two episodes of impaired circulation, North America would not be the source of the fresh water pulse. It would be more difficult to stop the ocean conveyor belt with the melting of ice from Greenland and the Arctic, because any cooling caused by a slowing of the conveyor would affect Greenland and the Arctic, slowing the further melting of ice in those areas.

However, factors other than salinity changes could help slow the overturning circulation. Water expands as it warms, and surface water density in the North Atlantic will therefore be reduced as temperatures rise there. Even if conditions remain acceptable for continued downwelling, the conveyor must remain strong enough to overcome an impediment on the ocean floor. East of Greenland, water sinks to depths of up to 3,700 meters. To move south from there and complete the circuit of the conveyor belt, the flow has to surmount the Denmark Strait, a ridge on the ocean floor between Iceland and Greenland that is only 600 meters below the surface. The conveyor will manage to continue hurdling that ridge only if its density remains greater than the water it displaces further south.

Over recent decades, observations of the rate of flow of the conveyor have differed substantially; no consistent change in trend has been established. The consensus view at present is that the variations in measurements are largely attributable to multiyear shifts of the North Atlantic Oscillation and other temporary climate patterns (IPCC, 2007). Although uncertainties are considerable, the IPCC predicted that the conveyor would gradually slow to about three-fourths its current speed by 2100 but was "very unlikely" to "undergo a large abrupt transition during the 21st century."

A RUNAWAY GREENHOUSE?

The possibility of a runaway greenhouse is sometimes raised in commentaries on climate change. Although interpretations differ, the formal meaning of a runaway greenhouse is a planetary warming that no natural mechanism can stop until all the planet's water has evaporated. Venus is the prime example. Soon after its birth, its water evaporated. Ultraviolet radiation high in its atmosphere then broke molecules of water vapor into separate hydrogen and oxygen atoms. The hydrogen escaped into space and, as a result, liquid water could no longer be formed. Without water, the carbon cycle shut down; CO_2 released by volcanoes could no longer be sequestered in oceans and sediment. The consequence is a Venusian atmosphere that is 97% CO_2. On the surface of Venus, the atmospheric pressure is ninety-three times that of Earth, and the temperature is 462°C.

Could it happen on Earth? Could greenhouse feedback loops accelerate into explosive temperature dynamics? As noted earlier, CO_2 and water vapor do generate amplifying feedbacks for climate change. In general theories about dynamic systems, amplifying feedbacks may be of two types: one in which the cycles of feedbacks gradually subside over time; and another in which each round of the feedback loop stimulates a response of greater amplitude. In the latter case, the dynamics are unstable, and the process becomes explosive and potentially catastrophic. Which of the two types of dynamics characterize our climate system?

First, consider CO_2 *feedbacks*. As noted earlier, when the ocean warms, it releases CO_2 into the air, thereby causing more warming. The size of the responses is critical. In an ongoing feedback loop process involving these CO_2 releases from the ocean, the warming caused by a new release of CO_2 turns out to be less than the warming caused by an earlier release of an equivalent amount of CO_2. The reason is that the more CO_2 present in the air, the less another molecule of the gas can affect temperature: New emissions have a harder time finding infrared radiation not already captured in the frequencies that CO_2 can absorb. The dynamics are similar to the concept of diminishing returns in economics. Each additional kilogram of CO_2 produces smaller and smaller warming effects. Put another way, it takes ever more CO_2 to keep raising the temperature the same number of degrees.

Unfortunately, we do not know with much confidence how much the planet's temperature will rise with given amounts of extra CO_2 in the atmosphere. The IPCC uses the estimate that a doubling of CO_2 will produce 3°C of global warming. This means that CO_2 would need to increase by a multiple of four to generate a 6°C temperature rise. (This estimate includes associated water vapor feedbacks but omits longer-term feedbacks related to the melting of major ice sheets.) According to that IPCC benchmark, then, CO_2 would need to increase from the preindustrial level of 280 ppm to 560 ppm to raise temperatures by 3°C and jump to 1,120 ppm to warm the planet by 6°C. Because of the importance of the estimated temperature response to a doubling of CO_2, it is called the "climate sensitivity." The IPCC indicated that its point estimate of a 3°C climate sensitivity is subject to considerable uncertainty and a skew toward the upside as well. It estimated a one-third probability that the warming from a doubling of CO_2 would lie outside the range of 2°C to 4.5°C.

The other side of this feedback loop also helps ensure that CO_2 would not cause a runaway greenhouse. Water releases about 4% of its remaining CO_2 when it warms 1°C. Thus, in successive rounds of warming and resulting further CO_2 releases from the ocean, the amount of CO_2 outgassed would gradually become smaller and smaller as the concentration of CO_2 in the ocean fell.

The stability properties of the *water vapor* feedback loop are not the same as those for CO_2. As noted earlier, warmer air can hold more water vapor (about 7% more for each degree Celcius). Also, as temperatures rise, roughly enough evaporation occurs to maintain relative humidity on average. When water vapor rises through the atmosphere or moves toward the poles, it cools, and if enough vapor is present, tiny drops of liquid or ice crystals form and are seen by us as clouds. An increase in cloud albedo effects tends to offset the greenhouse warming of additional water vapor. Although a precise calibration of water vapor feedback dynamics is not available, one study estimated that to get a runaway process going, the surface temperature of the Earth would first have to be raised to an incredible 373 °C (Kasting, 1988). The extra water vapor and CO_2 that would be present in the air at that temperature would raise the surface atmospheric pressure 220 times above the present. The conclusion of the study was that conditions on Earth are not and have never been favorable for a runaway greenhouse.

Indeed, despite a wide range of temperatures over Earth's history, no run-away greenhouse has occurred, at least since the early days of planetary formation. The oceans are still with us. Moreover, our best measure of the amplifying feedback of water vapor is already included in the estimated 3 °C "climate sensitivity" response of the global average temperature to a doubling of CO_2.

GHG CONCENTRATIONS UNDER BAU POLICIES

After assessing the likely interactions with the carbon cycle, a forecast of anthropogenic emissions of GHG can be translated into projections of the atmospheric concentrations of GHG. Future temperatures and other climate changes can then be projected. The IPCC reviews studies encompassing a wide range of BAU scenarios, with benchmark CO_2e concentrations in 2100 varying from around 600 to 1,550 ppm. For a forecast of continued emission growth at 1.5% per year through 2030 and just under 1% thereafter, a corresponding IPCC scenario indicates a CO_2e concentration in 2100 of 1,250 ppm. This level would be nearly 2.75 times the IPCC's estimate in 2007 of the CO_2e concentration (455 ppm) and about 4.5 times the preindustrial level of CO_2. In the absence of other factors, the estimated equilibrium temperature of the planet in response to such an increase in GHG would be more than 6 °C above preindustrial levels.

With similar BAU growth rates for CO_2 emissions, the studies prepared for the U.S. Climate Change Science Program forecast a range of concentrations in 2100 for CO_2 alone of 711 to 854 ppm. Currently, non-CO_2 gases account for about 75 ppm of the estimated CO_2e concentration. If 75 or 100 ppm were added for non-CO_2 gases as of 2100, the projections of GHG concentration in these U.S. studies would be somewhat lower than the benchmark IPCC scenario cited above. The reasons for the differences could include greater expected reductions in deforestation in the U.S. studies, somewhat lower starting emission levels, and perhaps greater natural sequestration. The variety of possible outcomes for a similar path of emissions indicates the extent of uncertainties involved in long-range climate forecasting. In any case, emissions after 2100 are also a concern, and the unrestrained emissions of BAU forecasts generally result in continuing increases in CO_2e concentrations and global average temperatures in the next century.

GREENHOUSE MOMENTUM

Any ratcheting up of the concentration of GHG creates a momentum for climate change. Feedback processes and changes in the global average temperature take decades and even centuries before they are completed. For instance, the IPCC (2007) estimates that, even if the GHG concentration were held constant at the level reached in 2000, continuing feedback responses and gradual climate adjustments would result in warming of the planet by an additional 0.6°C over this century. The effects of global temperature changes on ecosystems, weather, economic activity, and human health also take years to be fully realized.

The upward pressure on the planet's temperature from an earlier rise in the GHG concentration is not the only type of greenhouse momentum at work today. Further back in the process, a variety of forces continue to spur anthropogenic emissions. The *existing* capital stocks of the world's economy, including power plants and vehicles of all types, generate a momentum to sustain current emission levels. If current emissions are maintained, the concentration of GHG in the atmosphere will surge. Moreover, the world's power production and vehicle fleets are rising rapidly. Population growth and the natural human impulse to improve one's standard of living are a major impetus for ever more *increases* in our GHG emissions.

The engines of greenhouse momentum thus begin at the level of the individual and the family, and are boosted by numerous types of economic activity, institutions, and invested capital. They extend into the physical world through numerous amplifying feedbacks, from immediate water vapor responses to the slow albedo effects of melting ice. We are experiencing a vast juggernaut of climate change. What are the potential consequences?

SIX

Potential Impacts of Climate Change

Aside from the direct effects of changes in temperature and CO_2 concentrations in the atmosphere and the ocean, climate change could substantially alter sea levels, storms, floods, drought, and wildfires. Changes in the prevalence of disease vectors and pests are already being observed. Climate change could also potentially bring forced migrations, the destruction of ecosystems, and the extinction of many species. Again, identifying scenarios of possible outcomes is important, but weighing the associated uncertainties is also crucial though even more difficult.

SEA LEVEL RISE

In the Greenhouse climates that the Earth experienced over most of its history, sea levels were much higher than today. Indeed, by IPCC (2007) estimates, the sea level would rise almost 70 meters (230 feet) if the current ice sheets on Greenland and Antarctica melted entirely (after adjustment for the replacement of ice that is below sea level with water). The level of the sea over geologic periods depended not only on the amount of water stored in ice sheets but also on the depth of ocean basins and the span of continental land masses. Over the last 2.75 million years, sea levels have varied substantially because of the ebb and flow of ice sheets over North America and Eurasia. As noted earlier, the strong northern summer radiation of our last interglacial period around 120,000 years ago evidently melted enough ice on Greenland and, with amplifying feedbacks on West Antarctica as well, to raise the ocean about 5 meters (16 feet) higher than it is today. With the return of continental glaciation after 115 kya, sea levels dropped again. At the time of the glacial maximum of around 21 kya, the oceans were about 120 meters (almost 400 feet) lower than today. By the time the continental ice sheets had melted around 6,000 years ago, the sea level had nearly reached its current level. Over the last several millennia, the height of the ocean has edged up very slowly, if at all.

Estimates of the historical sea levels are made using a variety of proxy measures. Oxygen isotope records in marine shells and ice cores provide estimates of the amount of water locked up in polar ice sheets. Fossil coral that thrive only at certain depths in the ocean are another key indicator. A variety of proxy indicators, such as rock carvings and the height of ancient Roman fish tanks, has been cited to suggest little change in sea level over the last couple millennia (Church, 2006). In more recent years, direct measurements of the height of the ocean have been collected. As described below, they show fairly modest annual increases in sea level, but also suggest the possibility that the pace is picking up.

The ocean's surface is not a uniform height above the center of the Earth because of tidal forces, winds, storms, current flows, and an uneven ocean floor. Moreover, gradual subsidence or uplift of land can alter local sea height even if the global average level is unchanged. A coastal area tends to sink if it is near a subduction zone, where one tectonic plate plunges under another and into the Earth's mantle. Land surfaces may rise because of glacial rebound. As noted earlier, an ice sheet that is several miles thick is heavy enough to push the crust of the Earth down into the more fluid mantle beneath it. When the ice melts, the crust slowly recovers its previous elevation in what is called a "glacial isostatic adjustment."

A variety of effects need to be considered when calculating the possible vertical movements of land. For instance, when an ice sheet depresses the crust in one region, nearby regions that have no ice are pushed up as viscous matter squeezes under them. When the ice sheet melts, the borrowed material is returned. The adjustment and recovery process takes many millennia: Glacial rebound is still underway today in continuing response to the melting and drainage of ice sheets more than 6,000 years ago. Although the year-by-year effects on land elevation are small, they are important because the estimated annual changes in sea level are also fairly small.

Data collected since the late 1880s on high and low tides at various locations have been combined to try to construct estimates of the global average sea level. These "tide gauge" measurements are made using reference markers on nearby coastal lands. Corrections are made for estimated changes in the elevation of the land surface. The data indicate that the sea level rose an average of about 0.7 mm per year between 1870 and 1935 and at a faster rate of 1.8 mm per year since then (Church, 2006).

Since 1992, satellite data have become available, allowing sea level measurements that do not depend on nearby land reference points. The satellites bounce signals off the sea surface, thereby allowing direct measures of the height of the ocean. However, these data also require adjustment owing to the gradual decay of orbits. In addition, satellites have limited lifetimes and, after the launching of new equipment, distinct calibration is typically needed for the instrumentation. Arranging for overlapping periods of data collection among satellites of different vintages has also been a challenge because of budgetary constraints.

Nevertheless, scientists have greater confidence in the satellite altimetry data than in the tide gauges. The satellite data, supported to some extent by tidal measures as well, suggest that the sea level has been rising at average rate of around 3 mm per year since 1992 (see Figure 6.1 and Leuliette, 2004). The IPCC (2007) cautioned about the uncertainty of those estimates; it could only say, with 90% probability, that sea levels had been rising between 2.4 and 3.8 mm per year over that time.

As noted previously, the upper portion of the ocean (about 100 meters) is well-mixed by the wind; its temperature changes are therefore closely correlated with those of the lower atmosphere. Indeed, with oceans covering 70% of the Earth, observations of sea surface temperatures are important components of global-average temperature estimates. Below the well-mixed level, the sea temperature drops fairly rapidly until it reaches about 2.5 °C at about 1 km of depth. The temperature edges only a bit lower before reaching the ocean floor at depths that can exceed 4 km (Duxbury, 2000).

Because of the strength of the hydrogen bonds in a water molecule, the density of water changes very little when it is subject to increasing pressure. However, the ocean expands as it warms (Duxbury, 2000). At the average surface water temperature of around 16°C, an increase of 1°C would boost water volume by a modest 0.016%. The warming of the ocean since 1992

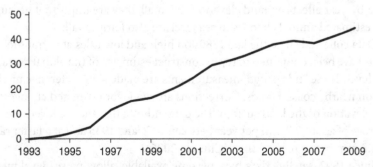

Figure 6.1. Relative global average sea level (millimeters, annual averages).

Source: http://sealevel.colorado.edu and Leuliette, E. W., R. S. Nerem, and G. T. Mitchum (2004), "Calibration of TOPEX/Poseidon and Jason altimeter data to construct a continuous record of mean sea level change," *Marine Geodesy*, 27(1–2): 79–94.

(amounting to 0.25 °C at the surface) has raised the average sea level by an estimated 16 mm. That is more than half the estimated total rise in the level of the ocean over that time (IPCC, 2007). At this rate, however, it would take more than 6 °C of warming for the thermal response of the ocean to raise the sea level by half a meter.

More than one-quarter of the recent rise in sea level is attributable to the melting of mountain glaciers and ice caps. However, all the water stored in mountain ice could raise the ocean by less than half a meter. The disappearance of mountain glaciers is of greater concern because of its implications for fresh water availability, as discussed later, than because of its effects on the sea level.

The melting of sea ice does not change the height of the ocean because ice sitting on top of the sea already adds its weight to the world's oceans. Thus, the dramatic reduction in summer sea ice in the Arctic Ocean in recent years has not directly lifted sea levels. However, it has lowered albedo and therefore spurred a further warming of ocean waters.

The IPCC (2007) estimated that perhaps 10% to 20% of the sea level rise since 1992 was attributable to the net melting of ice on Greenland and Antarctica. However, estimates of decreases in the size of the major ice sheets are subject to considerable uncertainty. The Greenland ice sheet holds nearly 3 million cubic kilometers (700,000 cubic miles) of ice – enough water, if melted, to raise global sea levels by about 7 meters. Solar radiation in summer is strong enough to melt the surface of some of the glaciers on Greenland. Some ice is lost directly because of melting and drainage. In addition, when water slides into crevasses in the ice, it can rapidly melt a path to the bottom of the glacier. The flow of water down such "moulins" and along the bottom of a glacier can lubricate its flow over the surface of the land. A moving ice sheet encounters varying frictional forces at different locations. When a large piece is shoved off a mooring, an "ice quake" can occur that is registered by seismometers. More rapidly flowing glaciers discharge greater quantities of ice into the sea, thereby boosting sea levels. New snowfall helps rebuild an ice sheet each year.

On Antarctica, two distinct ice sheets are present. West Antarctica carries about two-thirds as much ice as Greenland (about 2.2 million km^3), whereas East Antarctica holds almost 25 million km^3, about half the total fresh water on Earth. Melting of all the ice on Antarctica could raise the sea level by more than 60 meters (IPCC, 2007). Although a little melting of ice occurs every summer on Antarctica, the air is generally too cold for substantial meltwater to accumulate, even with twenty-four-hour summer sunlight.

On Antarctica, the greater risk is that outlet glaciers will speed up because of an unblocking of their passages into the sea. Many Antarctic glaciers extend beyond the mainland. Some are deep enough to rest on the floor of the continental shelf well below sea level, including a major portion of the West Antarctic Ice Sheet. When glaciers extend beyond their grounding points and float on the surface of the sea, they are called "ice shelves." Largely because of the warming of ocean currents around Antarctica, the thickness of these shelves has diminished in recent years and their grounding lines have shifted further back toward the continent. Ice sheets resting on the continental shelf are thought to be especially unstable because the ocean floor often slopes down close to the mainland, because the greater weight of ice there has caused a deeper depression of the crust. Therefore, when one grounding line melts away, the point of contact between the ice sheet and the land may jump back quite a ways, exposing a large new expanse of ice to ocean currents.

As in the case of sea ice, the melting of ice shelves or ice lying below sea level does not elevate the ocean, but it does reduce albedo, allowing the ocean to absorb more solar radiation. However, the portion of an ice sheet resting on the continental shelf that is above sea level would raise the level of the ocean if it melted. In addition, the dissolution of an ice shelf could unclog the path of glaciers heading into the ocean, thereby accelerating the loss of land ice, which would clearly boost sea levels.

Another potentially important factor for ice dynamics is the presence of a vast network of lakes under Antarctic ice. The largest of these, Lake Vostok, holds as much water as Lake Ontario. Water can persist in liquid form under the ice because of heat coming up from the Earth and the thick blanket of insulation provided by the ice sheet itself. Many Antarctic lakes are interconnected by streams that flow primarily because of differences in pressure from the overhead ice rather than because of gravity. It is unknown how changes in the rates of accumulation and the movement of these subglacial waters may affect future ice dynamics.

Projections of sea level are subject to multiple uncertainties. First, they depend on forecasts of the global average temperature decades ahead. Even if future temperatures were known with certainty, other factors affecting the responses of ice sheets would remain difficult to assess. Indeed, the IPCC (2007) declined to hazard a guess regarding the effects of ice sheet dynamics, noting that they were still too poorly understood to be included in climate models. However, dynamic factors such as the effects of moulins and grounding line retreat, as discussed earlier in the chapter, are likely only to boost the melting of ice sheets. Therefore, omission of such factors implies a downward bias to the IPCC's forecasts of sea level change. Under BAU policies, which would bring an estimated warming of 1.8 to 4.0 °C over the century, the IPCC projected a sea level rise of 0.2 to 0.6 meters (7 to 23 inches). The top of this range is about twice the annual rate of sea level rise observed since 1992, whereas the bottom is two-thirds of that pace. The IPCC attributes more than half of the projected sea level rise to the expansion of water as it warms and most of the rest to the melting of mountain glaciers and ice caps. It expects the major ice sheets to play only a minor role during this century.

Comprehensive studies have generally indicated fairly modest net losses in volume for the major ice sheets up to the present. For instance, one study estimated that Greenland has been losing about 100 Gt of ice per year and West Antarctica about 50 Gt (Shepherd, 2007). However, East Antarctica on net has been gaining about 25 Gt per year from increased snowfall. These annual ice losses represented just 0.003% of the existing ice on Greenland and 0.0001% of the ice on Antarctica and would cause a rise of only about 0.35 mm per year of sea level rise.

However, some signals of a speedup in ice sheet loss are now emerging. A recent analysis indicated considerable thinning in outlet glaciers on both Greenland and Antarctica, which speeds their discharge of ice into the sea (Pritchard, 2009). An updated comprehensive estimate put the range of annual ice loss on West Antarctica at about 30 to 200 Gt per year and the range of ice mass change on East Antarctica at minus 4 to plus 22 Gt/year (Chen, 2009). However, melting on Antarctica evidently dropped very low in the 2007–2008 and 2008–2009 summers, which has been attributed to the atmospheric oscillation called the Southern Hemisphere Annular Mode, the La Niña phase of the Pacific Ocean oscillation, and the stratospheric ozone hole over Antarctica (Tedesco, 2009).

As for Greenland, more rapid melting has been detected using laser mapping by airplanes as well as satellites (Hanna, 2008). In 2007, ice loss on Greenland may have reached as much as 300 Gt (Fettweis, 2008). A more recent study suggests a notable acceleration in the loss of ice from Greenland, from a contribution to global average sea level of about 0.3 mm/yr over 2000–2005 to about 0.75 mm/yr over 2006–2008 (Broeke, 2009).

A related concern is the extent of summer melting in the Arctic. Sea ice in the Arctic dropped dramatically in 2007, taking the scientific community by surprise. The minimum expanse of ice in September of that year was about 25% below the previous record low set in the summer of 2005 (based on satellite measurements since 1979). Along the northern coast of Canada, a Northwest Passage, so fervently sought by explorers centuries ago, finally opened for the first time in recorded history.[1] An unusually persistent, cloud-free, high-pressure system over the Arctic played some role in the record melting. However, the summer lows of sea ice recovered only slightly in 2008 and 2009, suggesting that greenhouse warming is also likely contributing to these developments (data from University of Colorado). The reduction in albedo because of a continuing loss of summer ice would warm Arctic waters and thus could hasten the melting of land ice on Greenland, increasing the risk of higher sea levels.

The uncertainties about the future elevation of the ocean are substantial. The risks seem skewed toward higher levels than are currently forecast by the IPCC. However, it is important to avoid exaggerating the extent of the potential danger over a period as short as a century or so. The melting of mountain glaciers and the prospective warming of the ocean, combined, can only raise the height of the ocean by about a meter (IPCC, 2007). The risk of a major sea level rise thus depends on the behavior of the ice sheets on Greenland and Antarctica. Although some net losses of ice seem to be occurring at present, they represent only a small increment to sea level change so far. The surfaces of the ice plateaus on Greenland and Antarctica are at such high elevations (and high latitudes) that, in most places, temperatures year-round remain well below the freezing point of water. Moreover, the calving of icebergs from outlet glaciers, though dramatic when it is captured on film, has been going on for thousands of years, serving mainly to offset ice sheet growth from new snowfall. Only minute fractions of those major ice sheets have been lost in recent years.

Although the chances of a major rise in sea level over the next century or so are fairly low, the risks over the longer-term are undeniable. We have become habituated to the current height of the ocean, but it is far from the only equilibrium setting. Levels much higher and much lower have persisted for long periods of Earth's history. As noted earlier, the ocean was about 5 meters higher than today for several millennia during the last interglacial period. That level was reached even without the help of any anthropogenic greenhouse gas (GHG). If the oceans rise that much over the next few centuries because of partial melting of both the Greenland and West Antarctic ice sheets, it would cause severe inundation of coastal areas.

---

[1] In the early 1900s, a passage across northern Canada was first navigated by Roald Amundsen using an icebreaker. In the late summer of 2007, an ordinary commercial ship could make the journey for the first time without the help of an icebreaker.

IMPLICATIONS FOR ISLANDS AND COASTAL AREAS

A higher level of the ocean is a threat to the existence of some small island nations, such as Tuvalu, Kiribati, Vanuatu, and Fiji. Many low-lying coastal areas around the world are also vulnerable to increased damage from flooding and storms. The potential future harm to society is likely to be enhanced because of the migration of people toward the coasts, which has been ongoing for years. Currently, about 1.5 billion people live both within 100 km of a coast and at less than 100 meters above sea level. Twelve of the world's sixteen largest cities are in such areas. Migration of people toward coastal cities is another type of momentum that could intensify the damages from climate change. The IPCC (2007) suggests that by 2100, perhaps 5 billion people will live in coastal areas. That would be a recipe for economic upheaval, domestic instability, and international conflict if the ocean level rises substantially (CNA, 2007). The IPCC estimated that a sea level rise of more than half a meter in this century would cause the loss of several hundred thousand square kilometers of coastal lands and displacement of more than four million people from their homes.

A variety of measures can be taken to reduce the potential damage to coastal areas from sea level rise and storms, including the construction of sea walls and improved disaster planning. Human activities can also worsen the prospective damages to coastal areas from future climate change. If mangrove stands are cleared from coastal areas to develop new land for settlement, a natural storm buffer is lost. Destruction of coral reefs would also remove some natural protection for coastlines. Creation of dams and overuse of upstream waters impair river runoff and the flow of sediment into delta areas. Coastal water drainage causes subsidence of land, and the reduced elevation of coastal lands increases susceptibility to penetration by salt water. The Mississippi River delta has provided one example of the consequences of human development activities: An estimated 1,600 square kilometers of its coastal marshlands were inadvertently converted to open water between 1978 and 2000 (Barras, 2003). The resulting increased vulnerability of such areas to storms and flooding has been dramatically evident in recent years.

WATER AVAILABILITY AND STORMS

Nearly 20% of the world's population relies on seasonal melting of mountain glaciers and snowpacks for their water supply. The flow of melt water is especially helpful in maintaining rivers and reservoirs in the late summer or dry season. Mountain glaciers and ice caps lost an estimated 5% to 10% of their ice between 1960 and 2004; the remaining mountain ice covers some 510 to 550 km² (IPCC, 2007). As these stores of ice and snow melt further in coming years, substantial amounts of water will be supplied to rivers and reservoirs. The risks of damage from flooding will increase, especially in cases where meltwater accumulates in large pools behind temporary ice dams. After a few decades, the shrinkage of mountain glaciers will mean reduced fresh water supplies and impaired hydroelectric power in many locations. In the extreme, some major river systems may dry up each year after the springtime melting has drained away the previous winter's snowfall. Construction of new catchment basins would likely prove to be only a partial remedy for these problems.

Water stress will also be caused by increased evaporation and changes in the regional patterns of rainfall. Because the air absorbs more moisture as it warms, today's semiarid regions will become more parched. Water tables, lakes, and reservoirs in such areas will recede, especially at lower latitudes and in the interior of continents. One study estimated that, because of increased evaporation, the level of the Caspian Sea will likely fall 9 meters by the end of the century (Elguindi, 2006). Extreme drought, which is now experienced on only about 1% of the world's land surfaces, is projected to increase to 30% under BAU policies (Burke, 2006).[2] Also, because of the desiccation of many areas, wildfires will become more frequent and more extensive. In addition, diminished river flow will abet the intrusion of salt water into coastal aquifers and deltaic plains.

Paradoxically, global warming could bring more flooding as well as more droughts. More intense storms, caused in part by warmer sea temperatures, could increase flash flooding and overwhelm existing drainage systems. Rainfall will generally intensify because of the greater moisture-carrying capacity of the air. In particular, more water vapor will be transported from tropical areas to higher latitudes. Also, wider differences between land and sea temperatures in summertime should intensify monsoon rains. Enhanced emissions of aerosols, however, could cool land areas and mask this effect. Although intensified monsoons would increase flooding in South Asia, they would be beneficial for the Sahel region of Africa. Equatorial and southern Africa, however, would experience drying.

It is unclear as yet whether global warming will bring more persistent El Niño conditions and a general weakening of equatorial trade winds. If it

---

[2]　An extreme drought is defined as less than 500 cubic meters of water resources per person per year. However, one-half to four-fifths of that resource is lost before it can be captured for human use. A person's water needs are less than 20 cubic meters per year, but agricultural and industrial needs are ten and three times higher per person, respectively (Stern, 2006).

does, the rains brought to the Amazon rainforest from the Atlantic Ocean will diminish. Some models predict a great sensitivity of the Amazon to a reduction in rainfall. For instance, one group of researchers forecast that, under BAU policies, reduced rainfall would convert much of the Amazonian rainforest to savannah (Cox, 2003). Increased wildfires and continued deforestation would speed the transition. However, this result is not a common finding among other climate models.

AGRICULTURE

The effects of higher CO_2 and temperatures on agriculture are complex. More CO_2 will promote photosynthesis and faster plant growth, increased agricultural yields, and shorter maturation times for plants. Moreover, the earlier arrival of springtime will lengthen the growing seasons at higher latitudes.

In many regions, however, water and nutrients are the limiting factors for plant growth, not CO_2 and temperature. In areas where climate change lowers the rate of precipitation or reduces the availability of melted snow from mountains in critical growing seasons, crop yields will fall. In addition, too much warmth can retard the growth of plants. As noted earlier, photosynthesis is impaired at temperatures above 35°C (95°F) and shuts down completely above 40°C (Brown, 2008). At such temperatures, the key staple food crops, corn and rice, lose the ability to develop pollen. To some extent, farmers may be able to alleviate such effects by switching crops and altering the times for planting and harvesting. The IPCC (2007) judged that yields would generally rise with a warming of 1°C to 3°C, except in tropical areas. For a temperature increase of more than 3°C above the 1980–1999 global average of 14.25°C, however, agricultural output would generally fall, even in some high-latitude regions.

Food supplies could also be impaired by lower yields from fishing. Marine life will be harmed, not only by rising temperatures, but also by a relative increase in acidity because of the ocean's absorption of CO_2, as discussed later. Finally, if the overturning circulation of the ocean slows, the reduced upwelling would mean fewer nutrients brought to the surface and therefore lower productivity for the world's fisheries.

HEALTH

Although climate change poses a risk to human health, other environmental factors will likely continue to be greater hazards. Additional effort will be needed to avoid the release of toxic and harmful industrial pollutants into the air and water, and to improve the quality of nutrition, sanitation, and health facilities. Indeed, vaccinations, mosquito control, and educational programs will be more effective in preventing disease than reductions of CO_2 emissions. However, global warming will aggravate health problems in most areas. More severe coastal storms, more frequent floods, and warmer water will increase the incidence of cholera and dysentery. For instance, a recent study in sub-Saharan Africa suggested that a 1 °C increase in temperature and a 50 mm increase in rainfall would increase the incidence of cholera by about 5% and 2.5%, respectively (Fernandez, 2009). Rising temperatures will allow mosquitoes and other tropical disease vectors to expand their ranges. Droughts and declining crop yields will impair nutrition in poorer areas, particularly in Africa. Increased heat waves, fires, floods, and storm damage will result in more injury and deaths.

The health effects of climate change are not all harmful, however. Disease and mortality in high-latitude areas are likely to be reduced because of less frequent episodes of extreme cold. One study predicted an overall net reduction in mortality and disease if the global average temperature rose by only 1 °C over the first half of this century (Bosello, 2006). Under business-as-usual (BAU) policies, however, considerably more warming would occur by later in this century. In the BAU outlook, according to the judgment of the IPCC (2007), any health "benefits will be outweighed by the negative health effects of rising temperatures worldwide."

EXTINCTIONS

A wide range of activities other than our GHG emissions are already adversely affecting the viability of many ecosystems. Water pollution, deforestation, and exploitation of resources without regard for environmental effects have jeopardized the prospects for many species. Higher global temperatures and ocean acidification are now also contributing to what seems likely to rank as another major extinction event for the planet.

Coral reefs are on the way to becoming an early casualty of our carbon emissions. Corals are animals that form chalky skeletons using carbonate ions in the ocean. As mentioned earlier, when the ocean removes CO_2 from the air, the dissolved gas combines with water and carbonate ions to produce bicarbonate. The hydrogen ions that remain, after the buffering by carbonate, reduce the pH of the ocean.[3] The resulting dearth of carbonate ions and lowered pH makes it harder for corals to grow. Also, these creatures are very sensitive to temperature changes.

Widespread bleaching of corals has provided dramatic early evidence of environmental stress. Reef-building corals obtain more than 90% of their nutrition from algae harbored within their tissues. The algae generate nutrients for the coral through photosynthesis and in return benefit from the CO_2 and organic wastes produced by the coral. The success of this symbiotic relationship is very sensitive to environmental conditions. The coral must grow within 60 meters of the surface of the ocean for enough sunlight to reach the algae. A change in ocean temperature or chemistry can disrupt the usual exchange of nutrients and induce the coral to expel (or digest) the algae. Some corals can cope by attracting alternative species of algae that are better adapted to the new environment (LaJeunnesse, 2009). Also, some coral varieties have shown a greater ability to recover from bleaching through asexual reproduction (Diaz-Pulido, 2009). However, for many corals, a persistent bleaching event results in death. The IPCC (2007) projects "widespread coral mortality" if the global average temperature rises more than 2.5 °C during this century. The risks extend to many species of fish and crustaceans, as well as turtles. About one-third of the species of the ocean make a livelihood amidst the coral, which are sometimes called the rainforests of the sea. In addition to climate change, pollution and overfishing have also damaged such ecosystems.

Lowered pH could also make it more difficult for plankton and other creatures at the base of the ocean's food chain to form their skeletons. Such creatures constitute more than a third of overall marine life. Ripple effects from the loss of such creatures would spread up the food chain.

A wide variety of other species are threatened by rapid climate change. In one high-visibility case, reductions in Arctic sea ice have led the U.S. Department of the Interior to place the polar bear on the list of species whose survival is threatened. One recent study projected that sea ice loss was likely to cause the death of two-thirds of the world's polar bears by 2050 (Durner, 2007). The wetland ecosystems of river deltas are also likely to be damaged by climate change, especially from more severe storms and

---

[3] Although this has been called "acidification," the ocean remains somewhat basic on average, with a pH of about 8.2. Nevertheless, the reduction of its average pH by about 0.1 since preindustrial times reflects more than a 25% increase in the hydrogen ions present in sea water on average.

flooding. Habitat destruction in these and other areas could lead to losses of some 950 to 1,800 of the world's 8,750 species of birds (Jetz, 2007). The IPCC (2007) projects that, overall, up to 30% of the world's species are at increasing risk of extinction due to climate change; the total could exceed 40% if the global average temperature rises more than 3.5°C over this century. While the Earth has been much warmer in the past, the rapidity of the current warming substantially increases the environmental stress and gives species little time to adapt.

It is unclear whether a global average threshold exists at which damage to ecosystems suddenly becomes far more severe. Indeed, even in assessing possible tipping points in local conditions, the vitality of an ecosystem depends, not only on temperature change, but also on the availability of water and nutrients, the contamination of other pollutants, the presence of invasive species, and many other factors. Continuing research is needed to reduce uncertainties regarding the prospective extinction of species.

SUMMARY OF POTENTIAL CLIMATE IMPACTS

Anthropogenic emissions of GHG, as measured by a standard CO_2-equivalent indicator, have been rising at an average rate of about 1.5% per year since 1970. Emissions from the production and use of fossil-fuel energy (for buildings, industry, and transport) have been growing at a slightly faster clip and are now responsible for approximately 55% of our GHG emissions. Agriculture and forestry, combined, account for about 30% of overall GHG emissions, whereas about 12% comes from industrial processing outside the energy sector, and a few percent from waste management.

In the absence of further initiatives, emissions could plausibly continue growing at a 1.5% rate through 2030. Many BAU forecasts project a slower pace of emissions thereafter because of diminishing population growth and a moderation in the rate of economic expansion. If emissions growth slows to an average of just below 1% between 2030 and 2100, and the natural takedown of atmospheric CO_2 by plants and the ocean follows a related IPCC scenario, the CO_2e concentration under this BAU scenario could reach 1,250 ppm by the end of the century. The global average temperature could then be 5°C higher than it is today.

A variety of alternative BAU projections could be constructed with either more or less global warming. Whether any one particular forecast is more probable than another is not the key issue at present. What matters more is the nature and magnitude of the risks involved. The lessons from climate history can be cited to help assess the uncertainties in the outlook.

One key risk is the potential for a major rise in sea level, especially considering the increasing concentration of population and economic activities in coastal areas. Over the last 125,000 years, the height of the ocean has ranged from around 120 meters below today to about 5 meters above. It is highly improbable that a major portion of the Greenland or West Antarctic ice sheets will melt in a time period as short as a century. However, the sea level was about 5 meters higher than now during the last interglacial period, and the global average temperature was not much different than today. Thus, if we sustain current or higher temperatures for a long enough time, the ice sheets would almost surely boost sea levels substantially. If it happened rapidly enough, major dislocations of population could occur.

Another episode from the past is also of relevance – the thermal maximum reached around 55 Mya. This event was apparently caused by the venting of GHG from an ocean rift as Greenland separated from Europe. The amount of gas released was less than the amount present in our current fossil fuel resources. A major extinction event occurred because of the rapid increase in the acidity of the ocean and the global warming of 55 Mya. However, that episode unfolded over a few thousand years – much slower than the pace at which we are currently emitting GHG.

Regional climate changes are in some cases more difficult to predict than global averages. Agricultural production could be substantially damaged in many areas because of seasonal water shortages owing to changing patterns of rainfall and diminution of mountain glaciers. Warming and drought could increase the prevalence and severity of wildfires. With a spread of tropical disease vectors, human health will likely be impaired on net from global warming.

However, it should be noted that our GHG emissions have not been entirely deleterious. Emissions related to the industrial revolution may have helped bring an end to the Little Ice Age. Those emissions, and perhaps others stretching all the way back to the agricultural revolution, may have helped prevent the gradual initiation of a new major Ice Age. Indeed, our GHG emissions could potentially allow us a prolonged interglacial period extending through another full 21,000-year cycle of the precession of the equinoxes – a fortuitous event that may not have happened in over 400,000 years. While contemplating such long-term possibilities, however, we should note that if we push our emissions too far, we could return the planet to the type of climate it experienced over most of its long history – a Greenhouse world with no permanent ice. That would imply sea levels around 70 meters (230 feet) higher than today.

PART TWO

CLIMATE POLICY CHOICES

The second half of the book draws from the lessons of Earth's climate history and outlook to assess alternative possible policy responses. It begins with a broad discussion of policy goals, including a review of efforts to assess the costs of the prospective damages from climate change. It then considers major options among policy mandates and market-based approaches. Market-based alternatives include taxes and cap-and-trade systems; the latter may take quite different forms, depending on their detailed design features. Existing and proposed options for cap-and-trade design are assessed and insights are drawn from the experiences with monetary management. The final portion of the book discusses existing and prospective frameworks for the international coordination of climate policies.

SEVEN

Climate Policy Goals

Climate change is already underway in response to rising temperatures and CO_2 concentrations. To mitigate the damages from future climate change, a substantial transformation of major economic sectors may be required. How much risk of damages should we permit and how much should we spend to try to offset the rest? To begin answering these questions, efforts to quantify the value of climate damages need to be considered. If we were confident of the damage estimates, we could compare them with estimates of the costs of mitigating and adapting to climate change in an overall cost-benefit analysis. But a point estimate is insufficient; the risks of being wrong about our cost forecasts also need to be weighed.

DAMAGE ESTIMATES

A wide variety of studies have tried to evaluate likely damages from climate change. Many have focused on specialized aspects of the problem, such as the effects on agricultural production in a particular region. Comprehensive studies are rarer, and even these efforts typically fail to include components that are especially difficult to estimate. Moreover, unresolved method-ological issues have potentially profound effects on the predicted monetary losses.

As noted in the previous chapter, the major impacts of climate change will be felt on coastal regions, agriculture, health, and ecosystems. Economic losses to coastal areas could come from sea level rise, increased storm dam-age, and forced migrations. Over wider geographic areas, the production of crops, livestock, and fisheries will be affected. The loss of livelihoods in these economic sectors, as well as damage to homes from flooding rivers, could also result in displaced populations. As mentioned earlier, climate change is not the most important factor for controlling the incidence of disease, but it will affect mortality, morbidity, and the demand for clinical services. Quantifying the monetary value of health effects and the prospective damages to ecosystems are daunting challenges. Estimating the effects of adaptation to climate change by humans and other species is also extremely difficult. In principle, the net losses from climate change should include the resources *spent* on adaptation but exclude the damages *avoided* through adaptation. Climate impacts also entail spillover consequences for economic sectors that are not directly affected, such as homebuilding, tourism, and infrastructure construction.

Most studies of prospective climate damage focus on particular sectors and geographic areas. For instance, Nordhaus (2006a) estimates the increased damages from hurricanes that would occur in the Eastern United States because of a doubling of CO_2 in the atmosphere. Using statistical relationships derived from storm records going back to the 1800s, he predicts an increase of 104% in annual damages, amounting to 0.064% of U.S. gross domestic product (GDP). Applied to the level of GDP in 2007, the incremental losses would be about $9 billion. The effects of rising sea levels, which would magnify the damages from a storm of a given intensity, were not included in the analysis.

Another recent paper explored the economic effects of a modest near-term rise in sea level (Bosello, 2007). It excluded storm damage, salt water intrusion, and losses of wetlands. Inundation and erosion alone, following a 25 cm rise in sea level, was predicted to result in a loss of 125,000 square kilometers of dryland areas. The study calculated the direct loss in agricultural output at only about 0.02% of GDP. This estimate did not include possible infrastructure damage, which could be much greater than the losses in agricultural output, especially for larger increases in sea level.[1] For the modest sea level rise assumed in the paper, protection of the entire coastline with dikes and landfill was estimated to be more expensive than enduring the agricultural losses. Finally, this paper emphasized the idea that the responses of the economy, including a boost to investment, would tend to offset a portion of the direct costs of climate damage or coastal protection.

These hurricane and sea level studies did not allow for the effects of possible forced migrations of people. The IPCC (2007) reported that under business-as-usual (BAU) policies, various analyses suggested that

---

[1] The paper merely commented that overall losses would double if the proportion of infrastructure capital lost in each of the world's eight regions were equal to the proportion of land that was lost. However, this is likely a substantial underestimate, given the concentration of cities, ports, and industries in coastal areas.

an additional 20 million people per year living in coastal areas could be flooded by 2050. However, the costs of moving and resettling people are only matters of speculation at present. Tol (2002) assumed an average emigration cost of three times per capita income and an additional cost of resettlement per person equal to 40% of the per capita income in the host country or region. Others have been concerned with potential social conflicts arising from resettlement pressures, which could greatly magnify the overall losses (CNA, 2007).

The monetary value of health effects are inherently difficult to estimate and to combine across countries. A common valuation method is based on the principle of "willingness-to-pay." For instance, if consumers are willing to pay $10,000 to avoid a 1% chance of death, then a premature death would be valued at $10,000/1% = $1,000,000. A related method is based on the willingness of workers to accept wage premiums for higher-risk jobs. Using studies based on such principles, one well-known climate model prices each year of life lost at twice the annual per capita income (Nordhaus, 2007). Another recent analysis valued a premature death at 200 times annual per capita income and a year of disease at 80% of income (Bosello, 2006). These monetary values are clearly not limited to the lost earning power of an individual; they attempt to measure the drop in total social welfare from disease or premature death.

Cross-country comparisons of the estimated value of health and other nonmarket effects of climate change pose a special challenge. Residents of rich countries are able to pay considerably more to avoid the risks of disease and death. The average per capita income in advanced economies is about six times higher than that in developing countries today.[2] To compute a global estimate of health costs, should lives in wealthy countries be valued six times higher than lives in poor countries? The ethical error seems obvious. An alternative approach is to apply an "equity weight" to the monetary value of climate damages in each country. For instance, before adding together the results for different countries, each country's net loss could be multiplied by the ratio of the world-average income per capita to that country's income per capita. Thus, monetized losses in the poorest countries would get a weight six times higher than the weight for the richest countries, and a human life would have equal statistical value, wherever it was lost. Rather than estimating regional values and then applying equity

---

[2] In comparing incomes across countries, purchasing-power-parity (PPP) exchange rates are generally used rather than market exchange rates. PPP exchange rates are based on equating the value of a benchmark basket of goods in different currencies (IMF, 2008).

weights, a global average statistical value could be used for each type of nonmarket damage, irrespective of where the loss occurred. Thus, the same world-average willingness to pay to avoid the risk of death would be used to value the net loss of life from climate change in both advanced and developing economies.

Revealed preference (willingness-to-pay) measures have also been employed to estimate the value people ascribe to using ecosystems. However, ecosystems also have non-use values, including the value of knowing that the ecosystem exists, the option value of possible future use, and the value as a bequest to future generations. Surveys are sometimes employed to estimate these non-use values, but no definitive measures are available. Rough estimates have been reported within a range of $9 to $107 per person in the advanced economies, with an average of about $50 in 1990 dollars (Pearce, 1993; Fankhauser, 1995). Correspondingly lower values are used for countries with less per capita income.

Tol (2002) found that economic valuations could be quite sensitive to the method used to combine nonmarket effects across countries. For a modest warming of 1 °C by 2050, a net *gain* of 2.3% of global GDP was computed based on a simple sum of benefits and costs over eight regions of the world. The main reason for this result was reduced mortality from cold weather in advanced economies. However, if global average prices were used for nonmarket items in each country, the outcome would flip to a net *loss* of 2.7% of world GDP. This change in sign occurred because global average values boosted the estimated losses in developing countries from displaced populations and premature deaths.

Clearly, a wide range of uncertainty surrounds estimates of the value of the nonmarket impacts of climate change. Using "best estimates" can be misleading if probability distributions around those forecasts are not symmetrical or if social welfare includes substantial risk aversion. The underlying risks may well be skewed to outcomes with greater damage. To handle such risks, some researchers estimate damage costs in various economic sectors, as shown earlier, and then add another cost for the chance of a catastrophic outcome. In one early example (Nordhaus, 2000), the catastrophe cost was derived by asking experts in the field what probability they would assign to the chance that climate change would cause a 30% loss of global GDP, about the same as occurred during the Great Depression. The physical nature of the catastrophe was not specified. The resulting probability-weighted estimate of catastrophic losses amounted to one-half to two-thirds of the total estimated value of climate change damages.

Uncertainty can be handled more formally by assuming a probability distribution for each unknown variable and then running numerous model simulations, each time selecting new values for those variables by making random draws from the assumed distributions. The result is a probability distribution of outcomes. However, historical data may not be available to help construct probability distributions for many key variables, and the shape of the distributions themselves may evolve with climate change and other future developments.

Aside from the measurement issues discussed earlier, the losses from climate change depend importantly on the horizon and on the amount of projected warming. As noted earlier, Tol (2002) found that, by some measures, the world economy could enjoy net benefits from a modest 1°C warming by 2050. However, in most forecasts, the damages from BAU policies ramp up sharply later in this century and in the next. Nordhaus (2007) develops a loss function from sector-by-sector estimates for two benchmark temperature levels. Including nonmarket effects and the chance of a catastrophe as discussed earlier, the BAU losses amount to about 2.5% of world GDP for the 3°C of warming he projects for 2100. However, by 2200, with warming of about 5.5°C, losses would exceed 8% of GDP. Stern (2006) forecasts higher baseline temperatures under BAU policies: about 4°C by 2100 and 7.4°C by 2200. The losses (again, including nonmarket effects and the chance of a catastrophe) are about the same as Nordhaus for the year 2100 (2.5% of GDP), but much higher at 11.3% of GDP by 2200.[3]

Even if economists could agree on estimates of losses at a future point in time, another major controversy would need to be resolved. Far-ahead climate damages need to be "discounted" to the present so they can be compared with the cost of current mitigation investments. Economists, and even philosophers, have debated the discount rate that should be used for such purposes; a higher discount rate implies that a given future value is worth less today. For instance, at the discount rate of 7% used by the U.S. government to evaluate public-sector projects, climate damage of $1,000 a hundred years from now is worth only $1 today. At a discount rate of 2%, however, the same future damage would be worth $133 today. The Nordhaus and Stern studies mentioned earlier used quite different discount rates. As previously noted, their BAU damage estimates for the year 2100 were similar at

[3] Stern (2006) estimates greater losses of 2.9% in 2100 and 13.8% in 2200 for a "high climate" alternative with more warming for the same GHG concentrations.

about 2.5% of GDP. However, differences in discounting resulted in major divergences in the present value of damages and the resulting policy prescriptions. In particular, Nordhaus used much higher discounting (a 1.5% time discount rate and a 5.5% equilibrium interest rate) compared with that used by Stern (a 0.1% time discount rate and a 1.4% equilibrium interest rate). For details, see Nordhaus (2006b). A more complete discussion of issues related to discount rates is given in the appendix.

DAMAGE ESTIMATES IN COST-BENEFIT ANALYSIS

The total welfare loss from climate change is not the most useful benchmark for calibrating climate policies. Our options are not limited to a single massive investment that would halt climate change in its tracks. We can consider incremental investments that would mitigate an increasing fraction of prospective climate damages. A standard cost/benefit analysis would assess the incremental ("marginal") benefit of each ton of reductions in emissions. The marginal benefit is the value of the damages that are avoided if that ton is not emitted. The cheapest projects to reduce ("abate") emissions would be implemented first. Increasingly expensive projects would go forward until the incremental cost of abatement (the "marginal cost") rose to the level of the marginal benefit. The efficient level of damages and emission reductions would then occur where the marginal cost and marginal benefit curves intersect, as depicted in the schematic diagram shown in Figure 7.1.

The vertical axis of that diagram shows the dollar value, per ton, of marginal costs and marginal benefits. The horizontal axis gives the tons of emission reductions. The intersection of the marginal benefit and marginal cost curves indicates the economically efficient outcome for the following reasons: Abating one ton less would mean enduring an incremental loss from climate damage greater than the cost of preventing it. Abating one ton more would mean bearing an incremental mitigation cost greater than the marginal benefit of avoided climate damage. On the vertical axis, the intersection point gives the price to pay per ton of emission reductions at the efficient outcome.

The marginal cost of reducing emissions is depicted as having a standard upward slope, reflecting the idea that a range of activities could reduce emissions, and the cheapest projects would be implemented first. However, the marginal benefit of reducing climate damages is shown as being fairly constant across the range of possible emission reductions in a single year. An additional ton of CO_2 in the air causes additional damage, but the amount of incremental damage from the first ton of emissions in a year

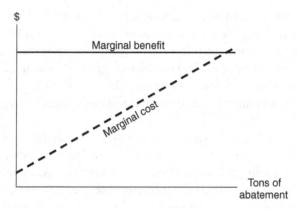

Figure 7.1. Schematic of emission abatement in one year.

is likely about the same as the damage from the last ton emitted that year. Incremental damages increase with rising temperatures and greenhouse gas (GHG) concentrations, but temperatures and GHG concentrations are boosted only slowly as additional emissions occur.

The marginal damage curve is also likely to be fairly flat because of somewhat offsetting effects on marginal damages from higher atmospheric concentrations of CO_2. At higher concentrations, the CO_2-absorption bands in the atmosphere would be more filled, as discussed in Part One. Another ton of CO_2 today would therefore cause less incremental warming. However, higher CO_2 concentrations would imply higher temperatures, which would mean that a given increment of warming would produce more damage. Because of the offsetting nature of these two effects, the initial level of CO_2 concentrations has been found to have little effect on marginal damage estimates (Hope, 2007). Nevertheless, as discussed earlier, higher CO_2 concentrations cause some damage directly, in addition to their effects on temperature.

The flat marginal damage curve, as a function of emissions of GHG, differs importantly from the case of many other environmental pollutants, which may have health effects that rise sharply depending on the amount of emissions in a particular year in a given location. Unlike other pollutants, GHGs are not toxic substances. Also, they disperse rapidly throughout the atmosphere and therefore do not have immediate local effects. The initial impact of GHG is on the global climate. Eventually, changes in the global climate do have differential effects in different locations, as discussed earlier.

Because of the relative stability of the marginal benefit of reducing GHG emissions, researchers have sought estimates that could be useful for policy making. The marginal damage estimate for a given year would indicate the efficient price to pay for the last ton of emission reductions in that year. If we imposed that price of emissions on private-sector firms, those firms would naturally try to minimize costs by reducing emissions until the marginal cost of abatement equaled that price. Thus, in principle, the economically efficient amount of abatement and residual climate damage would be achieved.

The marginal damage of climate change from GHG emissions in a given year is often called the "social cost of carbon." As might be expected given the difficulty of valuing the total damages of climate change, marginal damage estimates are also extremely uncertain. The social cost of CO_2 is calculated from the discounted present value of the predicted future damage from emitting one more ton of CO_2-equivalent GHG today. Estimates vary widely across studies in part because of the different approaches to computing the present value of damages. Based on a survey of one hundred peer-reviewed studies, the IPCC (2007, WGII) reported a range of values across the studies from around zero to about $130 per ton of CO_2e. This wide range actually underestimates the total uncertainty regarding the social cost of CO_2 because it does not take account of the confidence intervals around the estimates in each study.

The uncertainty about climate damages goes beyond the type of risks that are the typical subject of analysis in financial markets. Enough information is usually available regarding financial instruments to construct a reasonable probability distribution for the possible outcomes. In the case of potential climate damages, however, our knowledge is too limited to allow the identification of the probability distributions with any confidence. A deeper type of uncertainty, with unknown probability distributions, was originally discussed by the economist Frank Knight (1921) and is now often called Knightian uncertainty. It is not clear, however, that climate change is a pure case of Knightian uncertainty. We may not be able to convincingly quantify the probability distribution of climate outcomes, but we have some sense of its overall shape. In any case, we cannot afford to wait for climate damages to occur so that the uncertainties can be resolved. By then, it will be too late to act. Additional research to improve our estimates of future climate damage is an important priority, but policy judgments need to be made even with our current level of understanding.

The social cost of CO_2 is likely to increase slowly over time because of rising temperatures and GHG. In addition, the passage of time will bring us closer to the years when large climate changes will occur and discounting of the future will have less of an effect. The IPCC (2007) judged that the social cost of CO_2 will rise about 2.5% per year.

Despite the uncertainties in estimating the social cost of CO_2, the UK government has chosen to use such a measure in deciding on public-sector investment projects (DEFRA, 2007). The UK government specifies a price for carbon and that price is used to penalize high-emission projects when they are compared against low-emitting alternatives. The price began at £26 per ton of CO_2 in 2008 (corresponding to around US$48) and is rising by 2% per year above the general rate of inflation.

CLIMATE GOALS AND EVALUATION CRITERIA

In addition to the uncertainties about future climate damages, the costs of the low-emission technologies that may be developed in the future are also unknown at this time. Because of all the uncertainty, traditional cost-benefit analysis has not often been used in the formulation of climate policy prescriptions. Instead, policy recommendations are typically framed in terms of goals for the global average temperature, the atmospheric concentration of GHG, anthropogenic emissions, and even sea level limits.

These alternative indicators could be evaluated along the lines of two criteria that are often used to assess choices of policy instruments: controllability and closeness to ultimate concerns. A trade-off typically exists between these two features of a policy instrument; measures that are highly controllable tend to be farther removed from ultimate objectives. For instance, in monetary policy, short-term interest rates and longer-term interest rates could be evaluated as alternative policy instruments. Short-term interest rates are far more controllable by a central bank but probably have less effect on an economy than longer-term interest rates.

Trade-offs may also exist among the ultimate objectives of policy. In monetary policy, the fundamental purposes are low inflation and stable economic growth, which are at times in conflict in the short run. In climate policy, the objectives are stabilization of the climate and avoiding large regulatory costs, which also tend to conflict.

Some goals may be favored over others in part because of the assessment of relative risks. Although climate damage estimates are uncertain, the risks may be discernible enough to justify use of the "precautionary principle" in formulating policy. This principle may be expressed in many ways, some stronger than others. The general idea is: When an uncertain amount of harm may occur, policy should lean toward taking extra caution.

The precautionary principle is often cited as a rationale for the choice of a particular goal for temperatures, concentrations, or emissions. However, as discussed further, analysts may differ in their assessments of the thresholds at which significant harm could begin to occur and when, therefore, the precautionary principle should come into play.

A TEMPERATURE GOAL

Our ultimate concern is the damage that will be caused by climate change. The single measure that may most closely predict climate damage is the planet's average temperature. The regional impacts of climate change may vary considerably, but the global average temperature is often a key variable in predicting them. Shifts in precipitation and in the patterns of circulation of the atmosphere and the ocean are important aspects of climate change in their own right, but they are linked to some extent to global warming. The strength of amplifying feedbacks also depends on temperature movements. If we eventually learn to identify tipping points for climate damage or thresholds for major amplifying feedbacks, they will probably be indexed to the temperature level as well. For these reasons, a temperature ceiling might be an attractive choice for a quantitative climate objective.

A temperature goal may be preferred to a target based on GHG concentrations for several reasons. The global average temperature may reflect broad climate concerns better than the atmospheric concentration of GHG. Moreover, the link between atmospheric concentrations and the subsequent planetary temperature is uncertain. As noted earlier, the IPCC (2007) judged that a doubling of the CO_2e concentration would likely result in 3 °C of warming; however, with a probability of about one-third, the warming would be either less than 2 °C or more than 4.5 °C. Uncertainties about feedbacks heighten the risks because they generate a skew in the probability distribution of the climate sensitivity in the direction of greater warming (Roe, 2007). Thus, we could potentially meet a target for the atmospheric concentration of GHG and still find that the planet was warming too much. A temperature goal would avoid that problem by focusing directly on the variable of greatest concern.

Nevertheless, a temperature goal has several disadvantages. First, although temperature is fairly closely linked to the damages from climate change, it is not closely linked to the costs of mitigation. We are ultimately concerned about both damages and mitigation costs. Second, the level of the temperature alone is not a sufficient measure of prospective climate damages. The capacity of humans and other species to adapt depends in part on the speed of warming, not just the level of the thermostat. More fundamentally, global warming is not the whole story of climate change. As discussed in Chapter 6, increased CO_2, by itself, can cause mortality of corals, ocean plankton, and the creatures that depend on them.

In addition, the planet's current temperature may give a misleading signal of future climate change. It may take several decades before the planet's temperature fully adjusts to a change in GHG concentrations. Thus, the global temperature may seem comfortably below an agreed ceiling for years while extravagant energy policies are nevertheless making it inevitable that the ceiling will eventually be breached. Furthermore, many temporary factors may obscure a long-term warming trend. For instance, the global temperature may remain well below a target ceiling because of industrial releases of sulfate aerosols, which seed clouds and enhance the planet's albedo. When the aerosols are better controlled to prevent adverse health effects, very rapid warming may occur as the full effects of the accumulated GHG show through. Volcanic releases could also temporarily cool the planet. With a temperature goal, support for costly mitigation efforts might weaken if such temporary factors pushed the planet's temperature lower for a while. Moreover, because of the numerous factors that influence the global temperature other than anthropogenic activities, excuses might be offered, rather than increased mitigation efforts, if the temperature rose too high.

If a temperature goal were nevertheless the choice, what options could be considered? In 1996, the Council of Ministers of the European Union (EU) picked a global temperature ceiling of 2°C above preindustrial levels. Reflecting the precautionary principle, this goal was chosen because the risks of irreversible climate change were seen as unacceptable at any higher temperatures (EU, 2005). The 2°C temperature ceiling also gained the endorsement of the Group of Eight industrialized nations (G8) at a meeting in L'Aquila, Italy, in July 2009.[4] In September 2009, however, the importance of the G8 itself was downgraded, as heads of state of a larger grouping of nations, the G20, which includes major developing countries, announced in Pittsburgh that the G20 would henceforth take the lead role in international policy coordination. In the Copenhagen Accord, discussed later, most countries around the world signed on to the 2°C ceiling.

Despite some political momentum for the 2°C goal, it may not be realistic. By 2009, the planet had already warmed 0.8°C above the preindustrial level. As noted above, the IPCC estimated that the planet would be 1.4°C

---

[4] The G8 countries: Canada, France, Germany, Italy, Japan, Russia, the United Kingdom, and the United States.

above preindustrial levels by the end of this century, even if the atmospheric concentration of GHG were kept unchanged at the 2000 level. However, the concentration of CO_2 rose from 370 ppm in 2000 to 387 ppm by 2009 and continues to increase by about 2 ppm per year. According to the IPCC's central estimate of climate sensitivity, a 2°C goal would be associated with an atmospheric concentration of about 450 ppm of CO_2-equivalent GHG (though the uncertainties are considerable, as noted previously). We had already reached that concentration by 2007, according to the IPCC. Moreover, the pledges that countries have made for future emission reductions do not seem ambitious enough to achieve the 2°C goal, as discussed in Chapter 11.

If a tough temperature ceiling is set and then exceeded, it might help raise alarm bells and perhaps motivate greater sacrifices. However, the predicted damage might not occur soon after a temperature ceiling is exceeded. For instance, lags in the response of the ice sheets to global warming may make a temperature ceiling seem unduly alarmist in the years immediately after it is exceeded. The consequence could be a weakening of the motivation to make the sacrifices needed to cool the planet below the ceiling or even to adhere strictly to a new, higher ceiling.

The rationale for a hard temperature ceiling may lean too heavily on the idea of a threshold at which the curve relating global climate damage to temperature suddenly becomes much steeper. As noted above, no such threshold has yet been identified. Damages from climate change are not *de minimis* up to a particular temperature and then enormous thereafter; climate change is already causing some harm. The current melting of mountain glaciers and ice sheets, along with the risks to island nations and ecosystems, suggests that maintaining the current global average temperature would likely not be acceptable over the long run. As an alternative to a single temperature ceiling, therefore, a two-part temperature objective could be considered: one goal for an intermediate-term peak and a second, lower target for a long-run stable level.

Holding global warming to 3 °C above the preindustrial level by 2100 might be achievable. According to the IPCC's central estimate for climate sensitivity, this would imply a peak concentration of CO_2e of about 560 ppm. If the global average temperature remained that high for centuries, however, the ice sheets on Greenland and West Antarctica would probably melt. In the long run, therefore, we might eventually find it worth the cost to return the planet to a temperature at which some mountain glaciers would rebuild and the ice sheets could be more confidently stabilized. Returning to a temperature below the current level would therefore seem an appropriate objective for the longer-term beyond the year 2100.

GHG CONCENTRATIONS

As mentioned earlier, a goal for GHG concentrations might be preferred to a temperature objective because we have more control over them. Also, some climate damages occur as a direct consequence of CO_2 concentrations rather than as a result of their global warming effects. However, a GHG concentration goal has some limitations similar to those of a temperature objective. Natural processes will help determine concentrations. Volcanoes will spew GHG into the air and natural sinks will remove extra CO_2 at speeds that will vary over time and likely prove difficult to predict.

In addition, anthropogenic processes could alter the climate even without changing GHG concentrations. Sulfate and black-carbon aerosols, as well as land use changes, inadvertently affect the planet's albedo. We could even make deliberate efforts to increase the Earth's reflectivity with geo-engineering projects. These options for helping cool the planet, which are generally at a very preliminary stage of investigation, are discussed in a later section.

If we did choose to set a goal for the level of GHG, a variety of specifications could be considered. An objective formulated in terms of CO_2 alone would be easier to measure and monitor, but including the more powerful GHGs arising from agriculture, waste management, and other industrial processes would be more effective in limiting global warming. For a broader measure, the IPCC's definition of CO_2-equivalent could be used, or a still more comprehensive indicator of anthropogenic effects that included the roles of aerosols and ozone-depleting substances. When comparing actual concentrations with the goal, the temporary effects of volcanoes would need to be accounted for separately.

Similar to the case for the global average temperature, the atmospheric concentration of GHG can be linked, though with considerable uncertainty, to the damages from climate change. GHG is also somewhat more closely linked than temperatures to our other important goal related to the costs of mitigating climate change. However, mitigation costs are a function of the amount of emission abatement, not the amount of GHG in the air. It is fairly straightforward, though again subject to uncertainties, to estimate the connection between abatement and the residual emissions that will occur. However, more profound unknowns regarding climate feedbacks and the speed of the natural takedown of CO_2 make it difficult to connect our emissions to future GHG concentrations. In part because of the mismatch of the determining variables as well as uncertainties regarding climate damages and abatement costs, a long-run cost-benefit analysis is undermined. As stated by the IPCC (2007), our climate models and forecasts "do not as yet permit an unambiguous determination of an emissions pathway or stabilization level where benefits exceed costs."

Until further research allows improved analyses, the precautionary principle could again be called on in support of a ceiling on the GHG concentration. The charter of the United Nations Framework Convention on Climate Change, for instance, includes the objective of "stabilization of GHG concentrations in the atmosphere at a level that would prevent dangerous anthropogenic interference with the climate system" (UNFCCC, 1992). As in the case of other applications of the precautionary principle, however, the GHG concentration at which "dangerous interference" emerges is a matter of controversy. In the absence of a clear tipping point, the danger may just grow gradually as the GHG concentration continues to rise.

IPCC estimates have often been cited in support of particular concentration goals. As noted earlier, a peak concentration of 550 ppm of CO_2-equivalent might be achievable.[5] That would represent a doubling of preindustrial CO_2 and, with the central estimate for climate sensitivity, global warming of about 3°C relative to the preindustrial level. A tighter goal of 450 ppm is frequently advocated as a means of keeping global warming under 2°C. A 450 ppm goal could not be interpreted as a ceiling because we have already reached that concentration and are heading higher, year by year. However, it could be a target level at which we could stabilize the atmospheric concentration in time to avoid exceeding a 2°C temperature ceiling. A temporary overshoot of a concentration target would be less harmful than a temperature overshoot, because the climate system responds only gradually to the average GHG concentration. One group of scientists has suggested a difficult set of concentration goals, with a peak at around the current level and a target at least 35 ppm lower to be achieved by the end of this century (Hansen, 2008). In terms of CO_2 alone, the end-of-century target would be 350 ppm. The paper suggested that achieving this goal would require CO_2 capture for all the world's coal plants by 2030 and for any use of nonconventional fossil fuels, as well as significantly increased carbon storage in forests and soils.

---

[5]　Non-CO_2 gases currently contribute roughly 70 ppm to the CO_2-equivalent measure. In the near term, the effects of non-CO_2 gases would be about offset by a net boost to albedo from anthropogenic aerosols. Sulfates boost reflectivity, on net, more than black soot reduces it. However, aerosols are washed out of the lower atmosphere within a few years, and it seems reasonable to assume that emissions of aerosols will eventually be eliminated for local health reasons.

The forecasts prepared for the U.S. Climate Change Science Program (CCSP) suggest that lowering the CO_2 concentration to 350 ppm during this century could be very costly. The lowest target in that study was a CO_2 concentration of 450 ppm. To achieve even that objective, the marginal cost of reducing emissions (equivalent to the price of CO_2) would range from $130 to $230 per ton of CO_2 in 2050 (in dollars measured at their value as of 2000). This is higher than the range of estimates of the current social cost of CO_2 cited by the IPCC, but not higher than those for 2050 if the social cost of CO_2 rises by an estimated 2.5% per year. The CCSP study found much lower marginal abatement costs, ranging from $10 to $67 per ton of CO_2 in 2050, for a CO_2 concentration target of 550 ppm. Given the uncertainties about future technological developments, the confidence bands around far-ahead abatement cost estimates are extremely wide.

Because of the powerful greenhouse effects of non-CO_2 gases, as noted earlier, it is preferable to define a concentration goal in terms of CO_2-equivalent GHG rather than in terms of CO_2 alone. If an intermediate objective were formulated as a limit on the CO_2e concentration to 550 ppm during this century, the global average temperature would likely rise an estimated 3°C above the preindustrial level by 2100. In the longer run, a stricter target would be needed to avoid continued melting of the polar ice sheets and an enormous rise in sea level. A CO_2e concentration below the current level could be pursued beginning in the next century, consistent with a 350 ppm level for CO_2 alone. In the long run, an even lower level will likely be needed to rebuild mountain glaciers and ice sheets, unless geo-engineering provides additional planetary cooling.

A note of caution is perhaps the most appropriate bottom line regarding a GHG concentration goal. Given the uncertainties about future climate damages and the costs of emission abatement, it seems unclear where a concentration goal for the end of this century and beyond should be set. If such long-run goals are formulated, they should be considered aspirational rather than a hardwired commitment. Commitment to a concentration goal of a few decades may be reasonable to announce. But it would seem better to internalize more of the climate response uncertainties by articulating a longer-run objective in terms of a temperature goal.

EMISSION PATHS FOR CONCENTRATION GOALS

Relative to a temperature goal, a GHG concentration goal can be translated more easily into targets for anthropogenic emissions. In general, a stable GHG concentration requires that anthropogenic CO_2e emissions match the net rate of natural CO_2 sequestration. As discussed earlier, natural sequestration is faster at more elevated atmospheric concentrations of CO_2. Thus, a higher concentration level allows a greater level of annual emissions. However, it would be risky to rely too much on accelerating rates of natural sequestration as the atmospheric concentration of CO_2 rises. As discussed in earlier chapters, at very high concentrations, the terrestrial channel of natural sequestration would weaken because temperature and other adverse climate-related effects would undermine the plant growth stimulus provided by CO_2 fertilization. Also, although diffusion increases with a widening gap between the CO_2 concentrations in the air and the sea, the warming of the ocean and changes in circulation could slow that sequestration channel as well at very high concentrations.

The IPCC (2007) summarized the results of 177 studies designed to achieve a stable atmospheric concentration of GHG by the early twenty-second century. If CO_2e emissions continued indefinitely at their 2005 pace (44 Gt), the projected concentration would stabilize only at a level of around 700 ppm. To achieve CO_2e stabilization below 600 ppm, the IPCC estimates that emissions over this century would have to average less than two-thirds of the 2004 level and fall to less than 40% of that level by 2100.[6]

Once the CO_2 concentration in the atmosphere stabilizes, its concentration in the ocean will gradually catch up. As the gap in concentrations diminishes, the rate of CO_2 takedown by the ocean will slow. Terrestrial takedown of CO_2 will also slow after plant growth has adjusted to the stabilized concentration level. Therefore, maintaining an unchanged atmospheric concentration of CO_2 would require a gradual decrease in the rate of annual emissions. After some centuries, when the air-sea concentrations reestablish balance and the global average temperature has also become stable, net anthropogenic emissions would have to fall to zero to maintain the same atmospheric concentration of CO_2e. By then, we would need to avoid any material emissions or employ a method for removing the additional CO_2 we put into the air.

A faster rate of decline in emissions would be needed if GHG concentration objectives were formulated in terms of a peak in this century and a lower longer-run goal. After stopping the rise in the atmospheric concentration, our emissions would need to fall below the rate of natural sequestration if we seek to lower concentrations and temperatures below the peak levels that are achieved.

[6] This is based on figure 3.18 of IPCC's Working Group III report (2007), which indicates cumulative emissions over the century in CO_2, rather than CO_2e, and the IPCC estimate of CO_2 emissions of 38 Gt in 2004.

EMISSION TARGETS

Among the quantitative climate indicators, anthropogenic emissions of GHG are the most controllable but the least directly linked to climate outcomes. We are wholly responsible for our emissions. Although measurement is imperfect in some sectors, especially in agriculture, we are generally able to track emissions and can hold accountable the parties that are responsible for them. A goal for global emissions could be converted through a variety of possible formulas into abatement responsibilities for individual nations. The obligations of emitting industries, and even individual plants, could also conceivably be linked to overall emission targets. By contrast, the atmospheric concentration of GHG and the global average temperature are not wholly within our control. They depend not only on our emissions, but also on natural forces that we do not yet fully understand.

In contrast to goals for temperatures or concentrations, an emission goal can be linked rather directly to the costs of emission abatement. However, an emission goal is farther removed from assessments of the future damages from climate change.

Emission goals are often formulated in terms of their expected connection with objectives for temperatures and concentrations. For instance, 2°C of global warming is often linked to both 450 ppm of CO_2e and a reduction in global emissions to half the 1990 level by 2050. Central estimates from ranges reported by the IPCC (2007) are cited to support the connections among these objectives. However, each connection is subject to considerable uncertainties. Moreover, many possible paths for emissions could be consistent with limiting CO_2e to a particular concentration.

Emissions goals have also gained considerable political momentum. The G8 (and the European Union, Japan, and Canada separately) have endorsed a goal of reducing global emissions to 50% of 1990 levels by 2050. However, developing countries have not yet signed on to that objective. The UNFCCC treaty, which most countries around the world have signed, articulated the principle of "common but differentiated" responsibilities and capabilities for addressing climate change. In that context, the IPCC (2007) suggested that a goal of halving 1990 emissions by 2050 could be met by an 80% reduction, relative to 1990, for advanced economies. Developing countries, which currently account for around half of world emissions and most of the growth in emissions in recent years, would still have to make substantial reductions from BAU levels.

Shorter-term targets have also been formulated for emission reductions. The Kyoto Protocol, which is discussed in detail in a later section, set out emission reductions for developed countries for the 2008-to-2012 period. In aggregate, these goals represented a reduction in emissions to 5% below the 1990 level for developed countries over that period.

A successor to the Kyoto Protocol is now under negotiation, and the political accord reached in Copenhagen in December 2009, discussed later, is a key step in developing a framework for a new agreement. Countries have made pledges of emission reductions to be achieved by 2020, often conditioning their commitment on the achievement of an international treaty with goals of comparable stringency by other countries. For instance, the EU announced a unilateral goal of a 20% reduction, relative to 1990, by 2020. However, if other countries make comparable efforts, the EU indicated it would agree to a 30% reduction by 2020. The new administration that took office in Japan in September 2009 announced that it would reduce emissions to 25% of the 1990 level by 2020 if other countries also took strict commitments. These goals for the EU and Japan in part reflect the suggestion by the IPCC (2007) that advanced economies reduce emissions 25% to 40% below the 1990 level by 2020 to be on a path to stabilize the atmospheric concentration of CO_2e, after an initial overshoot, at 450 ppm.

In the United States, the recent bill sponsored by Representatives Waxman and Markey, which passed the House of Representatives on June 26, 2009, provided for the United States to reduce emissions about 3% to 5% below the 1990 level by 2020 and 80% below that level by 2050. The fate of similar bills in the Senate is unknown as of the time of this writing. The details of the Waxman-Markey bill are discussed later in the book.

It is important to note that the previously mentioned goals for advanced economy countries do not reflect emission reductions to be achieved only in their domestic economies. Under the Kyoto Protocol and presumably any successor treaty, as well as the Waxman-Markey bill, advanced economies achieve their emission reduction goals in part by buying offset credits from developing countries. Offset credits are discussed further in the next chapter.

Similar to the case for a concentration goal of 450 ppm, the goal of reducing emissions to half the 1990 level by 2050 would clearly involve a hump-shaped outlook for global emissions. According to IPCC estimates, global CO_2e emissions were about 40 Gt in 1990. Half that level would mean a global target of 20 Gt by 2050. CO_2e emissions are estimated to have been 44 Gt in 2005 and still rising rapidly (CAIT, 2010). Emissions have fallen in advanced economies during the current economic slowdown. However, as economic growth resumes, the emissions outlook will depend on the mitigation policies that are implemented.

Translating a global emission goal into emission reduction commitments of individual countries could in principle be accomplished through the use of an agreed formula. However, it will be difficult to secure wide agreement on a formula. Moreover, implementing an emission goal involves a domestic political commitment that itself requires extensive negotiation among domestic stakeholders.

A key issue for some countries is the base period against which emission reduction goals are to be measured. In the Kyoto Protocol, 1990 was used as the base year for most countries. There are a number of disadvantages of this selection. First, information sources for measuring emissions in that year were rather limited, and uncertainty bands around the estimates are therefore much larger than for more recent years. In addition, fairness issues have been raised regarding 1990 as a base year. Some national populations and economies have grown rapidly since then, whereas others have stagnated. If country emission targets were compared to more recent emission levels, strong economic performance in the past would not be penalized. However, fairness issues cut in two directions, as selection of a more recent base year would mean that earlier efforts to reduce emissions by some countries would not be recognized.

How do these emission goals and related concentration levels balance mitigation costs and the benefits of reducing climate damage? The economic estimates in Stern (2006) would support even stricter emission targets. By contrast, in the Nordhaus (2007) model, the optimal policy allows emissions to rise somewhat over the next few decades and the CO_2 concentration to stabilize at around 700 ppm. And, as noted earlier, the studies for the U.S. Climate Change Science Program predict sharply higher costs if emissions are reduced enough to push the CO_2 concentration below 550 ppm (Clarke, 2006).

The truth is that we don't know as of yet whether an emission goal equal to 50% of the 1990 level by 2050 is appropriate or not. An emission goal for this far into the future will likely need to be revised as uncertainties about climate outcomes and mitigation costs get resolved. If climate sensitivity is as high as a 4.5°C for a doubling of CO_2, and if new, low-carbon technologies are cheaper than expected, a stricter emission goal may be appropriate. However, if climate sensitivity is lower than the central estimate of 3°C, natural CO_2 takedown is greater than expected, and low-carbon technologies remain expensive, a looser emission goal may be appropriate. It may be difficult to build flexibility about emission goals into legislation or an international treaty. Limiting the horizon of legislation or a treaty to a decade or so ahead also has disadvantages, because cost-effective emission reductions require long-term investments in technology development and deployment. Uncertainty about future policies after the expiration of a law or a treaty would impair the incentives for undertaking such long-term investments.

INTENSITY TARGETS

At the individual-country level, other forms of emission targets have also been proposed. The trajectory of a country's emissions depends heavily on the growth of its population and economy. Emission "intensity" is the ratio of emissions to population or GDP. Intensity targets can also be established for industries or firms depending on their level of output. Intensity targets allow emissions to grow with the level of economic activity.

In the United States, the Bush administration set a target of reducing GHG emissions per dollar of GDP by 18% between the years 2002 and 2012. This target was to be met through voluntary measures only. Actual U.S. emission intensity was falling even faster before 2002 as the economy gradually shifted toward service sectors and away from manufacturing. With rapid growth of the U.S. economy between 1990 and 2002, emission intensity fell by 37%. The actual level of CO_2e emissions, however, grew nearly 14% over that twelve-year period.

In late 2009, China announced a goal of reducing the CO_2 intensity of its economy 40% to 45% below the 2005 level by 2020. According to some forecasts (EIA, 2009), this emission intensity goal is not far from what the country would achieve through nonclimate-related policies designed to modernize its economy. Indeed, China's current domestic development plan includes a goal of reducing energy use as a ratio to GDP (energy intensity) by 20% between 2005 and 2010; it seems well on the way to achieving this objective.

A broader group of countries in Asia (along with the United States) announced an agreement on an energy intensity goal in 2007. The twenty-one members of the Asia-Pacific Economic Cooperation (APEC) announced a "regional aspirational goal" of reducing energy intensity by 25% between 2005 and 2030 (the Sydney Declaration). For reference, the United States actually achieved a 40% reduction in energy intensity during the previous twenty-five-year period (EIA, 2009).

An intensity target has the advantage of not impinging on economic growth as much as a hard emission cap. However, as noted earlier, energy and emission intensities have been falling under BAU policies, and the intensity targets that countries have announced have not been very ambitious relative to a BAU outlook.

VARYING GOAL SPECIFICATIONS BY HORIZON

An insight from monetary policy frameworks could be of relevance for setting climate goals. In monetary analysis, the appropriate goal for the short run of a year or two differs from that needed over the longer term. In the short run, a central bank often must adjust policy to avoid recessions or severe economic downturns. However, a central bank has almost no influence over the long-run growth rate of the economy. Nevertheless, its policies do determine the rate of inflation over the long run. Therefore, for monetary policy, economic stabilization is an appropriate short-run goal, but the long-run goal must be keeping inflation low.

Climate policy is focused on an even more distant outlook than monetary regulation. However, as in the case of monetary policy, different climate goals are likely to be appropriate, depending on the horizon of analysis. The greater controllability of emissions makes them more suitable as targets for the short run of a decade or two. Over the span of fifty years to a century, a GHG concentration goal may be more appropriate because it is more closely linked to climate outcomes but still reflective of efforts to mitigate emissions. In the longer run of multiple centuries, however, a temperature goal would seem most apt because it would best characterize the desired climate and might be achievable in part through means other than emission mitigation over that long a period.

PROS AND CONS OF GOAL SETTING FOR THE CLIMATE

The global climate is an example of a public good; no one can be excluded from consuming it. Like any public good, a stable climate can be enjoyed both by those who sacrifice to achieve it and by those who do nothing about it – the free-riders. It is in everyone's narrow self-interest to be a free-rider, to convince someone else to solve the problem. This has been called the "tragedy of the commons," after a famous example of the destruction of commonly owned land because of overgrazing by multiple herds of cattle (Hardin, 1968).

Some observers have argued that the process of setting common goals will help the international community overcome tendencies toward free-riding. In particular, international goal setting will generate benchmarks for assessing global efforts and create structures within which the commitments of individual countries are recognized and mitigation efforts can be compared (Corfee-Morlot, 2003).

International goal setting could also have some disadvantages. Targets for the global average temperature, GHG concentrations, and emissions tend to focus on only one-half of our climate policy objectives: the potential damages from climate change. The cost of reducing emissions is not taken into account. A particular goal may prove inadvisable, not only because of developments in the climate, but also because of unexpected progress or setbacks in developing low-emission technologies. Moreover, goals formulated in terms of emissions and GHG concentrations may overlook the possibility of research breakthroughs regarding geo-engineering.

Indeed, the type of goal that is agreed on by the international community could, in principle, constrain the alternatives among policy instruments selected by individual countries. For instance, an international agreement based on emission reduction commitments might dissuade a country from implementing a domestic policy that is based only on setting a carbon price equal to the best estimate of the social cost of CO_2. The next chapter carries this theme further by moving from broader issues regarding climate goals to the choices among particular instruments for national climate policies.

EIGHT

Policy Mandates and Market-Based Instruments

A key distinction is often made between command-and-control and market-based instruments of policy. Command-and-control policies include government mandates regarding choices among technologies, processes, equipment, fuels, and standards. Government mandates and controls also include support for research, development, and demonstration of new technologies and could conceivably include major geo-engineering projects. Market-based policies, by contrast, seek to achieve public objectives by adjusting the price signals that are observed in the private sector, counting on individuals and business firms to find inventive low-cost ways of meeting those goals. The two major alternatives for market-based climate polices are carbon taxes and cap-and-trade programs.

GENERAL RATIONALES FOR POLICY MANDATES

In a pure command-and-control economy, government bureaucrats decide on the goods to be produced and the prices at which they will sell. History has shown that a market system generally delivers better economic performance. However, markets do not always achieve social objectives when left on their own. Incomplete information, diverging incentives between producers and consumers, coordination problems, and the presence of public goods can result in market failures. Command-and-control techniques can sometimes be used effectively in a targeted manner to overcome these problems. Indeed, some regulation of markets is needed to safeguard important social values aside from economic efficiency.

Coordination and information problems crop up in a variety of ways. For example, consider the differences in incentives between landlords and tenants. If a tenant is responsible for the costs of fuel and electricity, a landlord does not have an incentive to invest in improved insulation and weather-stripping. For another example, homebuyers may not have sufficient information to compare the eventual savings they will get by buying a more expensive but more energy-efficient home. Similarly, consumers may not have enough information about lifetime fuel savings from a more fuel-efficient vehicle. Uncertainties about future gasoline costs might make such calculations extremely uncertain. Finally, policy mandates are one possible way to address difficult measurement issues regarding greenhouse gas (GHG) emissions from landfills, forestry, and agriculture.

TRANSPORTATION MANDATES

Direct government investments have a major influence on the transportation choices of individuals and businesses. The quality of infrastructure provided through public investment largely determines the cost and convenience of travel and shipping by road, rail, public transit, airplane, and watercraft. The resulting private-sector choices have critical effects on the GHG emissions from the transport sector. In particular, increased public transit and rail traffic in place of road and air travel, as well as diminished suburban sprawl, could bring large reductions in transportation-related emissions.

Concerns about congestion and air quality have played a key role in the choice of transportation infrastructure in urban areas. Hazardous emissions from vehicle exhausts have been regulated for many years in some countries. The goal of limiting oil imports has also motivated standards for vehicles and fuels. Although designed to serve other purposes, these policies also have important implications for GHG emissions.

For many years, national governments have imposed standards on the production and sale of vehicles. The purposes have been safety requirements, control of health-related pollutants, and improvements in fuel economy that would help reduce dependence on imported oil. In the United States, auto manufacturers have been required to meet minimum corporate average fuel economy (CAFE) standards since 1975. Canadian standards have been generally comparable. The U.S. standard, averaged over vehicle types, is currently about 25 miles per gallon (mpg). A 2007 law would have raised the average fuel economy standard to 35 mpg by 2020, but the Obama administration announced a tougher national goal of 35.5 mpg by 2016. In Europe, the automobile industry accepted a voluntary agreement to limit emissions to 140 gm of CO_2 per kilometer by 2008, which would be equivalent to about 40.5 mpg. However, the industry will evidently fail to meet this target, and in response, the European Commission is now recommending legislation for mandatory emission standards. In Asia, fuel economy standards are generally applied to different weight classes (An, 2004). The requirements in Japan would result in an estimated average fuel economy of about 35.5 mpg in 2010.

Vehicle standards are a direct means of improving the efficiency of energy use in the transportation sector. Standards are used instead of increasing fuel taxes on the argument that consumers may not respond sufficiently to changes in fuel prices. In addition, the long development times for new vehicle offerings may make auto manufacturers slow to respond to fuel price movements if there are no compulsory standards. Vehicle standards have the disadvantage of making it cheaper to drive a car; they may therefore boost the total miles driven by consumers. In consequence, the overall environmental benefit of increased fuel economy is somewhat undermined.

The use of petroleum and the emissions of GHG from vehicles could also be limited through fuel standards. Many countries now require ethanol or other biofuels to be blended with petroleum-based gasoline. In the mid-1970s, Brazil initiated a program for the use of ethanol made from sugar cane. By 2007, ethanol represented about one-fourth of Brazil's total motor fuel consumption. In the United States, legislation stipulates the amount of biofuel that must be mixed into the nation's gasoline. The minimum is 9 billion gallons in 2008, rising to 36 billion in 2022. In the United States, ethanol is now derived mainly from domestic corn. By 2022, however, 21 billion gallons of the nation's biofuel must be obtained from products other than corn. Most U.S. cars can run on a fuel blend that includes 10% ethanol, although some can operate with "E85" fuels that are 85% ethanol (Worldwatch, 2006).

BUILDING STANDARDS

Building codes have regulated the construction of new homes and commercial buildings around the world for many years. Typically, model codes are developed by associations, such as the International Code Council, and then adopted in full or with modifications by national or local government bodies. Building codes have been used mainly to ensure structural and fire safety, as well as appropriate sanitation, but requirements for energy conservation are also sometimes included. For instance, the building code for California specifies minimum insulation levels of R-19 for ceilings, R-13 for walls, and R-8 for ducts. Judging by past practices, if building codes were modified to achieve climate policy goals, existing buildings would not be affected except when renovation work was undertaken.

Aside from mandatory building codes, voluntary standards have also been promulgated for energy efficiency in buildings. For example, in the

United States, the Green Building Council has devised a set of efficiency ratings called LEED (Leadership in Energy and Environmental Design). In addition, the Energy Star program of the EPA provides energy efficiency standards for buildings and many household appliances. The Energy Star symbol on appliances gives a potentially valuable signal of energy efficiency to consumers and therefore provides an incentive to businesses to produce qualifying products.

POWER SECTOR STANDARDS

In developed economies, the power sector has been subject to regulation for many years for the purpose of controlling air pollution. In the United States, the Clean Air Act, passed in 1963 and amended in 1970 and 1990, mandated controls on the emission of hazardous pollutants from coal-burning power plants. In 2007, the U.S. Supreme Court ruled that CO_2 emissions could also potentially be regulated under the terms of the Act. The monitoring systems that have been installed for enforcement of the Clean Air Act could also be used for regulating CO_2 emissions. In addition, as discussed in subsequent chapters, the power sector figures prominently in several cap-and-trade programs.

For the purpose of achieving climate goals, more direct restrictions on the generation of electricity are sometimes advocated, including a possible outright ban on new coal-based power plants that do not capture and store their carbon emissions (Hansen, 2007). Because the cost of coal plants with carbon capture and storage is currently much higher than other sources of energy, this policy would imply a halt in construction of new coal plants for some time. A similar approach would be the adoption of a strict performance standard, which might have a similar effect. For instance, California requires that new power generation facilities emit no more than 1,100 pounds of CO_2 per megawatt hour of electricity supplied. New fossil fuel plants could meet this requirement only if they used combined cycle gas technology or carbon capture and storage (Palmer, 2007).

Another alternative is a Renewable Portfolio Standard that requires retail power companies ("load-serving entities") to buy a minimum percentage of their electricity from renewable sources such as wind, solar, biomass, or geothermal. This has the effect of reducing the emission intensity of electricity generation and supporting the deployment of relatively new technologies. However, the availability of renewable sources and therefore the cost-effectiveness of such portfolio standards vary greatly by geographic area. The EU and numerous U.S. states have adopted such policies, sometimes more as an aspiration rather than a hard legal requirement.

In any case, before a new power plant is constructed in the United States and in most other countries, permits are required from local government authorities. Thus, even in the absence of a general climate policy, the greenhouse effects of new generating facilities could potentially be addressed on a case-by-case basis.

Electric utilities may also be subjected to standards for energy efficiency. Targets for improvement relative to a baseline may be achieved through replacement of transmission and distribution equipment with energy-saving alternatives. In addition, the utility may earn efficiency credits for promoting improved lighting and other applications among homeowners and businesses. Several U.S. states have implemented or are considering energy efficiency standards (Nadel, 2006).

REGULATION OF OTHER EMITTING SECTORS

Mandates designed to reduce GHG emissions could also be imposed on agriculture, forestry, waste management, and other industries. Highly specific practices could be mandated to reduce industrial emissions of potent GHGs including required recovery and destruction of HFCs, PFCs, and sulfur dioxide before they are released into the atmosphere.

In some countries, landfill management must conform to various regulations for health and safety reasons, including compulsory recycling and dumping restrictions that are designed to keep toxins out of groundwater supplies. Regulations could also be imposed to reduce greenhouse effects by requiring recovery of methane from suitable sites. Indeed, the difficulty of measuring methane emissions from landfills may make technology mandates particularly apt in certain cases. For instance, landfill sites above a certain size could be required to install and operate methane digesters.

In many countries, the agricultural sector is subject to numerous regulations designed to ensure the health of animals and plants, the quality and safety of food, and the conservation of natural ecosystems. Some of these regulations would also tend to limit agricultural emissions of GHG. For instance, the Nitrates Directive of the European Union (EU, 1991) limits the application of nitrogenous fertilizers on croplands. The main purpose is to prevent a buildup of nitrogen in rivers, lakes, and estuaries, which can result in algae blooms, oxygen depletion, and consequent mortality of fish and other aquatic life. This regulation also helps limit the emission of nitrous oxide from agricultural soils. Mandates could also be imposed on agriculture for the express purpose of limiting GHG emissions, such as the use of methane digesters on large dairy farms or cropland practices that foster retention of soil carbon.

Most of the world's forests are on government-owned land. In developing countries, concessions are typically granted to private companies to harvest timber. The terms of those concessions could include additional provisions to reduce CO_2 emissions from forestry operations, including restocking requirements and improved harvesting techniques that minimize damage to remaining trees.

Private forest lands are less often subject to regulation. California has the longest experience regulating forestry on private lands, with related legislation dating back to 1945 (Dicus, 2003). The purpose has been to foster sustainable timber harvests with preservation of regional environmental and economic values. The state must approve a timber harvest plan, which is required to meet Forest Practice Rules, including compulsory replanting. Such regulations could potentially be extended to promote greater CO_2 sequestration in forests. For instance, clear-cutting for land development could be restricted and the minimum age of trees eligible for harvest could be increased.

FUNDING OF RESEARCH AND DEVELOPMENT

Aside from mandates for the deployment of certain types of technologies, governments may finance research and development activities. Funding may be provided for basic research, applied research, precommercial development, demonstration projects, or deployment of specific technologies. Government financing may be advocated on the view that the benefits to society exceed the private rewards from research. This rationale is more applicable to basic and applied research than to commercial development. Also, government decision making is more suited to providing a technology base through fundamental research rather than trying to pick winners in the future marketplace. Joint public/private research could accelerate the transmission of results into commercial applications, but also, in some cases, could run the risk of putting proprietary limits on the diffusion of technology.

Additional research is especially needed to develop and improve low-emitting technologies in energy production. Considerable work also remains to be done to investigate the possibilities for carbon capture and storage. Finally, geo-engineering, discussed further in this chapter, also remains to be explored. Further research on the climate is essential as well, including data collection, model development, and forecasting of climate developments. Improvements in information and analysis on the climate might ultimately help steer policy formulation away from possible costly errors.

GEO-ENGINEERING

Geo-engineering generally refers to efforts to alter the climate other than by mitigating anthropogenic emissions of GHG. The idea is that we may find a much cheaper way to maintain a stable climate without having to endure a wrenching overhaul of our energy sector (argued, e.g., by Carlin, 2007). Alternatively, geo-engineering may be an option of last resort if we fail to slow our GHG emissions sufficiently. Geo-engineering proposals are still at a very early stage of formulation; considerable research is needed to investigate possible environmental side effects and to develop details of the schemes. Two types of approaches are being pursued: increasing the Earth's albedo and enhancing the natural drawdown of CO_2 from the air.

Albedo-changing schemes include putting a large sun shade in orbit or seeding cloud formation. Another leading idea involves mimicking an aspect of the behavior of volcanoes. The entire planet has been observed to cool noticeably for a year or two after a major eruption. The reason is the ejection of sulfate particles into the stratosphere, which help reflect sunlight. Deliberate seeding of the stratosphere with sulfate aerosols might provide a similar global cooling. One study found that the scattering of light by aerosols was most effective when using particles that were considerably smaller than those associated with volcanic releases. The analysis suggested that 1.5 million tons of sulfur per year could cool the planet by about 3 °C, thereby offsetting the global warming effects of a doubling of CO_2 (Rasch, 2008).

This geo-engineering proposal may seem strange at first glance, as our coal-burning power plants already inject sulfur dioxide (SO_2) into the air. However, these particles remain in the lower portion of the atmosphere and fall as acid rain within a few weeks, creating regional pollution of lakes and rivers. Particles injected into the stratosphere would spread widely around the globe before descending. Most of them would fall into the ocean, which covers 70% of the Earth. However, the full environmental effects of injecting sulfur into the stratosphere are not clear. Another recent study indicated that such particles could result in damage to the protective ozone layer (Tilmes, 2008).

Changing the planet's albedo would not mitigate the harmful effects of high CO_2 concentrations on marine life. Geo-engineering designed to remove CO_2 from the atmosphere include time-honored tree-planting projects, which have been undertaken in the past mainly to serve local environmental goals. Forests in tropical areas are especially useful in helping to cool the planet because they not only remove CO_2 but also substantially enhance the rate of evaporation, which directly cools the surface and also increases cloud cover. However, trees also reduce albedo because they absorb more sunlight than grasses or other ground cover. In boreal environments (high latitudes), planting additional trees would evidently warm the surface of the planet on net, as the albedo-reducing effects would overwhelm the cooling from enhanced evaporation and CO_2 takedown (Bonan, 2008).

A variety of new proposals have also been suggested for withdrawing CO_2 from the air. Fertilizing the ocean with iron particles, for example, could spur the growth of phyto-plankton, which extract CO_2. For permanent CO_2 storage, however, the carbon-containing remains of these plankton blooms would need to fall to the deep ocean or to the ocean floor rather than dissolve along the way, as may be the case more often. Moreover, it is unclear whether ocean fertilization would result in increased emissions of methane and nitrous oxide. Other environmental damage could also occur, including the hypoxia associated with algae blooms in coastal areas.

Other schemes have been suggested to enhance the rate of chemical weathering or the sequestration of carbon in the soil. A variety of chemical, electrical, or biological means could be used for taking down CO_2 from the atmosphere. However, our fossil fuel power plants will provide a highly concentrated source of gaseous CO_2 for many years to come; capturing CO_2 from such plants will be cheaper than capturing it from the air.

It is not clear yet whether some geo-engineering idea will turn out to be an inexpensive way to moderate global warming. However, the prospects are still highly speculative at this stage. No scheme provides enough confidence to warrant a relaxation of concern regarding our GHG emissions. Nevertheless, continuing geo-engineering research is surely advisable at least for hedging purposes; we cannot be sure at present that we won't need to use such extraordinary means sometime in the future to prevent a climate catastrophe.

GENERAL ADVANTAGES OF MARKET-BASED APPROACHES

A basic principle of welfare economics, tracing back to the "invisible hand" of Adam Smith, highlights the benefits of a market economy: Competitive markets will produce the amounts and types of goods and services desired by consumers in the most efficient possible way. This principle does not hold true in cases of "market failure." Because of the absence of private markets for public goods like clean air and climate stability, the market system does fail. In the absence of such markets, polluters do not pay for the environmental damages they cause. An "externality" is then said to exist, a social cost external to the signals indicated by prices in private markets.

The economist Arthur Pigou argued that public policy should try to estimate the value of externalities and then impose a tax or subsidy to correct the signal in market prices. He argued that a modification of market prices of this nature would be more efficient than behavioral mandates. He claimed that if market prices are corrected for the value of externalities, no further policy measures are needed or desired. The basic principle of welfare economics is then recovered, and private markets can be left to find the optimum level of production of each good or service.[1]

In the case of GHG, the climate is the public good that is impaired by emissions. Under a laissez-faire approach, a private firm imposes externalities in the form of climate damage costs on the rest of society. The private firm does not pay for the environmental costs it imposes on others; it responds to the incentives of the prices it observes, which place a value of zero on maintaining a stable climate under a business-as-usual (BAU) policy. But a stable climate has a value greater than zero. To correct market prices for the climate externality, each ton of emissions should bear the cost of the marginal climate damage it would inflict. A Pigou-type pricing policy would thus imply that firms should pay the social cost of CO_2 for each ton of their emissions. That payment could be made either through a tax on emissions or the purchase of an emission allowance at that price, as discussed later.

Caveats to a simple Pigou-pricing policy have already been discussed. We cannot place much confidence in our estimates of the social cost of CO_2. Moreover, the absence of a price on CO_2 emissions is not the only market failure affecting our use of energy and other emitting sectors. In some cases, as discussed earlier, specific mandates may be needed to overcome deeply embedded information and incentive problems. Nevertheless, even if some targeted policy mandates are employed, they could be combined with a broad GHG pricing policy. We do not know the "correct" price for

---

[1] Ronald Coase (1960) argued that such taxes or subsidies are not needed if property rights are precisely defined and private parties then negotiate compensation among themselves. However, coordination of such negotiations is often impractical, and especially so in the case of global warming, where the property rights of future generations are at stake.

GHG emissions (the value of the marginal environmental damage they will cause), but we can nevertheless make our best estimate. A general price on GHG will motivate adjustments across the widest possible range of economic activities. It will induce consumers to switch demand away from high-emission products; motivate producers to increase efficiency, switch production processes, and choose alternative inputs; and create an incentive for investors to fund research and development of alternative products and production processes. Unlike government mandates, a price signal will allow the private sector to invent new ways to reduce emissions, ways that bureaucrats may not have imagined.

SUBSIDIES ON ENERGY USE

For many years, energy policies around the world have generally been designed to support rather than discourage the development and use of fossil fuels. Governments have subsidized the exploitation of oil, natural gas, and coal resources, thereby keeping energy prices lower than would have been the case in an unfettered private market. One purpose for such subsidies has been the development of local energy supplies in order to reduce dependence on imports. In the United States, extraction and use of fossil fuels is supported by generous tax deductions, reduced tax rates, low-cost leases of mineral rights on federal lands, and low-interest loans to energy cooperatives (Fischer, 2000). An estimated 10% of the *revenue* from coal mining and 15% from oil and gas drilling (by independent producers) is regarded as a depletion allowance that is free of tax. This treatment is far more generous than the depreciation of capital equipment that is allowed for other business investments. Owners of coal leases also have the option of treating their royalty income as a capital gain. Any losses incurred on investment in oil and gas properties can be used to offset ordinary income without limitations that apply in other economic sectors. Fuel cooperatives escape tax as nonprofit organizations and can obtain low-cost loans from the Rural Electrification Administration, even if they sell mainly to wealthy suburbs that have many alternative sources of supply. Even the largest energy companies in the world can benefit from government-funded infrastructure investments and tax breaks for technology development.

Many other countries around the world have similar incentives for the development and use of fossil fuels. Oil-exporting countries typically keep domestic gasoline prices far below world price levels. A recent study estimated that energy subsidies around the world tallied up to more than $550 billion in 2008 (IEA, 2010).

A subsidy on the use of fossil fuels is also a subsidy on the emissions of CO_2 that result. It is the opposite of the Pigou-type pricing policy needed to correct for the climate externality. At a meeting of the G20 in September 2009, President Obama proposed, and other leaders agreed, to work toward elimination of energy subsidies.

WILL FUEL PRICES RISE ENOUGH ON THEIR OWN?

In recent years up through the summer of 2008, sharp increases in global fuel demands and fears that supplies may not keep up led to an extraordinary spike in energy prices. The price of petroleum, which averaged about $26 per barrel over 2001 and 2002, rose above $140 in July 2008. Natural gas prices tripled over the six years ending in April 2008. Coal prices rose by 50% over the five years ending in 2007 and then more than doubled over the first half of 2008.[2] These price increases had multiple causes, including rapid growth in demand for energy in China, India, and elsewhere, a limited amount of investment in the development of new oil supplies, and a surge of financial investment in energy commodities.

With the onset of financial crisis and global economic recession in late 2008, energy prices plummeted. Continued weakness in the global economy, and some important new discoveries of oil and natural gas, will likely keep energy prices below the peaks reached in the first half of 2008 for some time. However, conventional oil and gas supplies will become increasingly depleted in the coming decades. The resulting rise in energy prices will likely spur changes in consumption patterns and perhaps lifestyles. Choices in vehicles and modes of transportation will probably be affected, and perhaps also the size, energy efficiency, and location of residences. These energy efficiency developments will have the side benefit of reducing GHG emissions as well. In addition, increases in the market prices of traditional fossil fuels could also provide a boost for the development of renewable energy resources.

However, higher prices for conventional fuels could also bring some adverse consequences for GHG emissions because they may spur development of nonconventional sources of liquid fuels. As discussed earlier, the emissions of carbon per barrel of liquid fuel produced is much greater when using tar sands, oil shale, or coal-to-liquids technologies than when extracting oil from conventional sources. This risk underscores the need

---

[2] The price data are from the U.S. Energy Information Agency. The prices are for West Texas Intermediate oil, U.S. wellhead natural gas, and for U.S. bituminous coal.

to correct energy prices for the externality associated with CO_2 emissions, no matter how tight the market would get because of private supply and demand. The true social value of GHG emissions is not zero.

AN "UPSTREAM CO_2 TAX" ON FUELS

One alternative for implementing a Pigou-pricing policy is to impose a broad tax on emissions of GHG. The wider a tax burden is spread, the more options become available for reducing emissions and the cheaper it is to achieve an emission reduction goal. However, the wider the tax incidence, the greater the administrative cost of collecting it. A carbon tax on the producers of fuels would provide fairly broad coverage of emissions while also keeping the administrative burden of tax collection fairly low. A tax collected close to the point where fossil resources are extracted is called an "upstream" tax. By contrast, a "downstream" tax is collected from the final users of energy. Many intermediate points of tax collection are also possible.

An upstream tax may seem unfair. Why should industries that produce fuel be penalized when it is the users who actually emit the CO_2? However, in a competitive industry, consumers in fact pay for a tax even if it is collected from producers, because firms will raise prices to pass on their costs. The point at which taxes are collected can have vastly different implications for administrative costs. For fossil fuels, a fully downstream approach would be impractical, given the millions of residences and commercial buildings that use energy. However, there are also an enormous number of drilling rigs, so collecting a tax right at the point of extraction of oil and gas would also be an administrative burden.

The appropriate point for collecting a CO_2 tax has been reviewed in several analyses of U.S. industries. For instance, one early study (Hargrave, 1998) identified some 600,000 oil wells and thousands of distributors in the United States, but fewer than 200 oil refineries. Thus, administrative costs would likely be lowest if the tax were collected from refineries. The situation was similar in the natural gas industry, with some 300,000 wells but only about 725 processing plants. However, about 20% of U.S. natural gas is pure enough to enter distribution pipelines directly, bypassing the processing plants. Because there are only about 150 major pipelines, a tax could be collected when natural gas enters a pipeline. In the case of coal, there are about 550 preparation plants; these plants receive ore from the mines and assess its carbon content, providing the information needed for a CO_2 tax to be collected. However, the tax could also be collected from power companies, which are the main users of coal, including some that is shipped directly from mines, bypassing the processing plants. Also, power companies already provide data on CO_2 emissions (with other pollutants). Several other complications would need to be addressed if a broad CO_2 tax were imposed. Some oil refinery outputs, such as asphalt and petrochemical feedstocks, do not result in GHG emissions. Also, imports of finished oil products would need to be monitored and taxed. Finally, fuel exports would need tax rebates, especially if they would be subject to a CO_2 tax in the importing country.

An upstream CO_2 tax would raise fuel prices for all downstream users and thereby spur energy-efficiency improvements in buildings, vehicles, and industries. However, as noted above, fuel combustion is responsible for only about 60% of global GHG emissions. Other policies would be needed to address the GHG emissions of agriculture, forestry, and waste management. The revenues provided by a fuel tax could potentially be used to provide subsidies for nonfuel-emission-reduction projects. The tax revenues could also be used to support environmental research, to provide temporary assistance to impaired industries and regions, to reduce government budget deficits, and/or to allow reduction of other taxes in the economy. Indeed, replacing taxes that penalize investment and work with a GHG tax could provide a net boost to the overall economy, particularly after transitional adjustments to the price changes have been completed.

GASOLINE AND VEHICLE TAXES

Consumers are already required to pay taxes on gasoline in most countries. In the United States, for instance, the federal government tax was $0.184 per gallon in 2008. State governments impose taxes as well, averaging about $0.286 per gallon (API.org). The total U.S. gasoline tax thus averages $0.47 per gallon. In Canada, gasoline taxes are more elevated, averaging about C$0.93/gallon plus sales taxes of 8% (Dept. of Finance, 2006). European taxes are higher still. The rate was £0.50/liter in the UK in April 2008, equivalent to about US$3.80/gallon, plus a value-added tax of 17.5%. In Germany, the rate was €0.65/liter, equivalent to about US$3.90/gallon, plus a value-added tax of 19%. In Japan, a gasoline tax of ¥25/liter (about US$0.93/gallon) expired in April 2008; its possible reinstatement has been a major political controversy.

The revenues from such gasoline taxes are usually recycled for the construction and maintenance of roads and bridges that support the use of road vehicles. Therefore, these taxes do not have the net effect of discouraging driving. Although they likely do not alter total miles driven, they may help lower overall energy use somewhat by supporting the choice of vehicles with better fuel economy.

In advanced economies, gasoline is a necessity for many and its cost takes a bigger bite out of the income of the less well-off. A regressive gas tax therefore accentuates disparities in discretionary income. Some countries, such as Germany, promote biofuels by allowing them an exemption from fuel taxes. Most biofuels are currently produced from food crops such as corn, sugarcane, and oil palm. The energy-related increases in the demand for such crops have contributed to a sharp rise in food costs of late. Those price spikes have led to riots in Haiti, Bangladesh, Indonesia, and numerous African countries. Moreover, the atmospheric concentration of CO_2 has been boosted, rather than reduced, when tropical forests have been cut to cultivate such crops.

EFFECTS OF A CO_2 TAX ON CONSUMPTION

Because gasoline taxes are typically used for road improvements, they are not Pigou-type taxes that correct the market prices of fuel for the future climate damages they cause. A CO_2 tax that was not recycled to road users would create incentives to reduce driving and switch to lower-emitting fuels and vehicles with better gas economy. Although the tax would boost the attractiveness of biofuels relative to petroleum-based fuels, some tax might apply even to biofuels because of the lifecycle emissions involved in their production, processing, and transportation.

A new CO_2 tax might not translate into very large reductions in emissions from gasoline consumption. The tax would likely boost gasoline prices by only a fraction of the increases already seen over the last several years. Burning a gallon of gas releases about 8.8 kg of CO_2 (EPA), so a \$50/ton of CO_2 tax would add only \$0.44 per gallon. By contrast, market forces have pushed up prices at the pump by about \$3 a gallon over the six years ending in the summer of 2008. For small price increases, gasoline consumption is rather inelastic in the short run. Low-income consumers outside urban areas have limited transportation alternatives, whereas wealthier individuals spend only an insignificant share of their incomes on gasoline. Economic analyses suggest that a 10% increase in gas prices would reduce fuel consumption by about 4% to 7% (Parry, 2007). More than half of those reductions would occur only over the long run, when new vehicles were purchased. However, the introduction of new vehicles depends largely on the strategic investments made by auto manufacturers several years before the vehicles are actually available for sale.

In making vehicle choices, consumers may be especially responsive to incentives and taxes on vehicle purchases. In a "feebate" program, for instance, fees would be charged on high-emission vehicles, with the revenues distributed as rebates on cars with better gas mileage (McManus, 2007). The response would depend on the size of the tax and its coverage. The U.S. "gas-guzzler tax," introduced in 1978, has had very limited impact. The tax ranges only from $1,000 to $7,700 per vehicle and applies mainly to foreign luxury cars; SUVs, minivans, and trucks have been exempt (EPA. gov). However, the U.S. "cash-for-clunkers" program, which operated in July and August 2009, elicited a substantial response. In that program, enacted as part of the economic stimulus plan, consumers obtained a rebate of up to $4,500 on the purchase of a new vehicle with high fuel economy if they agreed to scrap their current low-fuel-economy vehicle. The Department of Transportation reported that almost 700,000 older cars were scrapped to earn rebates during the two months of this program. However, many of those cars may have been scrapped in any case over a longer interval of time, and the program is evidently not a cost-effective means of controlling GHG, judging by estimates of costs per ton of CO_2 of $240 or much higher (Knittel, 2009).

A variety of feebate approaches could also potentially be considered outside the transportation sector. An investment tax on new coal-burning power plants, for instance, could be recycled as rebates to lower-emitting alternative investments.

A CO_2 tax would have a greater effect on most electricity prices than on gasoline prices. As noted earlier, a $50/ton tax on CO_2 would increase gasoline prices by $0.44 per gallon. This would be only about a 10% increase over the average, regular-grade U.S. gasoline price as of July 2008. The percentage increase from this CO_2 tax would be smaller in other advanced economies because of higher gasoline prices. In the electricity sector, the effects would be more complicated because of the varying mix of sources of power generation. For coal-burning plants, which produce about 40% of the world's electricity, the effects would be notable. Each kWh from coal releases about one kg of CO_2.[3] The previously mentioned tax would thus amount to about $0.05 per kWh from coal, which was about 50% of the average retail price of electricity in the United States in 2007 (EIA). A CO_2 tax would therefore create strong incentives for utilities to switch to lower-emitting sources of power.

---

[3] As noted before, the carbon content of coal is about 26 kg/GJ. At an efficiency of 33%, it takes about .0108 GJ of coal to produce one kWh of electricity (as one kWh = 3,600,000 joules). This would release $26 \times .0108 = .28$ kg of carbon or $.28 \times 3.67 = 1$ kg of CO_2.

CAP-AND-TRADE PROGRAMS

The other major alternative for a market-based approach, aside from a tax on GHG, is a cap-and-trade program. In these programs, the government places an overall limit, or cap, on an activity, such as the emissions of GHG gas. The limit applies to the aggregate emissions of all firms covered by the program, not to each firm individually. The government issues a fixed number of permits, or "allowances," equal to the aggregate emissions cap. Regulated firms are required to surrender allowances for each ton of their emissions, and they are allowed to trade allowances among themselves, so that firms with excess allowances may make sales to those that are short.

Tradable allowances, without an explicit emissions cap, may also be used to help reduce the cost of implementing a performance or technology standard: A firm that is able to comply cheaply earns credits if it goes beyond the minimum standard. It can sell those credits to firms that find it more costly to comply. The buying firms then surrender credits to the government to cover their shortfall in meeting the standard. Systems of tradable permits have been proposed and employed for Renewable Portfolio Standards in the power sector and emission standards in transportation. In distinction from cap-and-trade, trading systems of this nature are sometimes called averaging, or baseline-and-credit programs.

The market for allowances helps reduce the overall cost of the program. Consider, for instance, a simple case in which mandates or market-based approaches are used to achieve a given amount of emission reductions in electricity production. In one case, a command-and-control approach is used, under which all power generators have to make the reductions. Alternative market-based approaches are a tax or cap-and-trade designed to achieve the same aggregate emission reductions in the power sector. Suppose the country's CO_2 emissions come entirely from two *identical* coal-burning power plants in a connected grid. One of the plants is in a location favorable for windmills, whereas the other has no option but to burn coal. The emission goal is a 50% reduction in the nation's overall emissions from the power sector.

Under the command-and-control alternative, the government mandates each power plant to cut its emissions in half. At one plant, windmills are installed to replace half the power output (thus, one-quarter of the national output). At the other plant, carbon capture and storage is installed. Suppose wind raises the cost of electricity from 10 to 12 cents per kWh, whereas carbon capture raises the cost from 10 to 30 cents per kWh.

The average cost of the command-and-control approach, per kWh consumed in the country, is as follows:

$$(12-10) \times 0.25 + (30-10) \times 0.25 = 5.5 \text{ cents.}$$

For a market-based approach, consider first an emission tax that raises the cost of electricity from coal by 3 cents per kWh. In this case, one plant would avoid any tax by generating all of its output with wind. The other coal-burning plant would maintain its output and pay the tax for its emissions. The overall 50% emission cut would be achieved entirely with cheap wind power rather than partly with more expensive carbon capture and storage. The average cost to the economy, per kWh, would be $(12 - 10) \times 0.50 = 1$ cent. The tax paid by the other plant represents no cost to the economy as a whole; it is merely a transfer from the private sector to the government. (Nevertheless, the cost of the tax to the firm, as well as the higher cost of energy to consumers under any carbon-control policy, raises political economy issues. These are discussed at the end of the chapter.)

Cap-and-trade achieves the same cost-effective result as the tax. Suppose the government auctions emission allowances equal to half of the current level of emissions. The plant with favorable wind would not buy an allowance for more than the equivalent of 2 cents per kWh. The other plant, however, would bid higher to ensure getting the allowances, thereby avoiding the need to capture its carbon. Again, wind power would replace coal entirely at one plant. The other plant would buy all the allowances and emit CO_2 as before. Again, total CO_2 emissions would be cut in half using the cheapest available means. The average cost to the economy would once more equal $(12 - 10) \times 0.50 = 1$ cent. The revenue from the government's sale of allowances to the other plant is again a transfer from the private sector to the government, not a cost for the economy as a whole.

Perhaps the most important benefit of a market-based procedure arises outside the context of the above example. All the possible emission mitigation activities are not generally apparent at the time a policy is implemented. Market pricing provides an incentive for producers and consumers to seek out innovative, cost-reducing mitigation measures that may go far beyond original expectations. To obtain the full benefits of tradable permits, a broad-based, multisector program to limit emissions is needed, because this increases the opportunities for the private sector to seek out the cheapest possible reductions in emissions across many economic sectors and many types of activities.

With cap-and-trade, the market price is determined by the overall supply of, and demand for, allowances. The total supply is fixed at the number of allowances issued by the government – the emission cap. The demand for allowances equals the residual emissions of regulated firms after all abatement projects are implemented. Demand varies over time, depending on economic growth and the resulting need for energy. In a competitive market, the actions of an individual firm would not have a noticeable effect on the overall demand for allowances and the market price. A firm would keep cutting emissions until the cost of further abatement would exceed the market price of allowances. Thus, the cost of the last ton of emission abatement (the marginal cost) would just equal the market price of allowances. Therefore, if cap-and-trade is designed to achieve a market price equal to the expected marginal damage from climate change, it would, in principle, realize the optimal result of a cost-benefit analysis, with marginal cost equaling marginal benefit.

In some cases, a performance or technology mandate may be imposed on industries that are also subject to a cap-and-trade program. In this case, the mandate does not generate additional emission reductions; it merely directs how some of the required reductions will occur. For instance, power companies may be subject to cap-and-trade and may also be required to use renewable resources for a given percentage of their power generation. If it is more expensive to reduce emissions through the use of renewable resources than through other means, the portfolio standard increases the overall cost of the program. Thus, the full benefit of a market-based system is not realized.

THE ISSUANCE OF ALLOWANCES

As noted earlier, with implementation of cap-and-trade, a market for allowances is created. The demand for allowances arises solely because firms are required to hold them. The government can supply allowances through auctions or distribute them for free; the choice could be interpreted as an assumption about property rights. In the past, the price of zero on CO_2 emissions has allowed any user of fossil fuels to assume implicitly an ownership right in the global climate. An emission allowance, however, is an explicit right to emit GHG and thereby alter the world's future climate. Allowances may be auctioned, generating revenues for government, or distributed for free. Potential recipients include firms that will be required to surrender allowances for their emissions and communities where jobs may be lost. In the past, jobs have been created and long-term investments have been made under the assumption that no restrictions will be placed on the use of fossil fuels.

A variety of arguments can be made to undertake some free distribution of allowances to the firms that will have to surrender them to the government in order to continue operating. Free distribution to emitting firms would benefit shareholders by protecting the rates of return on capital investments that were made in the past. Free distribution of allowances may also help sustain production levels, thereby helping maintain employment in such firms. Free distributions could also be structured in a way that helps preserve the competitiveness of emitting firms subject to international competition from countries lacking a similar price on GHG emissions.

If a program for free distribution of allowances is poorly designed, however, the shareholders of emitting firms may be overcompensated. Overcompensation can occur because, even if an industry receives free allowances, the price of the industry's output product typically rises to reflect the market price of allowances. The reason is that a free allowance has an opportunity cost: Even if a firm produces and emits nothing, it can sell the allowance in the market. By producing another unit of output, a firm gives up the opportunity to sell the free allowances needed to cover the emissions from producing that unit. A firm would therefore produce another unit of output only if it could sell that unit at a price high enough to recoup both the cost of production and the opportunity cost of using the allowances. For that reason, output prices rise to reflect the market value of allowances when cap-and-trade is implemented in a competitive industry, whether the government sells allowances or distributes them for free to emitters. The consumer pays firms for the usual costs of production plus the opportunity cost of allowances. Consumers thus pay even for the allowances that firms get for free.[4]

Researchers have generally found that firms, on average, need free distribution of only a fairly small portion of allowances to preserve shareholder values (see, e.g., Burtraw, 2008, references therein). If regulated firms are given a large share of the emission permits for free, they may earn "higher profits than in the absence of a permit system" (Goulder, 2008). Of course, low-emitting alternatives to users of fossil fuels also gain large benefits from a price on GHG emissions, but the incentive effect in those cases helps promote additional investment in low-emitting activities.

---

[4] The price of output would end up rising somewhat less than cost of allowances to the extent that consumption falls in response to the price rise. The marginal cost of production also therefore falls, similar to the standard analysis of a tax on output.

Allowances may also be distributed for free to communities that are adversely affected by a cap-and-trade program or as incentives for the development of low-emitting technologies (for instance, as bonuses to firms that capture and sequester their carbon emissions). To the extent that allowances are auctioned, revenue is generated for the government, which could also be used in a variety of ways, including support for technology research and adaptation to climate change. Economists have long emphasized that the overall costs to an economy of a cap-and-trade program may be significantly reduced if the auction revenue is implicitly recycled by reducing other distortionary taxes that affect the incentives for investment and employment (see, e.g., Dinan, 2007).

POLITICAL ECONOMICS OF MANDATES
AND MARKET-BASED APPROACHES

Any policy that restricts or penalizes GHG emissions will have winners and losers. The winners are energy-saving products and low-emitting technologies. The losers are mainly the coal and oil industries and related capital equipment producers. With shifts in production and consumption, jobs will be lost in fossil fuel industries and gained in renewable technology sectors. In a healthy, dynamic economy, as pointed out by the economist Joseph Schumpeter, some types of jobs are always becoming obsolete and whole industries sometimes disappear. However, the elimination of such jobs and industries are a result of progress because they are replaced by alternatives that meet human needs more efficiently. Who complains today about the absence of horse-drawn carriages and the phonograph machine?

The transition costs to a more sustainable future may not be trivial, however. A major turnover of jobs, as seems likely in the energy sector if we are to reduce GHG emissions, will probably boost the level of structural unemployment for a while. Structural unemployment is the portion of joblessness that does not rise and fall with the business cycle. It depends on how rapidly the economy is being transformed by new technology and on the mobility of labor between jobs and between geographic areas. The prospect of a thoroughgoing overhaul of energy industries has already brought considerable cross-currents of lobbying pressures on politicians. Potential losers will continue to resist a strenuous effort to mitigate climate change, whereas prospective winners will support it. Aside from diverging special interests, judgments about the common good for the future of society will continue to be disputed. In the midst of these conflicting forces, the strictness of climate policy will depend on political leadership and the level of concern of the general public about climate change.

As discussed earlier, a broad price on GHG, through a tax or cap-and-trade, has important advantages over specific policy mandates. The price signal may motivate extensive and unforeseen innovations in behavior by the private sector. A market-based approach helps ensure that the cheapest abatement possibilities are realized. It also spreads the burden of meeting the public policy goal across many economic sectors, reducing the impact on any particular industry.

However, energy price increases, and taxes per se, are not popular with the voting public, whereas the implications of a policy mandate are not likely to be clear to many consumers. Indeed, voters may believe that enforcing a policy mandate on an industry is "making the polluter pay." In competitive markets, however, enforcing an increase in costs on an industry through a policy mandate may reduce the industry's profits in the short run, but consumers will also pay higher prices. In the long run, the industry may shrink in size, but the rate of return on capital will recover to equal the economy-wide norm, whereas consumers will continue to pay more for the industry's output.[5]

Indeed, the irony is that a policy mandate is likely to impose larger costs on society than a market-based policy designed to achieve the same environmental goal. Those additional costs will be borne in part by consumers and in part by investors. In the short run, the costs are higher for a command-and-control approach because of the lack of flexibility about where and how the policy goal is achieved. Firms that find it cheap to comply have no incentive to go beyond the standard. Other firms that are required to comply find they can do so only at higher costs. In some cases, exceptions may be made for firms that find it technically impossible or unreasonably expensive to comply, but discretionary leniency of this type opens the door to special pleading and weakens achievement of the environmental goal. In contrast, trading systems allow avoidance of high-cost pollution abatement automatically (without any need for special pleading), and they also provide incentives for additional low-cost abatement beyond any fixed mandate. Economic costs are also likely to be higher and environmental benefits lower with command-and-control in the long run as well, especially if mandates lock in specific technologies or standards that eventually become obsolete.

---

[5] The effects on price and output would vary across economic sectors, depending on the short- and long-run elasticities of demand and supply.

Another political economy issue involves the flexibility that is built into a policy. The uncertainties about future climate outcomes and advances in low-emission technologies are profound. To cope with unexpected developments, climate legislation would need to build in considerable flexibility. However, legislators generally have not been willing to provide much flexibility to regulators when it comes to environmental issues. The reluctance may be even greater for regulating GHG emissions through a broad-based program that affects most sectors of the economy. Because of the difficulty of passing any sweeping legislation of this nature, supporters may not want to risk reopening the law after it passes for fear that it could be weakened or even rescinded. Thus, the legislative process itself provides little opportunity for flexibility. If the enabling legislation micromanages policies by specifying them in great detail for many years into the future, policy instruments could go badly off track if the future diverges significantly from expectations. It is a challenge, therefore, to build climate policies that can make course corrections as needed to cope with future developments while also creating confidence that environmental objectives will be met.

NINE

The Design of Cap-and-Trade Programs

Cap-and-trade systems have widely differing designs. The details determine how effectively emission mitigation goals are met and at what cost to society. They also affect how the large costs and potential gains from the program are distributed. This chapter begins by discussing the basic components of cap-and-trade systems. It then reviews the cap-and-trade programs that have been developed and proposed for the United States and the program created in Europe to implement the Kyoto Protocol.

CAP-AND-TRADE: WHO GETS REGULATED?

As in the case of a tax, an upstream or downstream approach could be employed for cap-and-trade. In a downstream system, any enterprise above a certain size or level of emissions would be required to surrender emission allowances. In an upstream system, oil refineries and natural gas pipelines would be required to submit allowances not only for their own emissions but also for the fuel they sell. Allowances would be required for fuel sales to cover the emissions that occur when downstream users burn the fuel. The refineries and pipelines could do nothing to abate the emissions associated with their sale of fuels. However, the requirement to surrender allowances would boost their costs and those cost increases would be passed on to downstream users in the form of higher prices. The resulting price signal would provide an incentive for consumers to increase energy efficiency. Spurring energy-saving activities by fuel users is a key advantage of this upstream approach, along with lower costs of monitoring and enforcement.

As in the case of a tax, there would be advantages of departing from a pure upstream approach by including coal-burning utilities in the cap-and-trade system. The utilities burn most of the coal, including some that they obtain directly from mines rather than from coal-processing plants. They

157

also already have systems in place to monitor the emissions of other pollutants, at least in developed countries.

Because an upstream approach broadens coverage, it motivates a wide range of emission-mitigation activities. It also helps reduce "leakage," which means an increase in emissions by firms outside the cap-and-trade system that is caused by the program. Cap-and-trade restricted to a limited number of economic sectors or geographic area makes it easier for emitting activities to shift to unregulated firms. For instance, with a downstream program, electricity prices would likely rise but the sale of fuel oil at refineries would be little affected. Therefore, industries and homeowners would have a greater incentive to use fuel oil for heating rather than purchase heat pumps. The reduced emissions from power generation would "leak" out through unregulated combustion of fuel oil.

EMISSION CAPS AS RATIONING

Unlike a tax, a greenhouse gas (GHG) emissions cap is a form of rationing. Although it rations only an undesirable byproduct, it nevertheless constrains the combined output of all regulated emitters. If the program includes a wide range of economic sectors, the rationing effects would be ameliorated because a greater diversity of activities would be available to reduce emissions. In addition, higher prices for consumers spread across a range of goods would stimulate numerous demand-reducing efficiencies.

Many of the emission-reduction adjustments involve investments with lead times of varying lengths. It takes years to plan and implement new industrial facilities and infrastructure. Also, it is costly to discard capital equipment and appliances that still have economically useful lives. However, unexpected rationing effects could emerge even within a particular year, which is the length of compliance period that has often been used. The demand for energy in a particular year depends in part on the weather. If the winters are especially cold, more fuel will be burned to heat homes. If the summers are especially warm, the demand for electricity may soar to run air conditioning units. In addition, the growth of the economy may vary substantially from one year to the next and the demand for energy would rise or fall commensurately. In years of mild weather and tepid economic activity, an emission cap might be easy to hit. However, with extreme weather and rapid economic growth, an emission cap could be reached well before the end of a year.

If the cap were inflexible, the rationing feature would then cause considerable hardship. To avoid breaching the cap, emitting activities would have to cease until the beginning of a new period. Imagine a country unable to use any coal, oil, or natural gas for a couple of months. No fuel would be available for cars, trucks, or planes. Industries and homeowners would be subject to extended brownouts and blackouts. Homes would go without heat. The economy would shut down.

The public would not tolerate a complete shutdown of fuel supplies; a rigid cap therefore could mean a quick demise of the system. To avoid such outcomes, the system needs to incorporate some flexibility. Design features that are often proposed to cope with temporary fluctuations of emissions, relative to caps, are the banking and borrowing of allowances.

ALLOWANCE BANKING

A regulated firm in a cap-and-trade system may end up with more emission allowances at the end of a compliance period than it needs to surrender to cover its emissions during the period. System rules may allow the firm to "bank" its excess allowances rather than discard them. A banked allowance can be used to cover emissions in a future compliance period. If banking is allowed, a regulated firm could benefit by borrowing money to buy an extra allowance in one compliance period if it could thereby avoid having to buy an allowance in a future period at a price above the principle and interest on the loan. In fact, anyone – not just regulated firms – could profit by borrowing money to buy allowances and then reselling them in a future period at prices above the loan payoff cost. Banking therefore creates an additional demand for allowances in the current compliance period to the extent that allowance prices are expected to rise in the future.

Consider what would happen if GHG emissions were lower than expected because of temporary factors affecting only the current compliance period. For instance, suppose the weather was mild and economic growth was weak. The economy's demand for energy would be below expectations. The CO_2 emissions of regulated firms would be lower than forecast. Allowance prices would begin falling. The outcome would be quite different depending on whether banking was allowed.

In the absence of banking, regulated firms would postpone or scale back their abatement projects. Firms with excess allowances would try to dump them on the market. Buyers would be few. At the end of the period, allowance prices would drop to zero and any excess allowances would have to be thrown away.

With banking, however, the market demand for allowances would not drop to zero at the end of the period. Additional buyers would enter the market as prices fell, based on their individual expectations for allowance prices in future compliance periods. Some buyers might be regulated firms seeking extra allowances as a "hedge" against higher expected compliance costs in the future. Others might be speculators seeking financial gains by buying allowances at low prices in one period and selling them at high prices in future periods. The extra buying demand in the current period because of banking would keep allowance prices from falling very low.

It is sometimes said that banking places a floor on the price of allowances. However, for a variety of reasons, the floor would not be a clearly identifiable or fixed level. If a banked allowance could be used in any subsequent period, a high price at any future time could provide a good payoff on a banked allowance. If prices were likely to rise over time, expectations about the distant future might become relevant. Future prices, however, would need to be "discounted" to the present. The discount rate would equal the interest rate that would have to be paid on the money borrowed to buy and hold the allowance until it was used or resold. Thus, the floor price would tend to be based on the highest discounted expected allowance price in any future compliance period. Indeed, the entire trajectory of expected prices would likely reflect the future compliance period in which upward price pressures were forecast to be strongest. The possibility of major changes in the program in the future would also need to be considered. Individual firms would vary in their views of the outlook. They could also differ in their borrowing costs and their willingness to add allowances to their balance sheets. Such idiosyncratic factors would affect the price at which a particular firm would become a buyer of excess allowances and the amount it would be willing to buy.

Uncertainty about future allowance prices would add to the demand for banked allowances. If a firm was risk-averse, it would seek to bank allowances for precautionary purposes even if the current price was above its highest discounted expected future price. The difference would be an implicit insurance premium against the risk that future prices might be higher than expected.

An expectation that future allowance prices would be subject to temporary fluctuations would also add to banking demands. Depending on the extent of such price volatility, opportunities could arise to sell allowances at very high prices. For that reason, a speculator would be willing to buy allowances at a price above the discounted expected future price. The difference would be the "option value" of the allowance. The speculator would have the option of cashing in the allowance on any temporary spike in prices. The allowance price floor created by banking would thus exceed discounted expected future prices by insurance and option premiums. Again, individual buyers would have different views about the value of these premiums.

The precautionary demand for allowances would likely be particularly strong in the early years of a cap-and-trade program. Emission caps would probably be scheduled to tighten over time. Firms would likely forecast rising allowance prices, but uncertainties would be great. To the extent that firms wanted to build allowance banks, they would have to accelerate emission abatement projects. This would help realize environmental goals. In later years, after firms had built sizable banks, their precautionary demands would largely be met.

A firm with a sizable allowance bank could use the bank to cover part or all of its emissions in a compliance period when prices were especially elevated. For instance, if extremes of weather and strong economic growth temporarily pushed up the demand for energy, allowance banks might be used rather than built further. The general use of allowance banks would tend to reduce the extent of upward price pressures. Thus, banking could eventually help keep prices from rising very high in addition to its role in keeping prices from dropping too low.

Once firms have built sizable allowance banks, they have a stake in the continuation of the cap-and-trade program. If the program ended, the firms would lose a valuable asset. Creating this vested interest might help the program survive shifting political winds over the long period needed to affect the climate outlook. Banking could thus help support political sustainability.

Banking has some limitations, however. The efforts of firms to build allowance banks would add to price pressures. Also, in the early years of the program, the banks would not be large enough to help restrain allowance price spikes. The program's political sustainability could be especially fragile in those years, and high or volatile allowance prices could lead to calls for ending it.

In addition, banking would not help cope with a divergence of allowance prices from expectations that was thought likely to persist. For instance, if prices dropped because the entire schedule of allowance distributions turned out to be too generous, there would be little incentive to build allowance banks. Similarly, if prices rose because of pessimism about technological progress, firms probably would be reluctant to draw on their allowance banks. In the absence of other program flexibilities, the path for emission caps might have to be adjusted in either of these cases. If legislation had to be amended to adjust emission caps, however, the entire program might come into jeopardy, depending on the strength of various lobbying interests at the time. Even the possibility of wholesale changes in the program could reduce the incentives for longer-term investments in emission abatement.

ALLOWANCE BORROWING

Another design feature that can be used to limit temporary fluctuations in prices is the borrowing of allowances. Borrowing in this sense means using an allowance from a future period to meet a compliance obligation in the current period. The extra supply of allowances from such borrowings would restrain a temporary surge in prices. Allowance borrowing would be attractive if a price increase was not expected to continue in the future period when the borrowed allowances would need to be repaid. Although allowance borrowing can restrain a price increase in the period in which it occurs, it adds to price pressures in the period in which it has to be repaid. Often, borrowings must be repaid with some "interest" in the form of additional allowances, which would also add to price pressures in the repayment period.

If a price increase is caused by forces that are not temporary but are likely to persist, borrowing would not be helpful. The repayment of borrowings and interest on those borrowings could drive prices up to very high levels, particularly if the emission cap had become much tighter by the time of the repayment period. In that situation, new borrowing might be needed in the repayment period itself. If borrowings were renewed and increased, period after period, achievement of the program's intended emission caps could be indefinitely postponed. To reduce the risk of such outcomes, limits are often proposed on the amount of allowances that can be borrowed.

OFFSETS

At a personal level, anyone can invest in an emission offset, a project to reduce emissions implemented by someone else. For instance, suppose I was a frequent flyer and wanted to pay for someone else's emission reductions in order to offset the environmental effect of the emissions attributable to my air travel. A neighbor, who was less well off, heard of my interest in buying offsets and therefore came to me with a proposition. He was considering acquiring a hybrid-electric car but was concerned about the cost. He estimated the difference in lifetime CO_2 emissions was about 20 tons.[1]

---

[1] Assuming a standard, combustion-engine car would average 30 mpg and the hybrid 50 mpg, and that each vehicle would last 150,000 miles. Lifetime gasoline consumption with the standard car would then be 150,000/30 = 5,000 gallons, and only 3,000 gallons with the

If I bought 20 tons of offsets from him at a price of $15/ton, he would buy the hybrid. Otherwise, he'd go ahead with a standard, combustion-engine vehicle. At that time, $15/ton matched the price of offset credits from developing countries that were being sold under the terms of the Kyoto Protocol. Should I take my neighbor's proposition?

I ought to consider, first, whether my offset purchase would result in real and additional emission reductions. Would my neighbor in fact buy the hybrid even if I didn't purchase his offsets? Also, had he already sold those offsets to someone else? If I satisfied myself on such grounds, I should still ask whether the emission reductions would be sustained over the life of the vehicle. I would need to make sure that my neighbor didn't sell the hybrid after a year or so and then buy a combustion-engine car after all.

The same issues arise for offsets in organized markets. It is a challenge to verify that offset projects result in real, additional, and permanent reductions in emissions. If they do, offsets can lower the cost of achieving the emission-reduction goal. In some cases, emission reductions through offsets may represent low-hanging fruit compared with abatement projects in capped industries. Offsets also bring new economic sectors into the program that cannot conveniently be included in cap-and-trade. Monitoring and enforcing caps on the GHG emissions of agriculture and landfill management would be prohibitively expensive. However, methane capture projects in those sectors generate easily verifiable emission reductions, making them good candidates for offsets.

Even if well designed and administered, however, an offset program is not a panacea. Offsets may need to be limited to ensure that regulated firms have the incentive to make long-term investments in research and development on emission-reduction opportunities in their own industries. Also, offsets are not an effective means of coping with temporary fluctuations in allowance prices. Limits on offsets could be relaxed in response to a temporary rise in allowance prices, but it would take a while before additional projects could earn credits and, by then, the price spike might be over.

CAP-AND-TRADE IN THE UNITED STATES

The Leaded Gasoline Program

The United States pioneered the use of cap-and-trade to control environmental pollutants. One of the earliest examples was the program to control

hybrid. Given the EPA's estimate of 8.8 kg of CO_2 per gallon, the lifetime emissions from gasoline would be about 44 and 26 tons in the two cases.

emissions of lead from the combustion of gasoline. Lead had been used as an additive to boost the octane of gasoline beginning in the 1920s. With the Clean Air Act of 1963, the federal government began taking a role in air pollution issues, mainly by providing support for research. With heightened awareness of the health hazard posed by lead aerosols, the Clean Air Act was amended in 1970 to require reductions in the lead added to gasoline among other things. Also, unleaded fuel was required for catalytic converters, which were mandated to control other exhaust pollutants on new vehicles. In the early 1970s, gasoline typically contained 2.4 grams of lead per gallon. In 1975, the EPA required each refinery or importer to reduce the lead content to 1.7 gram/gallon.

When the limit was tightened to 1.1 gm in 1982, the EPA permitted firms to trade lead credits (the first time such transactions were allowed without prior regulatory approval). Refineries averaging less than 1.1 gm could thus sell credits to those still above that level. This was not an emissions cap but an averaging program in which the trading of credits lowered the cost of the gradual phase-out of lead additives. In 1985, the standard was tightened to 0.5 gm/gallon and the EPA also began allowing firms to bank credits for use in a future compliance period. By 1987, trading accounted for 40% of total lead credits and banking was being used by 90% of the firms. About half of the trades were between refineries owned by the same firm. Trading has been estimated to have reduced costs by about $250 million per year, a reduction of about 20% from the costs that would have been incurred with a command-and-control approach (Kerr, 1997).

To enforce compliance, the EPA required refiners and importers to report the lead content of each sales transaction and checked on the accuracy of those reports with random testing. Although most transactions were evidently reported accurately, several dozen cases of fraud were identified (EPA, 2001).

The Acid Rain Program

In the absence of mitigation measures, coal-burning power plants release considerable sulfur dioxide (SO_2) and nitrogen oxides (NO_x). In chemical reactions in the atmosphere, NO_x form ground-level ozone and other components of smog. Ozone has powerful greenhouse effects, and all of these gases are harmful to breathe. Sulfuric aerosols seed cloud formation. In addition, SO_2 and NO_x generate sulfuric and nitric acids that are eventually washed out of the atmosphere, polluting rivers and lakes.

The 1970 amendments to the Clean Air Act developed a considerable structure of regulation for air pollution (McCarthy, 2005). Under EPA administration, National Ambient Air Quality Standards (NAAQS) were developed for air quality control districts. State governments have the main responsibility for achieving and maintaining the standards, but the EPA must approve the State Implementation Plans (SIPs) that are designed to do this. The EPA also determines performance standards for new emitting sources (while states have more discretion in how those standards are applied to existing facilities). In particular, the EPA's New Source Performance Standards (NSPS) imposed a limit on the SO_2 emissions of new coal-burning power plants.

By the late 1980s, most air districts were in compliance with the provisions of the Clean Air Act, but those provisions had proved inadequate to solve the problem of acid rain. In 1990, the Clean Air Act was again amended. Under Title IV, a cap-and-trade program for SO_2 emissions was mandated. In the first phase of this program, from 1995 through 1999, the 110 highest-emitting coal plants were required to surrender emission allowances. In phase II, allowances were required from existing plants in excess of 25 MW and all new coal plants. Most of the allowances were "grandfathered," meaning they were distributed for free.[2] Annual auctions, conducted by the EPA, have amounted to only about 2.8% of the allowances. Allowances can be banked indefinitely; they never expire. Under phase I, about 30% of the total allowances issued were banked; under the tighter regulations of phase II, the level of banked allowances has gradually declined. The NO_x portion of the program was not cap-and-trade, but rather an averaging program: The EPA did not distribute tradable allowances for NO_x, but let utilities meet their emission targets by averaging the performance of their boilers.

Regulated utilities under the Acid Rain Program must send the EPA quarterly reports with hourly emissions data, made possible because of the widespread installation of "Continuous Emissions Monitoring Systems" on their smokestacks. These systems amass data on more than 200 variables, importantly including the emissions of CO_2 as well as SO_2 and NO_x.

The Acid Rain Program has been successful in reducing regulated pollutants in the power sector. SO_2 emissions were cut from about 15.7 Gt in 1990

---

[2] A plant received free allowances depending on its energy consumption during the base period of 1985 through 1987. In phase I, grandfathered allowances amounted to 2.5 pounds of SO_2 per million Btu; in phase II, it was 1.2 pounds. Firms could obtain extra allowances for energy conservation activities.

to about 10.2 Gt in 2005 (EPA). Firms accomplished this largely by install-
ing flue gas desulfurization equipment (scrubbers) and by switching to
low-sulfur coal sources. The trading of allowances resulted in an estimated
cost-saving of $1 billion per year, some 30% to 50% of the costs that would
have occurred with a command-and-control approach (Stavins, 2005). NO_x
emissions fell from 6.7 Gt in 1990 to 3.6 Gt in 2005. Tighter requirements
under new "Clean Air Interstate Rules" (CAIR) are being implemented over
2009 and 2010, although there are some uncertainties about their long-run
legal standing.

Despite the availability of banking, allowance prices under the Acid Rain
Program have been quite volatile. Since 1999, NO_x allowances have traded
in a range from around $500 to $7,500. The highest prices were seen early
in the program, when compliance costs were very uncertain. Prices for
SO_2 allowances have varied between $68 and $1,600 since trading began in
1994. The lowest SO_2 price was an EPA auction in 1996 when Enron bought
heavily. The high price was reached toward the end of 2005, a year of rapid
price increases following announcement of the tighter CAIR rules. Large
purchases by financial traders also evidently contributed to the price surge
at that time (FBR, 2006). Prices were also rather volatile during 2008 owing
to an initial court judgment against CAIR in July and a suspension of that
judgment in December.

Aside from 2005, the prices of SO_2 allowances have generally been far less
than anticipated. At the inception of the program in 1990, the EPA expected
allowance prices somewhere around $800 per ton (in 2004 prices). However,
the actual allowance price averaged less than $200 per ton through 2004. By
contrast, estimates of the health effects of SO_2 and NO_x have increased substantially over time, especially including the respiratory and cardiovascular
risks from associated air pollution (even more so than the acid rain). If
prices had been higher, deeper emission cuts would have occurred and the
resulting improvements in health could have resulted in net welfare gains
worth billions of dollars per year (Burtraw, 2006).

The RECLAIM Program

A cap-and-trade program was created for controlling SO_2 and NO_x emissions in Southern California in 1993, called the Regional Clean Air Incentive
Program (RECLAIM). All allowances were distributed for free. Until 2000,
an excess of allowances was supplied, because allocations were based on
the highest emissions over the 1988–1993 period. Allowances could not be
banked for future use, so their prices were very low and, as a result, only

limited mitigation investments were made by regulated firms. Also, firms were allowed to buy offsets for retiring old cars that would otherwise contribute to general air pollution. The offsets program was cancelled before long because many of the cars apparently would have been scrapped even in the absence of the program. When California energy prices skyrocketed in 2000, the price of NO_x allowances rose to more than \$45,000/ton. To avoid power outages because of allowance shortages, electricity producers were excluded from the program in 2001. Despite the many problems, the program did eventually result in significant reductions in SO_2 and NO_x emissions. In 2006, for instance, SO_2 emissions were about 50% of the 1994 level and NO_x emissions were about 34% of the 1994 level (SCAQMD, 2008).

The Regional Greenhouse Gas Initiative

In 2009, ten northeastern states initiated a cap-and-trade program for the power sector called the Regional Greenhouse Gas Initiative (RGGI).[3] The objective is to reduce the CO_2 emissions of the power sector by 2015 to the average level of the 2002–2004 period. Emissions are to be cut another 10% by 2020. Allowances are required to be submitted for all plants with a capacity greater than 25 MW covering emissions over a three-year compliance period. Most of the allowances are auctioned and can be banked without limit. Compared with estimates of the social cost of carbon, the price of RGGI emission allowances has been very low. The initial auctions have had a minimum price of \$1.86, and actual allowance prices ranged between \$2 and \$4 per ton through most of 2009. The reduced demand for power because of the economic downturn has kept allowances well below earlier expectations. Offsets are limited to 3.3% of a power company's emissions, but this limit will be eased to 10% if the allowance price averages above \$10 in any twelve-month interval within a compliance period (RGGI, 2007, 2008a).

Because the power sector in RGGI states has been deregulated, the price of electricity will increase to reflect the value of allowances. In principle, that would boost the profits of existing nuclear or hydroelectric plants and spur the development of low-emitting renewable sources to meet future power needs. Increased power supply from outside the RGGI region could potentially result in emission leakages. However, such effects are unlikely to become significant at the low allowance prices observed to date.

---

[3] The states are: Connecticut, Delaware, Maine, Maryland, Massachusetts, New Hampshire, New Jersey, New York, Rhode Island, and Vermont.

POSSIBLE FUTURE U.S. PROGRAMS

California and several other U.S. states and Canadian provinces are planning to implement a cap-and-trade program for GHGs called the Western Climate Initiative (WCI). Planning for the program suggests that states and provinces will be able to distribute some allowances for free whereas others will be auctioned through centralized facilities. The objective of this program would be to reduce emissions in the WCI region to 15% below 2005 levels by 2020. The WCI cap-and-trade program is scheduled to begin in 2012. However, a U.S. national cap-and-trade program for GHG may be in operation by then. If so, it would likely preempt any state or regional program within the country. Another regional cap-and-trade program is being discussed by several Midwestern states, but progress has been limited in the expectation of preemption by a national program.

At the federal level, numerous legislative proposals to reduce GHG emissions through cap-and-trade programs have been introduced in Congress in recent years. The Lieberman-Warner bill (S. 2191 and S. 3036) made it to the floor of the Senate in 2008 but was defeated there. The Waxman-Markey bill (H.R. 2454) passed the House of Representatives in June 2009, the first success for a GHG cap-and-trade bill in either house of Congress.

The bill provides that regulated firms will reduce GHG emissions to 17% below 2005 levels by 2020 and 42% below by 2030. The program extends out to 2050, when emissions of regulated firms will be 83% below the 2005 level. Coverage will be phased in, with power generators and oil refinery products subject to the emissions cap in 2012, followed by most other industries (including emissions at oil refineries themselves) in 2014 and natural gas distributors in 2016. After full implementation in 2016, 87% of the country's emissions would be subject to the cap.

In addition, the Waxman-Markey bill provides that large sources of methane emissions, which are not subject to an emissions cap, will be regulated under the terms of the Clean Air Act. That act requires new emission sources, or existing sources undergoing significant modifications, to implement best available technology to control pollutants.

The nominal emission cap under Waxman-Markey does not indicate the actual stringency of the program for regulated firms. Firms will be allowed to exceed the cap to the extent that they purchase offset credits. Up to 2 billion tons of CO_2e emissions can be covered by offset credits, which represent a large fraction of the cap on emission allowances, even in the early years of the program. However, the supply of offsets is likely to be well below that limit until developing countries establish qualifying programs to earn credits from reduced deforestation, as envisaged under the bill. Caps on offset use by individual firms will also make it difficult to reach the 2-billion-ton offset limit.

Under Waxman-Markey, emission allowances average 5 billion tons a year in 2012–2020 and 4.1 billion, 2 billion, and 1.6 billion a year, respectively, in the succeeding three decades. In the first decade or so of the program, the bill auctions off only about 15% of the allowances; the rest are distributed for free. Electricity distribution companies receive the largest share (about 40%); they are required to pass the benefits of these allowances on to their customers, under the guidance of their state regulators. Some allowances are provided for low-income consumers and displaced workers, whereas other allocations support, inter alia, the development of energy efficiency and clean technologies, domestic and foreign adaptation to climate change, and reduced deforestation programs in developing countries.

Industries that are heavy users of energy and subject to international competition receive up to 15% of the allowances in the early years of the program. Allowances are given to these industries to prevent the loss of domestic production (and jobs) and to avoid leakage of emissions to countries lacking comparable GHG control programs. Allowances are granted based on multiplying an emission factor times the level of current production. This output-based approach has quite different effects than free distribution through "grandfathering," which is based on actual emissions in a historical base period. With output-based distributions, firms receive a subsidy in the form of free allowances when they produce more output. However, they still have to submit allowances for their actual emissions and therefore have an incentive to reduce emissions per unit of output (emission "intensity"). They may be able to reduce emission intensity by, for example, shifting to lower-emitting energy sources and production processes. If a firm can produce with lower-than-average emissions per unit of output, it may end up with extra allowances to sell in the market. This is not a windfall profit, but a reward for the environmentally beneficial emission reductions of an efficient firm.[4]

---

[4] In the Waxman-Markey bill in particular, free allocations to internationally competitive industries are based on the average output of a firm over the last two years. The emission factor is the average emission intensity of the industry over a four-year period (which is updated every four years). Industries are defined at a very disaggregated level (a six-digit level of the North American Industrial Classification code). In addition, there is a separate calculation of the additional carbon costs to the firm from the use of electricity, for which free allowances are also granted.

Output-based allowances have a key disadvantage, however. The effect on output prices of the opportunity cost of the allowance surrender requirement tends to be offset by the output-subsidy of the free distributions. As a result, the price of output may not rise, or if it does, it will not increase by the full amount of the price on GHG emissions. Consumers therefore do not observe a price signal that reflects the full carbon content of the goods produced by the industry. Because consumers do not have an incentive to shift consumption toward lower-emitting substitute goods, the full benefit of a market-based approach is not realized. However, output prices might not have risen much in any case in an industry subject to stiff international competition from firms in countries that have no price on carbon. In sum, output-based allocations have some rationale to protect a domestic industry until competing economies implement comparable emission control programs. A more cost-effective achievement of global environmental goals would occur, without altering competitive balances, if countries could agree on a coordinated approach that creates a common carbon price signal for firms and consumers around the world.

The Waxman-Markey bill envisages a phase-out of free allowances to industry between 2025 and 2035. With the increasing proportion of auctioned allowances, additional funds will be devoted to consumer rebates. If internationally competitive industries continue to face competition from firms in countries lacking a comparable emission-mitigation program, a border adjustment program will begin in 2020: The imports of goods in such industries will be subject to an emission-allowance requirement. There are risks, however, of legal challenges under the World Trade Organization (WTO), retaliation by other countries, and an impairment of trade flows more generally. Clearly, it would be preferable to alleviate concerns about competition through a coordinated approach to carbon policies among countries rather than resorting to free allowances to competitive industries or border adjustments.

The Waxman-Markey and Kerry-Boxer bills include unlimited banking of allowances and also provide for borrowing of allowances by regulated firms. Year-ahead allowances may be borrowed without restriction or interest, but borrowing from more than one year ahead is subject to an interest charge. Also, a firm must hold the future vintages of allowances that it will "borrow" (some future vintages are to be distributed in advance). The Lieberman-Warner bill (2008) allowed firms to borrow without actually holding any future vintages of allowances; firms could borrow by merely making up a shortfall in their current compliance obligation in a future year.

In addition, under Lieberman-Warner, a government board could relax the limits on allowance borrowing if necessary to avoid "economic harm."

The Waxman-Markey bill includes another feature to protect the economy from high and volatile prices of carbon allowances. About 2.7 billion allowances are removed from the annual emission caps and placed in a "Strategic Reserve." A portion of these allowances is to be sold in auctions each year, but only if the allowance price rises high enough. The threshold price for release of these allowances is $28 in 2012 and rises to $31 in 2014 (in 2009 dollars). This is more than twice the EPA's estimate of the price of allowances under the bill in those years. Beginning in 2016, the threshold price is 60% above the average market price of allowances in the preceding thirty-six months. Given these high threshold prices, the Strategic Reserve is unlikely to be used unless a sudden change in the outlook for the carbon market causes a spike in prices.

Waxman-Markey also has a minimum price for the regular auction of allowances, which is $10 in 2012 and rises by 5% per year (in 2009 dollars). In addition, the bill allows unlimited banking of allowances. Banking gives some value to excess allowances because it permits them to be used for compliance in future years. Thus, in addition to the minimum price in regular auctions, banking will help keep allowance prices from dropping very low.

Nevertheless, allowance prices could fluctuate considerably under Waxman-Markey. The price could range between $10 and $28 in 2012 without hitting the minimum level in regular auctions or the threshold for the Strategic Reserve. The range would be similar (though somewhat higher) in the next two years. Thereafter, the "price collar" may become tighter. Under the EPA's price forecast, the threshold for release from the Strategic Reserve would drop to about $20 in 2015 (in 2009 dollars). However, if market prices began moving up closer to that threshold price, the threshold itself would begin rising under the terms of the bill. Indeed, prices could grow at a 25% annual rate in real terms without ever triggering a release of the reserve.

In late September 2009, Senators Kerry and Boxer released draft legislation in the Senate that is similar in many respects to the Waxman-Markey bill. In particular, it preserves the idea of an allowance reserve, but the threshold price does not rise with market prices. However, the allocation of allowances and the ultimate fate of a cap-and-trade bill in the Senate are undetermined as of the time of this writing.

If no comprehensive climate bill passes the Congress, the United States may resort to a more expensive command-and-control approach to the regulation of GHG. In the absence of modifying legislation, policy mandates would be required under the terms of the Clean Air Act. The Bush administration did not choose to implement the terms of that Act for the purpose of regulating GHG. However, in *Massachusetts v. the Environmental Protection Agency*, the Supreme Court ruled in 2007 that the EPA had to decide whether CO_2 was a threat to public health and welfare under that Act. In late September 2009, the EPA issued proposed regulations for GHG under the Clean Air Act. It would begin by requiring the best available control technologies to be used by all new sources emitting more than 25,000 tons of CO_2e, as well as sources undergoing major modifications. The United States would almost surely achieve better environmental benefits at lower cost by employing a market-based approach rather than implement these command-and-control regulations.

THE INTERNATIONAL CONTEXT

A major effort to reduce emissions by one country, or even a group of countries, would not be sufficient to halt increases in the concentration of GHG in the atmosphere. Indeed, some studies have projected that the BAU emissions of developing countries would cause global average emissions to rise even if advanced economies put a $100/ton price on CO_2 or cut their emissions to half the 1990 level by 2050 (MIT, 2007; Paltsev, 2007). A global effort is required. Moreover, the worldwide cost of mitigating climate change will be substantially reduced if all countries participate in the effort, for then the cheapest abatement projects across the planet will be implemented.

Worldwide cooperation on climate change achieved an important success at the Rio Earth Summit in 1992, where agreement was reached on the United Nations Framework Convention on Climate Change (UNFCCC). This treaty has been ratified by nearly all countries around the world. It articulates the goal of stabilizing GHG concentrations to prevent "dangerous interference with the climate system." It notes that countries have "common but differentiated responsibilities" and capabilities for achieving this goal. Countries with advanced economies would take the lead in combating climate change and would reduce GHG emissions to the 1990 level. This goal lacks specificity, however, as it would be achieved either "individually or jointly" and no date is given for its accomplishment. Advanced economies also agreed in principle to provide financing and technology transfers to help developing countries meet emission reporting, mitigation, and climate adaptation objectives. All countries would complete "inventories" of their emissions, and advanced economy countries agreed to do so annually.

Subsequent conferences of the parties to the treaty were expected to work out the detailed protocols needed to achieve these goals. The first was the Kyoto Protocol, signed in December 1997 and made effective in February 2005.

THE KYOTO PROTOCOL

Under the Kyoto Protocol, thirty-seven countries with advanced economies accepted GHG emission limits. The limits apply to a single, five-year commitment period, 2008 through 2012. On average across countries, the annualized emission cap is 5.2% below the 1990 level of emissions. Allowances were issued to countries under the Kyoto Protocol, and trading of those allowances is permitted, but there was no effort to build a liquid global market.

In line with the idea of differentiated responsibilities, developing countries (DCs) have no emission commitments under the Kyoto Protocol. Instead, DCs are allowed to develop offset projects and sell them to countries that are subject to emission caps. DCs thus earn a profit from the Kyoto system, whereas capped countries benefit from the offset program to the extent that it lowers the cost of achieving their emission targets.

A major weakness of the Kyoto Protocol is the small number of countries that are subject to emission limits. All are in Europe except for Japan, Canada, Australia, and New Zealand.[5] The absence of limits for developing countries was the main reason for the refusal of the United States to ratify. The disparity in compliance costs across countries is another problem. Some countries received far too many allowances and others too few. A key reason for the disparity was the choice of the past performance period on which allowance allocations were based. In addition, generous allotments were made to Russia and some other Eastern European countries to ensure that the minimum number of participants was reached for the treaty to go into effect.

The base-year problem is familiar to anyone who has received golf or bowling "handicap": An unusual performance in the base period can have a huge effect on subsequent adjusted scores. In the Kyoto Protocol, allowances (called Assigned Amount Units) were allocated based on emissions in 1990. However, with the collapse of communism, many inefficient and highly polluting factories in Eastern Europe were closed after 1990, making it easy to reduce emissions there. The development of oil and natural gas facilities in the North Sea also allowed the United Kingdom and Scandinavian

---

[5] Australia ratified only in 2007, more than two years after the protocol had entered into force.

countries to shift away from coal-burning power plants. Moreover, stagnation of populations and slow economic growth restrained the demand for energy in many countries. Some of these developments were known when allowance allocations were negotiated, but some were not (see Cooper, 2006; Shapiro, 2007).[6]

Because Russia and other Eastern European countries have not made any special emission mitigation investments, their huge surpluses of allowances have been dubbed "hot air." The sale of these allowances could potentially involve transfers of tens of billions of dollars and reduce the mitigation efforts of the purchasers. To ensure some gains for the environment from such allowance sales, selling countries are now expected to invest the proceeds in "Green Investment Schemes" (projects that generate environmental benefits). By mid-2009, only about 100 million tons worth of Assigned Amount Units had been traded.

The Kyoto program for offset projects in developing countries, called the Clean Development Mechanism, initially generated considerable hopes for international partnerships to generate emission reductions in developing countries (Stewart, 2000). However, the results have been far below expectations. At the end of September 2009, the UNFCCC had issued 333 million credits (each representing one ton of emissions) and it forecast that the cumulative credits between 2005, when the program began, and 2012 would total only 1.3 billion.[7] Administration of the Kyoto offsets program has been contentious. An Executive Board, drawn from parties to the protocol, develops methodological standards for project types, approves individual projects, and issues emission-reduction credits after verification. It also authorizes private firms, nonprofit organizations, and government agencies to appraise and monitor projects. Some of those entities have not performed up to expected standards. Market participants complain that the approval process has been long and costly. Environmentalists have been concerned that many projects would have been implemented even in the absence of an offset program; in the technical jargon, their emission reductions were not "additional." Moreover, some types of projects have been poorly conceived; for instance, refrigerant producers in China have sold offsets at prices far exceeding actual mitigation costs (Wara, 2007). In the summary judgment

---

[6]   The allocations, relative to 1990 emission levels, are: +10% for Iceland, +1% for Norway, unchanged for Russia, Ukraine, and New Zealand, −5% for Croatia, −6% for Japan, Canada, Poland, and Hungary, and −8% for other European countries.

[7]   Note that, unlike the Waxman-Markey bill, the Kyoto Protocol does not allow credits for reduced deforestation, which could significantly increase the supply of credits.

of the IPCC (2007), the program "has faced methodological challenges in terms of determining baselines and additionality" for offset projects.[8]

KYOTO IMPLEMENTATION IN THE EUROPEAN UNION

When the Kyoto Protocol was signed, the original 15 members of the EU accepted a group-average emission target equal to 8% below their 1990 emissions and then agreed among themselves on the parceling out of individual country targets under a burden-sharing agreement.[9] Since 2003, the EU has grown from fifteen to twenty-seven member countries, and most of the new entrants have their own emission limits under the Protocol.

The European Commission has the overall regional responsibility for managing progress toward Kyoto targets and longer-term climate goals. For that purpose, it established the European Climate Change Programme that includes policies and measures designed to help reduce emissions. For instance, countries are encouraged to more than double energy generation from biomass sources over the seven years ending in 2010. Numerous energy efficiency measures in building construction and transportation are also recommended (ECCP, 2006). The community's overall climate change goals are framed as 20–20–20 by 2020: by that year, GHG emissions are to be cut by 20% relative to the 1990 level, energy intensity is to fall by 20%, and the share of electricity generation from renewable sources will increase to 20%. The EU will agree to a greater, 30% reduction in GHG emissions if other countries commit to comparable actions.

A major component of Europe's climate program has been a cap-and-trade arrangement called the Emissions Trading System (ETS). Allowances are allocated to firms by individual countries, with auctions limited to a maximum of 10% of total issuance. The National Allocation Plans have to be approved by the Commission. The plans also specify limits on offsets (generally up to 10% of emissions). The general principle is that offset credits should not be used for more than half of the country's emission reductions. The allocation plans were implemented in two phases, the first

---

[8] Offsets can also be earned for projects in countries subject to emission limits (so-called Annex I countries) under what is called the "Joint Implementation" mechanism. Under this mechanism, emissions of the country financing the project would be offset, but the abated emissions would be added back to the total emissions of the country in which the project was located. This program has been slow to develop.

[9] In percentage change relative to 1990 levels, the targets are: Portugal (27), Greece (25), Spain (15), Ireland (13), Sweden (4), Finland (0), France (0), Netherlands (-6), Italy (-6.5), Belgium (-7.5), UK (-12.5), Austria (-13), Denmark (-21), Germany (-21), and Luxembourg (-28).

between 2005 and 2007, and the second between 2008 and 2012, the years of the Kyoto Protocol.

National governments monitor the emissions of private firms, which must surrender allowances at the end of annual compliance periods. The EU ETS is a downstream system in that industries are responsible only for their own emissions. Oil refineries and natural gas pipelines do not need allowances for the carbon content of the fuel they sell. The major regulated industries are electricity generation, oil refining, steel, cement, glass, brick, ceramics, and paper/cardboard. About 5,000 companies with a total of roughly 11,500 separate plants are involved. They represent a little less than half of the total GHG emissions from the EU.

Allowance trading began in March 2005, but a forward market existed as early as 2003. Allowance prices peaked at about €30 in early 2006 amidst concern about the ability of firms to meet targets. Given the free distribution of allowances, those prices resulted in large windfall profits, especially for the power sector in Germany. However, prices dropped sharply when data were released showing that actual emissions were well below the allowances that had been issued. Indeed, in the Phase I period of 2005 to 2007, allowances exceeded emissions by about 7% (CAN-Europe, 2007). Allowances could be banked from one year to the next, but not from Phase I to Phase II in most countries. A surfeit of Phase I allowances in 2007, the year of their expiration, caused prices to drop under €1. At the same time, Phase II allowances were trading at around €16 in futures markets (Kopp, 2007). Over the last year or so, prices have fluctuated over quite a range, largely because of changing prospects for the economy. Prices peaked at more than €30 in mid-2008, then plummeted with the weakening of the global economy, hitting a low point of less than €9 in February 2009. The market has recovered somewhat since then, with allowance prices averaging about €14 over the second and third quarters of 2009.[10]

The EU intends to continue its cap-and-trade system after 2012, and it sees the ETS as the primary means for achieving its emission-reduction goals for 2020. In the post-2012 period, National Allocation Plans will be eliminated. Allowance auctions will gradually replace the free allocation of allowances after 2012. Similar to the United States, however, industries that are subject to international competition will be granted free allowances. These allowances are designed to prevent a loss of profits, production, and jobs, and to avoid a leakage of emissions. However, in the EU, the free

---

[10] Price data are for the December 2009 futures contract from the European Climate Exchange website.

allowances are based on historical data (they are "grandfathered") rather than based on current output as in the United States. The consequence is that output prices will tend to rise in the EU because of the opportunity cost of those allowances, unless a price rise is completely stifled by foreign competition. The price increase will induce some reduction in demand for high-emission products, but it could also generate windfall profits for those EU industries because they will in effect be compensated for allowances they did not have to buy.

TEN

Prices, Quantities, and Lessons
from Monetary Policy

Central banks have been managing the supply of money for many decades. Similarities between regulating the supply of money and regulating greenhouse gas (GHG) emissions suggests the possibility of deriving lessons for climate policy from central banking. Differences between the two types of policy problems also need to be identified to discern how climate policy approaches should differ from monetary methods. The amount of discretionary authority for a legislature to allocate to an independent policy-making body is an important concern for each type of policy framework. Monetary policy can also provide lessons regarding the methods used to manage markets in a way that facilitates the implementation of policy.

MONETARY POLICY GOALS AND
INSTITUTIONAL FRAMEWORKS

Several cap-and-trade proposals, including the 2008 Lieberman-Warner bill, have called for the establishment of an independent board modeled on the Federal Reserve to assist with the implementation of the program. This chapter addresses the need for such a climate board and other lessons that can be drawn from the experiences of monetary policy. The chapter begins by explaining how the context of monetary policy compares with the framework of a cap-and-trade program for GHG.

Consider the policy challenge faced by a monetary authority. With a single primary policy instrument, it must try to achieve two key economic objectives: low inflation and full employment of resources. In the short run, there is a trade-off between these objectives. Stimulating the economy maximizes employment and production, but if overdone, it can lay the seeds for future price inflation. And once inflation gets going, it is difficult to control and reverse without causing an economic recession and high unemployment. The effects of monetary policy on production and employment are fairly rapid (within six months or a year), but its effects on inflation take longer to emerge and are more lasting.

In making monetary policy decisions, considerable professional expertise and judgment are needed to weigh alternative possible scenarios for the economy. Forecasts of future outcomes must be constructed and evaluated, separating transitory developments from newly emerging trends. Short-run trade-offs among policy goals need to be evaluated and weighed against longer-term implications. Risks on either side of policy choices must be identified and assessed, including judgments regarding both probabilities and the magnitude of consequences associated with alternative possible scenarios. These assessments need to be continually updated, because the economy is always changing and often, despite best efforts, in entirely unexpected ways.

What are the implications of this policy challenge for the independence and discretionary authority of a monetary authority? A key risk is that policy making becomes myopic, pursuing short-term gains in employment and production while placing insufficient weight on the longer-run inflationary effects of easy money. For this reason, it is essential for a monetary authority to be independent from political influences that may be more focused on the next election than on the longer-term inflationary consequences of monetary policy. Many episodes of excessive inflation around the world have been attributed to political interference in monetary policy making (see, e.g., Eijffinger, 1996).

However, if a central bank is given complete independence, questions may be raised about its accountability (see, e.g., Walsh, 2005). In recent decades, the dilemma of ensuring accountability while also granting independence has been addressed by providing an explicit legislative mandate for a central bank, often in the form of an inflation target (see, e.g., Bernanke, 2001). Because an inflation goal for monetary policy is set by legislation, the central bank is said to have "goal dependence." Outcomes relative to that goal are measurable, however, and the central bank is therefore accountable. The central bank is then empowered to make its own selection of the means to achieve that legislative mandate. It is granted "instrument independence" – discretionary authority over the setting of policy instruments (Fischer, 1995). A central bank needs the authority to adjust policy instruments according to its best professional judgment in order to be fully accountable for the achievement of its mandated goal.

Issues have been raised over the adequacy of an inflation target as a constitutional guide for monetary policy. In particular, an inflation target may give insufficient weight to the other component of the job of a central bank: ensuring full employment of the economy's resources. Unlike inflation, it is difficult to quantify this objective because it depends not only on policy preferences, but also the underlying condition of the labor market and the economy, which evolve over time. Because of the difficulty of quantifying this component of the duty of a monetary authority, a policy mandate that includes both goals may be left in qualitative terms.

For instance, the legislative mandate of the Federal Reserve is to achieve the objectives of "maximum employment" and "price stability." Without a more concrete, quantitative mandate, the Federal Reserve (the "Fed") has sometimes been pressured by presidential administrations to pursue an easier monetary policy, which would boost employment in the short-run at the expense of the longer-term price stability goal. The Fed has usually managed to resist such pressure. Its independence from presidential administrations is attributable to several features: It is formally accountable only to the Congress, not to the President. Twice a year, it presents Congress with a report on its monetary policy decisions, along with accompanying testimony. In addition, unlike cabinet departments and other administration officials, the board of the Fed does not serve "at the pleasure of the President." Board members have long, fourteen-year terms of appointment (although the Chairman's term is only four years). In addition, the Fed's policy-making committee includes the presidents of twelve regional Reserve Banks, which each include some participatory role for the private sector.

COMPARISON OF MONETARY AND CAP-AND-TRADE GOALS

Like the economy, the climate system is extremely complex. Controlling GHG emissions also requires professional forecasting, judgments about probabilities, and assessments of the consequences of alternative possible outcomes. Projecting climate developments under different policy scenarios is truly daunting, because the forecast horizon is decades ahead and the uncertainties include not only the climate system and behavioral responses to policy changes, but also longer-run technological advances.

As in the case of monetary choices, a cap-and-trade program involves a short-run trade-off between two objectives. With cap-and-trade, the goals are the level of GHG emissions and the market price of emission allowances. Other things being equal, at a higher market price, implying greater costs for the economy, emissions will be lower. At lower allowance prices, *ceteris paribus*, abatement will be more limited and emissions will therefore be higher.

As this type of trade-off is observed on a year-to-year basis, it will become more predictable, at least for a year or so ahead. The real purpose of the emission reductions – reducing damages from future climate change – requires much longer forecasting that will continue to be extremely challenging.

Cap-and-trade programs can be designed with varying degrees of emphasis on ensuring either a given emission cap or a given price of emission allowances. Some cost-containment features, such as a safety valve, can keep the price of allowances below a specified ceiling. Other devices can keep prices above a given floor level. Hard price limits of this nature may be achieved through a willingness to relax or tighten an annual emission cap as needed.

The parallels with monetary policy go beyond the mere existence of a short-run trade-off between two goals. Political economy considerations also have some similarities. An easy monetary policy (with low interest rates that help boost the economy in the short run) tends to be a popular choice when it is implemented. However, continuation of such easy policies can have very harmful longer-run inflationary consequences. Correspondingly, with cap-and-trade, a low carbon price (signifying plentiful emission allowances and offsets) is easy on the economy in the short run and may therefore be preferred by many at the time. However, continued high GHG emissions may bring enormous longer-run economic harm and social costs from climate damages. Although the long run for the climate forecasting is much more distant than that for inflation, the pressures that favor a myopic policy are analogous.

In light of the similarities in trade-offs among goals and the need for professional judgments that take a longer-run perspective, it is worth considering whether to create a climate policy framework that resembles the structure that has proved successful for central banks. For instance, a cap-and-trade program could adopt some of the features of inflation-targeting frameworks. Inflation targets are the legislative mandates that keep a central bank focused on a long-run goal and therefore constrain and guide its exercise of discretion in addressing shorter-run concerns about financial stability and employment of resources. The administrator of a cap-and-trade program could also be given some discretionary authority to address short-run trade-offs between annual emission caps and carbon prices within the context of a longer-run goal. The constraining mandate for a cap-and-trade authority, parallel to a central bank's inflation target, could be achievement of an intermediate-run target for emissions. For instance, the level of emissions eight or ten years ahead might serve as a hard constraint on any intervening discretion to be exercised by the administrator. A national emission target of a decade or so ahead would also match the horizon relevant for international negotiations. National legislation and international treaties could each conceivably be structured in a way that facilitates consideration of new emission targets each decade, without the need to reconsider the entire architecture of climate policy.

When seen from the perspective of the general mandates given to central banks, legislative proposals for cap-and-trade programs appear to be guilty of overspecifying the details of program design to the point of micromanagement of future policies. For example, it is difficult to imagine that the U.S. Congress would not revisit over the next thirty years the emission caps for 2040 and 2050 that have been embedded in draft legislation. Also, most legislative proposals allow little discretionary authority in the implementation of cost-containment features that address the short-run trade-offs between prices and annual emission caps. The issues of discretionary authorities and the independence of an implementing institution will be addressed more fully toward the end of this chapter. Before doing so, key aspects of the implementation of cap-and-trade programs need to be discussed further.

Other parallels can be identified in the implementation of a monetary policy and of a cap-and-trade program. In particular, carbon prices and emission caps are not merely potential policy goals; they are also instruments through which climate policy is implemented. They bear a close resemblance to the price and quantity instruments of monetary policy. The short-run trade-off between the monetary policy goals of low inflation and full employment of resources was reviewed earlier. There is also a choice between two possible instruments through which monetary policy is implemented: a price instrument represented by an interest rate; and a quantity instrument represented by the amount of the money supply. If a monetary authority fixes the level of interest rates, the money supply will be uncertain. If it fixes the money supply, interest rates will be uncertain. It cannot determine with certainty both the price and the quantity instrument. The same is true for cap-and-trade: An implementing authority can determine with certainty either the price of allowances or the quantity of emissions in a given year, but not both. Therefore, in both monetary policy and cap-and-trade implementation, a choice must be made between using a price instrument (thereby making prices certain) or a quantity instrument (thereby making quantities certain). An informed judgment could usefully take advantage of the deep experience of monetary policy with such instrument choices. To do so, it is useful to begin by exploring key similarities between the markets through which monetary policy and cap-and-trade are implemented.

CARBON MARKETS AND MONEY MARKETS

A cap-and-trade program and monetary regulation each typically involve the creation of a new market because of government regulation. In these types of markets, the *government* simultaneously determines both the quantity of supply and the market price, one by choice and the other by implication and with some uncertainty. With cap-and-trade, the government creates a carbon market by requiring firms to surrender allowances. It also determines the supply of allowances that it releases into the market. If it increases the supply, the price of allowances will fall. If it restricts allowance supply, prices will rise. Thus, depending on its choice regarding the supply of allowances, the government also indirectly controls the price of carbon.

The carbon market is related to the broader private markets for energy commodities. Similarly, even in the midst of vast private-sector money markets, a government can create a regulated market in that area by imposing a reserve requirement on banks. This is an obligation on commercial banks to redeposit in the central bank a certain percentage of the deposits they get from their customers. Thus, a reserve requirement creates a demand for reserves, which are deposits at the central bank. A central bank itself controls the total supply of reserves, which is a base form of money that can determine the overall quantity of money in the economy. Commercial banks have to bid to buy reserves in government auctions or in trading among each other. An increase in the government's supply of reserve money reduces its price, which is the overnight interest rate. A reduction in the supply of reserves raises the overnight interest rate. Thus, by adjusting the supply of reserves, governments can indirectly control overnight interest rates.

Quantities and prices are thus closely linked in both monetary policy and cap-and-trade because, in each case, the government creates a market by regulation and then controls the total quantity supplied in the market. Selection by the government of a quantity to supply means picking off a particular point on the demand curve (for either reserves or allowances) and therefore realizing a particular price. If the demand curve is known, there is no real difference between a quantity or price instrument. Picking a quantity determines the price and vice-versa. Unfortunately, the position of the demand curve is unknown in both the market for reserves and the market for allowances. This uncertainty creates a distinction between the effects of fixing a quantity (i.e., using a quantity instrument) and fixing a price (using a price instrument).

PRICES AND QUANTITIES

Consider, for instance, an extreme quantity instrument case in which a cap-and-trade program enforces a strict annual emission cap. The alternative is a pure price instrument (either a carbon tax or a policy of adjusting the supply of emission allowances as needed to achieve a given target price). If the demand for allowances is known with certainty, these policy instruments can deliver an identical result – a given level of emissions and carbon price. If the market price (or tax rate) is set at the point where the marginal benefit of emission abatement equals the marginal cost (the intersection point shown in Figure 7.1), the optimal result of cost-benefit analysis would occur. If there is an error in estimating the level of the marginal benefit curve (the social cost of CO_2), each policy instrument would make the exact same mistake.

However, if there is an error in estimating the demand for allowances, the two policy instruments give quite different results. Because of the flat marginal benefit curve associated with a stock pollutant like GHG, uncertainty tends to favor a price instrument over a quantity instrument, as explained further in the chapter (and more formally by Weitzman, 1974; Weiner, 1999; and others).

Suppose that a global cap-and-trade program is implemented with an emissions cap of 40 Gt of CO_2e. This cap is chosen, say, because it is expected to result in a $50 per ton price of allowances, which is the best estimate of the marginal value of future climate damages.

If we are right about abatement costs, a 40 Gt emission cap and a $50/ton price would be equivalent policies. A 40 Gt cap would result in a $50/ton allowance price, whereas fixing the price at $50/ton would result in emissions of 40 Gt. However, if climate damages are actually worth $100/ton, we would have failed to reduce emissions enough using either the price or the quantity instrument. If climate damages are worth $25/ton, we would have invested too much in emission abatement. The policy mistake would be the same with either a cap or a price instrument.

The instruments would give different results, however, if we are right about the value of climate damages but wrong about abatement costs. Suppose abatement costs are cheaper than expected and the 40 Gt emission cap can be achieved with a price of only $30/ton. We would have failed to reduce emissions enough. Each ton of additional emission reductions would have saved the planet $50 worth of damages, a good return on an investment of $30/ton. Indeed, we should have kept investing in such projects until their costs rose to $50/ton. If a price policy of $50 per ton had been imposed instead of a rigid emission cap, those additional abatement projects would have been implemented.

Alternatively, suppose abatement costs are higher than expected and a 40 Gt emission cap results in an allowance price of $70/ton. Some of our abatement projects would have cost much more than the climate damages of $50/ton. A better policy would have been to let those emissions occur. The cap therefore proved too tight to balance the costs and benefits. With a price policy of $50/ton, those additional emissions would have occurred and the policy error would have been avoided.

Thus, a quantity and a price instrument have the same error if we are wrong about climate damages, but only the quantity policy makes an error if we are wrong about abatement costs. What if we are wrong about both abatement costs and climate damages? These two types of uncertainties could offset each other or combine to make policy errors even more egregious. If they are positively correlated (i.e., climate damages and abatement costs are both likely to be higher under the same circumstances), the price policy is arguably less favored (Stavins, 1994).

Other considerations are relevant to a price-versus-quantity instrument choice beyond the simple effects of uncertainty discussed earlier. There may be more political momentum for an emission cap than a pure price policy. A tax is a hard sell for both the public and politicians. Moreover, an emission cap can be combined with free distribution of some allowances, making it more acceptable to fossil fuel industries, which have formidable lobbying power.

Environmentalists may also favor a cap if they fear that a tax or price target will not result in enough emission reductions. The responses of firms and consumers to price signals may indeed prove weaker than expected. In that case, the tax or price target would have to be raised to achieve the intended emission reductions. It is inaccurate to claim, however, that a GHG cap delivers "environmental certainty." An emission cap for a hazardous local pollutant can do so. However, limiting the GHG emissions of regulated firms in one country or region does not deliver certainty about the future climate. Even if a worldwide cap-and-trade program could be implemented, some emitting sources would not be included. The emissions of homeowners, small businesses, and perhaps also the agriculture, forestry, and waste management sectors would be too costly to monitor and control. And even if global emissions were controlled, environmental certainty would still not be achieved. As discussed in Part One, our scientific understanding of natural CO_2 sinks and the response of global temperatures to GHG concentrations is too limited to justify any claim of certainty.

A better argument for an emission cap is based on the structure of the risks that we face. With a price target, the probability distribution of outcomes is not in symmetric balance. If the price is set too high, we would pay somewhat more costs for mitigation than would be optimal. However, if the price is set too low, climate change could become unmanageable and the damages could become catastrophic. The risks are thus skewed. The probability distribution has a "fat tail" on one side but not on the other. Unlike a price target, an emission goal, if globally enforced, may lop off the fat tail on the distribution of climate damage risks and thereby balance the structure of residual risks.[1] Although a geographically limited emission cap would be inadequate, a cap in some countries could have a role-model effect that would help spread similar emission caps more broadly throughout the world. That is what has been hoped for the Kyoto Protocol and subsequent international agreements.

A LESSON FROM MONETARY HISTORY

As noted earlier, we do not face a stark choice between a carbon price target and a rigid emission cap. Moreover, different types of policies may be appropriate at different times. An example from a monetary policy episode in the United States may provide some insight in this regard.

Central banks have long faced a trade-off between prices and quantities as policy instruments. They cannot strictly control both the level of interest rates and the quantity of money. If a strict target is placed on the interest rates, the quantity of money will be uncertain. If a strict target is placed on the quantity of money, it is unclear what interest rates will result. Because there are many interest rates in a market economy, central banks do not have the option of implementing a pure price policy like a carbon tax. Central banks can therefore exert only indirect control over interest rates; they are more able to control the supply of money. This favors the use of a money supply instrument rather than an interest rate instrument. However, as the financial sector of an economy develops, numerous alternatives emerge for

---

[1] This argument envisions a welfare loss function that is the sum of abatement and adaptation costs, plus the residual damage from climate change. The probability distribution around the expected welfare losses would be more skewed with a price target than with an emission cap in part because producers and consumers might not reduce emissions as much as expected in response to a rise in CO_2 prices. Of course, a flexible policy that could adjust price targets or emission caps in a timely way would be able to narrow the distribution of potential outcomes and offset skews in the risks. This is one possible argument for discretionary authority in the implementation of a cap-and-trade program.

bank deposits (the main component of the money supply). Therefore, the relationship of the supply of money to a central bank's ultimate economic objectives – low inflation and full employment of resources – becomes less predictable. Also, in mature financial markets, interest rates become fairly closely linked through arbitrage relationships and have a more predictable relationship to a central bank's ultimate policy objectives. For these reasons, central banks now generally place greater emphasis on interest rates than on the quantity of money.

However, interest rates have not always been the instrument of choice for monetary policy. An episode from U.S. monetary history provides an example of an alternative situation with intriguing political economy lessons for climate policy. Over most of its history, the Federal Reserve (the "Fed") has formulated monetary policy in terms of interest rates rather than the quantity of money. However, during the "Great Inflation" episode of the 1970s, policy makers failed to raise interest rates enough to keep inflation in check.

In 1979, as the inflation rate was breaching 13%, Paul Volcker took over as Chairman of the Fed. He believed that the usual policy approach, based on targeting interest rates, would not succeed in controlling and reversing inflation. If he tried to raise interest rates enough to do the job, fierce political opposition might force him to stop. He believed that a change in the framework of policy was therefore needed. Under his leadership, the Fed stopped targeting interest rates and instead set goals for the quantity of money. Volcker could then argue in Congressional testimony that he was not responsible for interest rates because they were determined in private markets. All the Fed could do, he argued, was control of the supply of money. And strict control over money was needed to reduce the rate of inflation. The Fed was reluctant at this time to talk about the close link between the supply of money and the interest rate.

Under this policy, Volcker had the political cover he needed. The overnight interest rate rose to a record high level of 20%. As a result, the economy plunged into a deep recession. But inflation dropped from double-digit levels to around 4% and remained there for most of the rest of the 1980s. The Great Inflation episode was over. Gradually, the Fed returned to its usual policy of focusing on overnight interest rates rather than on the quantity of money.

In climate policy, similar political economy concerns may arise. It may be impossible to legislate a high enough price on GHG emissions to prevent serious climate damage. Politicians who enact a high carbon tax may soon need to look for another job. Legislative proposals for carbon taxes therefore will likely be considerably weakened before becoming law. That was the fate of the broad-based "Btu tax" sponsored by the Clinton administration in 1993. Originally designed as an upstream tax on all fossil fuels, it finally emerged from Congress as a narrow and modest transportation fuels tax.

Politicians and voters alike need to be unusually far-sighted and altruistic to accept an explicit cost now to prevent uncertain climate damages in future decades. Shifting the focus of the debate to the quantity of emissions, rather than the level of a tax, places attention on the climate problem itself rather than on the costs to be borne today. The effect may be similar to the policy reframing that Paul Volcker engineered at the Federal Reserve in 1979. Legislators may be able to enact strict emission caps to achieve environmental goals if they can avoid direct responsibility for an explicit increase in the price of energy.

PREDICTABILITY OF ALLOWANCE PRICES

Because of the complexity of modern financial systems, the supply of money no longer has a very close relationship to economic outcomes. Central banks around the world therefore generally focus on interest rates as the channel through which they affect the economy. (An exception occurs when the overnight interest rate has been reduced to its lower bound of zero. Even then, however, a central bank may target longer-term interest rates rather than the quantity of money it supplies.)

The climate system is also complex, and the level of GHG emissions, especially for an individual country, has a very uncertain relationship to climate outcomes. Unlike in the case of monetary policy, however, switching from a quantity target to a price target would not necessarily reduce uncertainties about climate outcomes. Indeed, the response of emitters to a CO_2 price signal is itself unclear.

Nevertheless, making GHG emission prices predictable could have salutary effects. A market-based policy achieves cost-effectiveness by sending the same price signal to every regulated firm. All abatement projects costing less per ton than the market price of CO_2 will then be implemented and all higher-cost projects will be avoided. Thus, environmental goals will be achieved at the lowest possible cost to the economy.

Many emission abatement projects take considerable time to implement, and their emission reductions are spread over many years. In planning such projects, regulated firms will need to forecast emission prices. If the uncertainties about future emission prices are too large, firms will tend to postpone investment decisions. Lower levels of investment will mean less reduction in emissions and a poorer outcome for the environment.

Uncertainty about future prices also increases the overall economic cost of a cap-and-trade program. Some firms will forecast high prices and implement abatement projects that are too costly. Other firms will forecast low prices and fail to implement projects that should go forward. Thus, the cost-minimizing effects of a clear price signal will be lost.

It is impossible to remove all uncertainty about future CO_2 prices in a cap-and-trade program. Indeed, as climate outcomes become better understood, emission reduction goals may need to be modified. We can only guess at the cost of future low-emission technologies. Even though these fundamental uncertainties cannot be removed, there are other types of uncertainty that are avoidable and arise solely because of the design of a cap-and-trade program.

PREDICTABLE PRICES WITH CAP-AND-TRADE

Several approaches can be used to make the price of carbon more predictable. One alternative is a tax. The tax rate need not be kept constant, but could rise over time while still remaining predictable. Of course, the legislature could change the law, which is an inescapable unpredictable aspect of a tax or any other government policy. Environmentalists often object to a tax because of uncertainties about the response of taxpayers and therefore the emission reductions that are achieved. A possible fix is a tax rate that changes over time depending on environmental results (Metcalf, 2009). For instance, the Stark bill (H.R. 594) provides for a CO_2 tax that begins at $10/ton and then rises by an additional $10 per year until U.S. emissions are 80% below 1990 levels. The Larson bill (H.R. 1337) gives the EPA some discretionary authority over annual increases in a carbon tax. The tax begins at $15/ton and then rises either $10 or $15 a year, depending on whether the EPA estimates that sufficient progress is being made to reduce U.S. emissions to 80% of 2005 levels by 2050. Note that a tax with these types of contingent dynamics can reduce uncertainties about emission reductions, but only at the expense of introducing some unpredictability about future tax rates. Other advantages of a GHG tax are administrative simplicity and avoiding the cost of market infrastructure. However, carbon taxes have rarely mustered the political support needed for implementation.

A variety of design features can be used to make cap-and-trade similar to a tax. In one alternative, included in a bill by Representative McDermott (H.R. 1683), allowances are sold by the Treasury department at fixed prices that rise in a predictable manner over time. Every five years, the Treasury can alter the price path if needed to meet cumulative emission goals. In this proposal, allowances cannot be traded among firms; hence, no market is created. Given the absence of any trading, the key difference between this approach and a tax is the discretionary authority given to the Treasury to alter the allowance price path. The legislature could not constitutionally give the Treasury as much discretion over the selection of future tax rates.

Another type of cap-and-trade program places a ceiling on allowance prices. Firms are allowed to meet compliance obligations by paying a fee for each ton of emissions rather than surrendering an allowance. The fee is called a safety valve. Because firms would not be willing pay more for an allowance than the safety-valve price, the safety-valve level acts as a ceiling for allowance prices. A safety-valve mechanism was included in the 2007 Bingaman-Specter bill (S. 1766). A safety valve is a substitute for the high-cost noncompliance penalties typically used in other approaches. In a year in which a safety valve is used, the emission cap is exceeded. If a safety valve is set at a very low level, it will be used year after year. In this case, the cap-and-trade program becomes indistinguishable from a modest tax and emission reduction goals are unlikely to be achieved.

ALLOWANCE RESERVES

An allowance reserve is a limited version of a safety valve. As mentioned in the previous chapter, an allowance reserve is included in the Waxman-Markey and Kerry-Boxer bills. It was also a provision of the 2008 Lieberman-Warner bill (S. 3036). With an allowance reserve, a specified amount of allowances may be released if prices are at or above a given threshold price (see, e.g., Murray, 2009). The extra supply helps restrain a rise in prices. However, the threshold price does not provide a hard ceiling for prices: After the reserve is fully released, allowance prices could continue to rise. Unlike a safety valve, however, the total amount of emissions remains capped because the allowances used to stock the reserve come from within the cap level.

Key issues regarding the operation of an allowance reserve are the level of the threshold price and the amount of allowances that can be sold from the reserve in any given year. Waxman-Markey and Kerry-Boxer take different approaches to these issues. In Waxman-Markey, the threshold price adjusts upward to remain well above average market prices. The threshold begins at $28 in 2012, but after 2014, it is 60% above the average market price in the previous thirty-six months. These upward adjustments in the threshold could allow rapid growth and wide fluctuations in market prices without any release of allowances from the reserve. Also, in Waxman-Markey, the maximum amount of allowances that can be released from the reserve is relatively low (5% of a year's total allowances before 2025 and 10% thereafter). At the EPA's estimated allowance prices under this bill of about $13 in 2015 and rising each year by about 5% in real terms, the reserve would not be used. Permanent storage of allowances in the reserve would merely serve to tighten the effective emission cap and raise prices a little.

In Kerry-Boxer, the threshold for release of the reserve also begins at $28 in 2012, but then rises at a fixed real rate of 5% per year. The EPA forecasts allowance prices under this bill to be similar to the Waxman-Markey case (less than $14 in 2015 and rising by 5% per year). However, if the emission cap proves harder to meet than forecast by the EPA, given the fixed price threshold for release of the reserve under Kerry-Boxer, there is a greater chance that it would be used than with the Waxman-Markey threshold specification. Under Kerry-Boxer, the maximum amount that can be released from the reserve is 15% of a year's total allowances until 2025 and 25% thereafter, substantially larger amounts than under Waxman-Markey.

As market prices begin to move closer to an allowance reserve's threshold level, adverse market dynamics could occur. As noted earlier, unlike in the case of a safety valve, there is no further restraint on prices after the full allotment of allowances from a reserve has been released in a given year. Thus, prices could rise well above the threshold price (as noted, e.g., in Elmendorf, 2009). If market participants believe that such an outcome could occur as market prices move up toward the threshold level, they may be willing to bid for allowances from the reserve at the threshold price. An expectation that the threshold price may be reached in an auction could push the general market price up to that level as well. Fears that the reserve could be fully drained may lead to aggressive bidding in the auction and a self-fulfilling hypothesis. (This type of phenomenon has been observed in currency markets with fixed exchange rates – see, for example, Eichengreen, 1994.) In the bidding for reserve allowances and shortly thereafter, prices could rise sharply. Market expectations alone could drive these results. As in the case of other trading dynamics arising from market psychology, if the expectations turned out to be largely unfounded, the price rise could prove to be a "bubble" that would soon collapse. The swings in prices caused by such shifting expectations could impair the incentives for investment in emission reductions. They could also arouse suspicions among the public and policy makers, rightly or wrongly, regarding possible manipulation of markets and speculative excesses. The rationale for creating a carbon market through legislation could be called into question.

The persistence of a strategic reserve and the provisions for restocking it, if used, have also varied across the legislative proposals. Under Lieberman-Warner, the reserve was to be discontinued in 2028 and no restocking was allowed (any allowances released from the reserve would lower the caps over 2030–2050). In Waxman-Markey and Kerry-Boxer, the initial stock of allowances is drawn from within the caps over all years of the program, and the allowance reserve continues in operation throughout the program's life. If the reserve is depleted, it is refilled through the purchase of offset credits. The purchases of offsets by the government to restock the reserve would not count toward the 2 billion per annum limit on offset use by regulated firms. Some observers are concerned that the pressure to refill the reserve could lead to acceptance of low-quality offsets that do not have real environmental benefits (Chan, 2009).

CAP-AND-TRADE WITH MANAGED PRICES

With another type of design, a cap-and-trade program can avoid unnecessary price fluctuations and possible adverse market dynamics associated with an allowance reserve. This alternative has been called a managed price approach (Elmendorf, 2009). It allows emissions to be higher or lower than expected in a given year in order to achieve a specified carbon price. The government publishes a multiyear path for allowance prices and issues as many allowances as needed to achieve its target price in a given year. To the extent that annual emissions are higher or lower than expected because of temporary factors, those misses should average out over time, allowing a cumulative emission goal to be met. In this type of approach, the government's announced multiyear path for prices is not immutable. If emissions depart from expectations for reasons that are likely to persist, the path for prices is adjusted to ensure achievement of a cumulative emission goal. Thus, the government makes future prices as predictable as possible, given cumulative emission goals, but not absolutely certain.

One version of a managed price approach was adopted in the McDermott bill, as discussed earlier. In that version, there is no carbon market; the Treasury Department merely resets the implicit tax on carbon every five years. Allowances must be purchased from the Treasury at the given fixed price and then returned to the Treasury to cover emissions. No trading of allowances is permitted.

Alternatively, a managed price approach can be implemented using the procedures employed by central banks to manage interest rates. This is the approach taken in the Doggett-Cooper bill (H.R. 1666). This version of a managed price approach allows the development of a deep and liquid carbon market without risking the volatility that often occurs in other commodity markets. The prices at which allowances trade are kept fairly close to a target price, just as central banks are able to keep private market interest rates close to a target interest rate.[2] Central banks use auctions to keep interest rates close to the target level. The auction procedures used by central banks could be adapted to manage allowance prices, as discussed further.

HOW A CENTRAL BANK MANAGES INTEREST RATES

Similar to the case of many other central banks, the Federal Reserve implements a monetary policy by setting a target for the level of overnight interest rates. In overnight lending markets, several hundred billion dollars of transactions occur every day among large banks and other private companies (Demiralp, 2006). Despite the very large amount of private trading, central banks are generally able to keep the overnight interest rate fairly close to the target. Unlike commodity markets, price swings due to shifts in speculative expectations and scandalous episodes of market manipulation do not occur. Central banks are able to achieve these results without frequent interventions that could disrupt the flow of private trading. They do not compete with brokers and market makers by posting bid and ask prices throughout the day. Their market interventions are limited to occasional auctions.

Central banks achieve their target interest rates in part by announcing the target rate in advance. The announcement guides market participants as they trade among themselves, helping keep interest rates close to the target. If a borrower believes that it can get the central bank's target interest rate, it will not borrow money from a lender that charges much higher rates. The drying up of the demand for funds at interest rates above the target rate helps restrain rates from rising much above the target. On the other hand, if interest rates drop well below the target rate, borrowers will rush in to get a good deal. The extra demand for funds helps restrain interest rates from dropping far below the target.

These responses occur only because market participants are confident that a central bank can generally achieve its target interest rate. A central bank reinforces this confidence by conducting auctions called open market operations. The auctions adjust the supply of overnight money that market

---

[2] For early work on applying central bank procedures to stabilize emission allowance prices, see Newell (2005).

participants have to trade among themselves.[3] As mentioned earlier, the more money the central bank makes available, the lower the interest rate that market participants will be willing to pay to borrow from others. By adjusting the overall supply of money, the central bank can influence market prices without having to intervene in the market throughout the trading day. The Federal Reserve, for instance, typically intervenes in the market just once a day, injecting or removing only a few billion dollars in an auction. Nevertheless, this intervention is sufficient to enforce its target despite total transactions that are hundreds of times larger over the course of a day. Interest rates do stray from the target at times owing to transaction costs, market frictions, unbalanced distributions of funds, and risk aversion. However, on the average day, the Fed misses its target interest rate, across all private trading, by less than one-tenth of one percentage point (Demiralp, 2006). The control of the overnight interest rate is imperfect but nevertheless fairly remarkable given the size of the daily private market.

Some aspects of these central bank procedures could be adapted to manage cap-and-trade prices while still fostering the development of a carbon market. Several adjustments are needed, because the allowance market has a longer time horizon than the overnight market. The allowance market is subject to an annual or longer compliance period, whereas overnight borrowers are trying to avoid an overdraft on their deposit account at the end of the day. Also, central banks announce a target interest rate that may change from month to month, but allowance prices need to be stabilized over an entire compliance period. With an annual compliance period, therefore, the government could announce a target price for allowances for the coming year. Allowance auctions would not be needed on a daily basis; four auctions a year would probably suffice to promote private trading and allow the government to achieve its target allowance price.

The same type of expectation effects that occur in the overnight loan market would help the government achieve its target price in the allowance market. If private firms expect the target price to be achieved in the auctions, their self-interested behavior would help keep prices close to the target throughout the year. If prices started rising notably above the target, buyers would tend to disappear. The weakening of demand would restrain the rise in prices. If prices fell below the target, buyers would come in to

---

[3] The Federal Reserve typically increases the money supply by buying Treasury securities in "reverse auctions." Market participants offer securities and the Fed pays for them by creating a deposit for the seller. As mentioned earlier, the deposits held by market participants at the Fed are a form of money (reserve money); the overnight lending market involves trading ownership in these deposits.

snap up the bargains; this response would help boost prices back toward the target. The above expectation effects would be strengthened if the last government auction is set close to the date when allowances need to be surrendered for compliance purposes. Traders would look to the expected price in that auction as the ultimate enforcement device for the target price during the year. As in the overnight market, some trades would nevertheless take place at prices differing from the target because of transaction costs, discounting, risk aversion, and temporary imbalances and illiquidity conditions.

To achieve a given target price, the government would need flexibility in the amount of allowances to be released in each auction. Unless the allowance demand curve is perfectly predicted, it is not possible to hit both a price and an emission target in a given year. How could such a system be designed to help ensure achievement of emission goals? In part, through the procedures used to set target prices each year. One alternative is to set each year's price target to achieve a specific level of emissions in that year. Another approach is to announce a multiyear price forecast intended to achieve a specific emissions goal several years ahead.

For instance, a smooth, multiyear price path could be constructed to achieve an emission goal for 2020. Emissions in any particular year might differ from expectations because of transitory factors, but these differences should average out if prices are kept on a path that would lead to achievement of the 2020 emission goal. If emissions moved off track for reasons that were likely to persist through 2020, an adjustment could be made in the entire future path of prices. Thus, the multiyear price path would be modified only because of permanent factors, not temporary influences such as unusual weather or swings in economic growth. This is the approach of the Doggett-Cooper bill, which is explained further in Whitesell (2009).

Cumulative emission goals could be ensured in part because adjustments would be made in the forecast price path as needed to achieve the emissions goal for 2020. In addition, any cumulative excess of emissions in the years leading up to 2020 could be made up by lowering the emission budget for the subsequent ten-year period.

A managed price approach could be particularly helpful in the initial years of a new cap-and-trade program even if it were not intended to be continued indefinitely. Stable and predictable carbon prices would be especially important in those early years when a new market was taking shape. Regulated firms and regulators themselves would be learning about the market, and predictable prices in those years could relieve possible suspicions about the functioning of the market. A similar case could be made for the early years of conversion of a cap-and-trade program from a framework where most allowances are distributed for free to one in which allowances are auctioned (as will occur in the EU ETS after 2012). Conversion to auctioning would greatly expand the role of the market in redistributing allowances among firms and would significantly boost the importance of limiting price volatility.

In addition, in the early years of a new carbon market, firms would be planning their new emission reduction programs. If future allowance prices are very uncertain, errors could be made in investment choices. Some firms might believe that future prices would be very low, or that uncertainty was too great, and therefore fail to undertake even moderate-cost abatement projects. Other firms might expect that prices would be very high and therefore choose to implement some high-cost projects. Thus, the efficiency gains of a market-based approach would not be achieved because of substantial uncertainty about future allowance prices. A managed price approach would help avoid such investment errors. Another key advantage of a managed price approach is that it would eliminate incentives for market manipulation and excess speculation, as discussed further.

MARKET MANIPULATION AND SPECULATIVE
BOOMS AND BUSTS

Despite the huge volumes of trading in the overnight U.S. lending market and the heterogeneity of firms that participate, from the largest financial institutions to small local credit unions, the market is virtually free of manipulative behavior and excess speculation. The Federal Reserve's management of interest rates removes the ability of firms to manipulate the price. No one can corner the market, because if the interest rate starts rising, the Fed adds more money to the market to get the interest rate back on target. The expectations of speculators cannot get carried away because the Fed can bring interest rates back to the target with its next open market auction. The market requires very little direct surveillance by regulators to police against manipulation and speculative excess because interest rate management itself virtually eliminates the opportunities and incentives for such behavior.

Similar benefits could occur if a managed price approach were used in emission allowance markets. The government would issue the number of allowances needed to keep allowance prices close to the target level in any year. It would be impossible for anyone to corner the market. Attempts to manipulate prices would fail. It would still be necessary for an institution such as the Commodity Futures Trading Commission to monitor markets to identify fraud and other types of illegal activity. However, by largely removing the incentives for such behavior, the burden on regulators charged to police the markets would be substantially reduced.

Even in the absence of manipulative behavior, prices in financial and commodity markets often go through boom and bust cycles. Some fluctuations in prices are unavoidable, as they are responses to new information about supply and demand. For longer-term assets, changes in expectations about future supply and demand can have a pronounced effect on current prices. However, expectations about the future are often contagious; the resulting herd behavior in financial and commodity markets, even in the absence of manipulative activity, can nevertheless generate wide swings in prices.

In addition, innovative financial products and mechanisms can open up markets to substantial flows of "hot money." The wide swings in the prices of crude oil and other commodities in recent years are an example. New mutual funds were created with the purpose of tracking the performance of one of many broad indexes of commodity prices. Pension funds, endowments, and hedge funds (private investment pools) began investing heavily in these commodity index mutual funds. These investments were generally not an attempt to manipulate the market, but rather an innocent means of diversifying financial portfolios (Buyuksahin, 2008). As a result of the large financial inflows, the managers of these mutual funds had to invest in the underlying commodities, including crude oil as an important component. This flow of financial capital from institutional sources helped push crude oil prices to more than $140/barrel in mid-2008. With the global financial collapse and sharp economic downturn in late 2008, along with the withdrawal of institutional capital from commodity investments, crude oil prices dropped below $40 a barrel in December 2008.

A similar scenario could occur in a carbon market. If the United States implemented a cap-and-trade program, the market would likely become large and liquid enough for GHG allowance prices to be included in an index of commodities. Pension funds, endowments, and hedge funds with no particular interest in carbon markets might then implicitly invest in GHG allowances merely by buying shares in a commodity index mutual fund. The managers of those mutual funds would need to buy GHG allowances to faithfully track the index of commodity prices. The resulting flows of institutional capital into and out of the carbon market could induce wide swings in allowance prices, increasing uncertainties for regulated firms that are planning emission abatement projects and perhaps raising public concerns about the wisdom of using carbon markets to implement climate policies. If so, the future of the cap-and-trade program could be at risk. If discouragement about the market led to adoption of a command-and-control approach instead, such as that mandated by the Clean Air Act in the United States, the costs to the economy for a given amount of emission abatement would be considerably higher.

A managed price approach would help prevent speculative booms and busts in carbon prices. The stabilization of prices at close to target levels in any given year would remove incentives for "hot money" flows and eliminate their ability to move prices if they did occur. Another design feature that could constrain speculative behavior is limits on allowance banking. The experience of central banks is instructive in that regard, as discussed further.

A CENTRAL BANK'S APPROACH TO
BANKING AND BORROWING

The Federal Reserve and some other central banks regulate commercial banks in part by imposing reserve requirements on their customer deposits. As mentioned earlier, requiring commercial banks to hold reserve deposits at the central bank is similar in some respects to requiring GHG emitters to surrender allowances in a cap-and-trade program. In one case, the requirement limits the customer deposits of commercial banks; in the other case, the requirement limits emissions.

In the regulation of deposits, "banking and borrowing" is called "carryover" of excess reserves or deficiencies from one compliance period to the next. Because central banks use other methods to manage interest rates, they do not rely on carryover as a means of controlling the overall volatility in the market. The Fed allows carryover of deficiencies mainly so that individual firms can avoid paying very high prices if they discover they are short on their compliance obligation at the end of a period when the market is illiquid. The Fed allows carryover of excess reserves mainly so that individual firms can avoid taking losses if they discover an excess at the end of a period and have to dump the balances at low prices in an illiquid market.

However, the Federal Reserve and other central banks do not allow unlimited carryover privileges. If carryover was unlimited, firms could game the system and create difficulties for the implementation of monetary policy. Firms could buy large amounts of excess reserves when they were cheap and get credit for them in a later, more expensive period. This would undermine the compliance regime and the central bank's ability to manage interest rates. To prevent such outcomes, the Fed limits carryover to 4% of the compliance obligation. In addition, a firm cannot carry an excess ("bank") in two consecutive periods, nor can it carry a deficiency ("borrow") in two consecutive periods.

If a managed price approach is used for an emission allowance market, the banking of allowances would also need to be limited. A small amount of banking would still be useful so that firms do not need to purchase allowances equal to the exact number of tons they emitted during the year. Otherwise, firms trying to dump any excess allowances at the end of the period (after the last auction) might get very low prices.

Limits would be useful on allowance banking even if a managed price approach were not being used. With unlimited banking, allowances could be hoarded by financial firms and others. Large buyers could then more easily manipulate the market. In addition, unlimited banking may not always help stabilize prices; it can even enhance price volatility in some instances. Banking links allowance prices in one compliance period to expected prices in future periods. When expectations about the future change, banking causes feedback effects on current allowance prices. For instance, under the Acid Rain Program, which allows unlimited banking, the tighter CAIR rules for sulfur dioxide were announced in 2005 but were not scheduled to be implemented until 2010. Because banking provides a link between the allowance markets in those two years, the expected tightening of the program in 2010 caused a sharp rise in allowance prices in 2005. Sulfur dioxide prices also swung widely during 2008 when a court at first overturned the CAIR rules in July and then reinstated them in December (McCarthy, 2009).

Allowance borrowing can help stabilize prices when a temporary spike occurs. However, as noted earlier, borrowing creates a problem for subsequent compliance periods. In a period in which firms must repay their borrowings, the demand for allowances is increased to make the repayments, thereby putting upward pressure on allowance prices. Moreover, if emission caps are gradually tightened over time, allowance prices might already be quite high in the repayment period. Other price stabilizing methods are more effective and have less risk of adverse side effects than allowance borrowing. In particular, borrowing would be unnecessary if a managed price approach were used.

COMPLIANCE PERIODS

In implementing reserve requirements, central banks have experimented with compliance periods of various lengths. In some countries, the requirement must be met each day. In other countries, the compliance period is a month (and a bank fulfills its obligation if its average daily reserves exceed the requirement). The Federal Reserve has used compliance periods of one and two weeks. Central banks have found that longer compliance periods have both advantages and disadvantages. The price of reserves (the overnight interest rate) is not very volatile early in a compliance period. The reason is that traders expect the central bank to achieve its target at the end of the period, and inter-temporal arbitrage then helps keep market interest rates close to what is expected for the end of the period. With a long period, therefore, interest rates will remain fairly smooth for many days.

However, the longer the compliance period, the more volatile the interest rates will be toward the end of the period. A long period can also make a firm's compliance obligation less certain at the beginning of the period. Firms that are risk-averse will front-load their purchases of compliance instruments. Other firms with greater risk tolerance will postpone their purchases of compliance instruments until the need for them becomes clearer. The distribution of compliance instruments among regulated firms therefore tends to get more out of balance with the ultimate distribution of needs when there is a long compliance period. The result is often a scramble at the end of the period and heightened uncertainty about interest rates at that time. An imbalance in the distribution of compliance instruments at the end of a long compliance period also tends to increase the frequency of noncompliance events.

In an emission allowance market, there are good reasons for the compliance period to be at least one year in length. Any shorter period could create sizable swings in the need for allowances from one period to the next merely because of seasonal fluctuations in energy demand. However, a three-year compliance period, as in the RGGI program and as has been proposed for the Western Climate Initiative, is likely too long. Although a multiyear compliance period would smooth out some year-to-year fluctuations in energy demand, it runs the risk of volatile prices at the end of the period and frequent noncompliance events. Other means could be used to stabilize allowance prices without running the risks of a multiyear compliance period.

AN INDEPENDENT CLIMATE BOARD?

With the benefit of the previous review of implementation issues, what further comments can be made about the possible need for an independent climate board to implement a cap-and-trade program? Two separate questions are involved: (1) How much discretion should the legislature leave to the administrator of the program? (2) Should this discretion be exercised by the presidential administration or by an independent professional board similar to a central bank?

As mentioned at the beginning of the chapter, one extreme of discretionary authority would be for the legislature to lay down a national emission goal a decade or so ahead, consistent with an international treaty commitment, and then leave it up to the administrators of the program to work out the cost-containment mechanisms that would be used to reach that goal. The legislature would conduct regular reviews of the program but would only be required to reopen the legislation when new emission goals were needed in future decades.

Alternatively, the enabling legislation could specify many of the details of the cap-and-trade program while still leaving some discretion in its administration. Existing programs and legislative proposals have indicated some examples. The European Commission, for example, exercises some authority in approving National Allocation Plans, identifying competitive industries, and setting benchmarks that help determine the amounts of free allowances firms will receive. In the United States, future carbon prices are determined in part by judgments of the EPA (under the Larson carbon tax bill) or the Treasury (under the McDermott cap-with-no-trading bill). The Doggett-Cooper bill, and other types of managed price approaches, would give discretionary authority to an administrator to adjust a target price path within the constraints of achieving medium-term and cumulative emission goals. The Lieberman-Warner bill gives authority to an independent board to adjust limits on allowance borrowing.

Some types of flexibility have also been built into cap-and-trade programs through automatic trigger mechanisms rather than the exercise of discretionary authority by an administrator. For instance, the RGGI program relaxes limits on offsets if the allowance price reaches a certain level. The Bingaman-Specter bill included a safety-valve price at which an unlimited amount of extra allowances would be released. The Lieberman-Warner, Waxman-Markey, and Kerry-Boxer bills specify a threshold price at which a limited amount of additional allowances are released. Whereas those bills used automatic mechanisms to set thresholds for release of the allowance reserve, others have proposed giving a climate board some discretion to set the thresholds (USCAP, 2009).

In general terms, each of the above options has some potential disadvantages. Inflexible legislation can generate persistent policy errors;

discretionary authority can be misused; and trigger mechanisms can be gamed and can create adverse self-fulfilling hypotheses. Measures can be deployed to help address such concerns: Legislation can be subjected to periodic review, and revisions can be passed using expedited procedures. Discretionary authority can be circumscribed within an explicit mandate. Trigger mechanisms can require discretionary approval before they are implemented.

When a new cap-and-trade program is passed, a legislature must listen to many voices. Professional testimony must be heard as well as the concerns of those who may be impacted by the program. However, there is sometimes a tendency to underestimate the abilities of firms and individuals to make cost-effective adjustments in the early years of a program. If the fears of economic harm are exaggerated, the legislation may end up codifying fairly weak targets. Indeed, similar to the experience with monetary policy, the incentives for politicians may be weighted in favor of fairly easy settings for policy instruments. As a result, in the early years of several cap-and-trade programs, emission caps have proved much easier to achieve than was expected. The consequence is a buildup of sizable emission banks which will weaken the achievement of environmental goals later on.

Monetary analysis has also wrestled with the idea of using automatic mechanisms in the formulation of policy. In particular, a variety of "monetary policy rules" have been proposed that generate predictable policy responses to varying economic conditions (see, e.g., Taylor, 1999). However, a wide range of possible rules can be used and they tend to give differing policy prescriptions. Moreover, policy rules often work well within a limited range of situations but go badly off track when conditions depart significantly from those used in the original construction of the rule. In light of these considerations, the practice among central banks has been to review the recommendations of numerous rules and then to exercise discretionary judgment when making actual policy choices.

Because of the limited experience with economy-wide cap-and-trade programs, it is likely advisable for a legislature not to try to micromanage the program by over-prescribing automatic response mechanisms. Some flexibility may be especially useful in administering the trade-offs between allowance prices and annual emission caps. These "cost-containment" procedures may eventually need to be harmonized with those of other countries if a common global carbon market is to emerge through linked cap-and-trade programs. Moreover, it is unrealistic to expect that a legislature will arrive at the optimal design of all details of a program, especially when the program includes some features that have never been fully tested.

A mid-course review of cap-and-trade programs is one means of handling the design uncertainties. In addition, an implementing authority could be granted some flexibility to learn from experience and improve its implementation techniques over time. The experience of central banks shows that considerable learning by doing is likely to occur and that procedures may need to be adjusted over time to deal with differing circumstances that may arise.

If discretionary authority is given to an implementing body, there are advantages of creating a semi-independent institution to exercise that authority. Some aspects of a cap-and-trade program, such as the monitoring of emissions of regulated entities, are appropriately housed in an EPA, or similar government body, that is already well-equipped to handle such tasks. However, an independent, nonpolitical board is useful when major discretionary decisions need to be made. Independence would be strengthened if board members have long terms of appointment. The board could be accountable directly to the legislature and be supported by a professional staff. With this type of structure, a board would likely develop its own culture of responsibility for its mission, just as central banks have developed an institutional ethic of their own as stewards of the value of the nation's currency. This institutional culture, as well as the legal mandate itself, would help to insulate the institution from political influences.

If an independent board is created to exercise discretionary powers in a cap-and-trade program, its authority needs not be as wide as those of central banks. For instance, a legislature could prescribe ranges for both emission goals and allowance prices and allow a board some discretion to tailor cost-containment mechanisms as long as the outcomes remained within those prescribed limits. Indeed, the distinction between goal dependence and instrument independence, so important in central banking, is not so clear for cap-and-trade. Emission caps and carbon prices are both goals and instruments. The ultimate goal of avoiding climate damage is too far into the future to be a measurable basis for institutional accountability.

A specialized climate board would also be useful to help coordinate and oversee the many institutions involved in implementing cap-and-trade. The functions of monitoring emissions, ensuring compliance, approving offset projects, allocating allowances, tracking allowance and offset ownership, conducting auctions, regulating the carbon markets, and assessing progress toward environmental goals will require the participation of many government agencies. In the United States, the EPA would certainly play a large role, but the Departments of Agriculture, Energy, and the Treasury may also be involved, as well as the Commodity Futures Trading Commission, the Federal Energy Regulatory Agency, and others. A climate board could usefully provide a coordinating and oversight role among these government bodies. As an institution independent from the presidential administration, it could play a useful role in making regular reports to Congress on the overall effectiveness of the program and recommending any needed changes in program structure or administration.

HUBRIS IN DESIGNING POLICIES

Given limited experience with economy-wide cap-and-trade programs, we do not at present have the full information needed to calibrate program designs with any special wisdom. However, we cannot afford to wait until all uncertainties are resolved before taking action. We need to create a policy framework for the long-run future. How can that be done without locking in an overspecified approach that may prove to be far inferior to the eventual best practice? A lesson from monetary policy might be applicable to this issue. In the 1960s, monetarists at times criticized the Federal Reserve for trying to "fine-tune" the economy (Friedman, 1968). The central bank was overconfident about its ability to smooth out the business cycle. Insufficient appreciation of uncertainties about the economy and about the effects of adjusting its policy tools were said to be contributing to adverse results. The business cycle was not being eliminated by the fine-tuning of policy, but perhaps amplified. The Great Inflation of the 1970s finally ended any remaining hubris among policy makers of the time. The financial collapse of 2008 has provided another such lesson.

It would be advisable to avoid overconfidence in the design of climate policies as well. The limits in our understanding about the climate are considerable. We are forced to consider climate prospects many decades ahead at levels of GHG that have not been seen on this planet since well before our species evolved. We need to be cautious about any particular point forecast. In addition, we have not had enough experience with carbon regulation and carbon markets to be confident that we know what will prove to be the best approach. For these reason, it seems advisable to build initial policy frameworks with some caution. A review of the policy design after a few years of operation would be useful to assess the need for improvements or even a major restructuring. Unless the administrator of the program is given the flexibility to adjust design features, accelerated legislative procedures may be required to make the necessary changes. We also lack real knowledge of the appropriate level of emission caps several decades ahead. If caps for those years are written into legislation, they will need to be reviewed in light of the progress made in abating emissions, new developments regarding the climate, technological advances, and treaty negotiations. We should expect to be surprised by the climate, by technology, by markets, and by the effects of our policy instruments. In this area, as in others, wisdom will likely always be a work in progress.

ELEVEN

The Outlook for Climate Policies

In the absence of a geo-engineering miracle, the world's climate problem cannot be solved by one large country or a limited group of countries. A substantial effort by all major emitters is needed. A coordinated international effort is essential to promote vigorous efforts by all parties and to avoid causing competitive imbalances through climate policies. However, the appropriate degree of homogeneity among policy approaches across countries at the current time is debatable. Although a uniform price on carbon would promote a cost-minimizing solution to the global climate problem, capacities and responsibilities differ across countries, as do the potential impacts of climate change. In the absence of a common, top-down approach, considerable progress could nevertheless be made through decentralized, national programs that are increasingly linked and harmonized, over time.

A SUCCESSOR TO THE KYOTO PROTOCOL

As noted in Chapter 9, in the Kyoto Protocol, thirty-seven countries with advanced economies agreed to reduce greenhouse gas (GHG) emissions to an average of 5.2% below the 1990 level during the years 2008 through 2012. Part of the emission reductions will come from offset projects located in developing countries (DCs). This distinction between the roles of advanced economies and DCs at Kyoto reflected the principle of "common but differentiated responsibilities" to respond to the climate change problem, which was included in the broader treaty – the United Nations Framework Convention on Climate Change (UNFCCC). In particular, the responsibility of advanced economies is greater because of their larger share of the historical emissions of GHG since the industrial revolution.

Expiring in 2012, the Kyoto Protocol was intended to be the first in a series of agreements to implement the UNFCCC. Negotiations on a new international agreement for the post-2012 period have been underway for some time. Two separate working groups have been established: one to extend and perhaps modify the Kyoto Protocol and a second to discuss long-term cooperative actions by all countries, not just those taking emission reduction commitments at Kyoto.

A key issue for the negotiations is the meaning of the principle of "common but differentiated responsibilities." At present, many advanced economy countries prefer to fold elements from the Kyoto Protocol into a single new agreement that includes emission reduction actions by all parties, including developing countries. However, DCs want to ensure a differentiated approach by making a successor agreement to the Kyoto Protocol a separate instrument that includes enforceable emission reduction commitments only for advanced economies. They prefer to specify any new mechanisms or instruments in a separate overall agreement. It had been hoped that a new treaty would be hammered out during the negotiations in Copenhagen in December 2009, but the accord that was reached lacked some specifics and did not take the form of a binding international agreement. It did enshrine a ceiling of 2°C for global warming, provided financing from advanced economies for DC climate activities of $30 billion through 2012 and $100 billion a year by 2020, and secured agreement for enhanced DC reporting on emissions and climate activities, which will be subject to international "consultation and analysis." However, much work still lies ahead if negotiators are to create a new international architecture for post-2012 climate policies (IISD, 2009).

Components of a new framework have been under discussion for some time. Although DCs are not yet willing to accept binding national emission targets, they are willing to pledge "Nationally Appropriate Mitigation Actions" (or NAMAs) that are measurable, reportable, and verifiable. That was the outcome of the "action plan" agreed upon in Bali, Indonesia, in December 2007. Three levels of NAMAs may be involved. First, DCs may take unilateral actions, such as those described later by China, Brazil, and Mexico. Second, they may agree to undertake more difficult actions if they receive financing and technical support from advanced economies. The Bali Action Plan specified that rich countries would commit to measurable amounts of financing, technology assistance, and capacity building to support climate mitigation in DCs. Contingent NAMAs by DCs that are undertaken with financing from the governments of advanced countries, and technology assistance arranged by them, would thus implement both aspects of the Bali Plan. These NAMAs could include reduced deforestation aided by support for administrative capacity building and economic alternatives in DCs. They could also include some higher-tech projects, such as Integrated Gasification Combined Cycle power plants and carbon capture and storage.

The third type of NAMA involves emissions baselines for particular industrial sectors that could be used as benchmarks for earning offset credits. The baselines would be below the business-as-usual (BAU) levels. The DC would make a contribution to the environment if it achieves the baseline. It would incur no penalty for excess emissions but would earn offset credits to the extent that emissions come in below the baseline. Thus, unlike the project-based offsets of the Kyoto Protocol, which were cumbersome to approve and regulate, an entire industrial sector could be involved in earning offset credits under this approach. "No-lose" sectoral programs of this nature could, in principle, generate greater gains for the environment and more financing of mitigation activities in DCs than project-based mechanisms (Helme, 2006). In some DCs, they might include credits relative to baselines of reduced deforestation. In addition, programs for industrial sectors in DCs could help alleviate the risk of emission "leakage" from the relocation of industries that are subject to an emission cap in advanced economies.

A number of challenges still need to be overcome to specify how a NAMA mechanism will actually work. A crucial step is for advanced economies to make commitments to provide finance in return for contingent NAMAs. A procedure for matching financing sources with the contingent NAMAs pledged by developing countries needs to be arranged. A procedure needs to be developed for determining the crediting baselines for no-lose sectoral programs in developing countries. Indeed, it has been difficult to develop reliable, plant-level emission data even in advanced countries. It may be some time before sectoral emission-crediting baselines can be created in DCs. Because of measurement problems, sectoral programs in DCs may for some time have to be based on technology deployment goals rather than verifiable emission reductions.

ANNOUNCED NATIONAL PLANS

Key ingredients to the international negotiations have been the goals and targets for new climate actions announced by countries. These actions are now being appended to the "Copenhagen Accord." Some countries are committed to substantial cuts in their nation's GHG emissions, often conditional on the actions of other parties. For instance, as noted earlier, the EU intends to reduce emissions to 20% below the 1990 level by 2020, or 30% below if comparable efforts are taken by other parties. The new administration in Japan has announced a goal of a 25% reduction by 2020, relative to the 1990 level, if a strong global treaty is signed. Similarly, Australia and New Zealand have announced ranges for their 2020 climate goals, depending on the commitments of others. Norway has announced a willingness to reduce emissions 40% below the 1990 level by 2020, conditional on the actions of others.

In other countries, however, emission pledges have been less ambitious. Russia has also announced a range for emissions, but at levels that are widely seen as not much different from BAU scenarios. In the United States, the Waxman-Markey bill would reduce emissions 17% below the 2005 level, although another 10% of emission reductions are being sought through a special program to reduce emissions from deforestation in developing countries.

In sum, using the lower portion of the previously mentioned ranges, the announced 2020 targets from Kyoto parties are about 8% below the annual target for the 2008–2012 Kyoto period and thus about 13% below the 1990 level (UNFCCC, 2009). Using the upper portion of the announced national ranges would bring the 2020 emission goal to about 20% below the 1990 level. The United States, which had about 60% of the total emissions of Kyoto parties in 2006, would reduce emissions to about 3% below the 1990 level by 2020 under the Waxman-Markey bill. According to IPCC (2007) estimates, a reduction of emissions from advanced economy countries to some 25% to 40% below the 1990 level, along with a substantial reduction from BAU levels for developing countries, is needed to return the world to a CO_2e concentration level of 450 ppm after some initial overshooting of that goal. This concentration level is estimated to be associated with keeping global temperatures below 2°C, the agreed goal from Copenhagen. Thus, the announced emission reduction targets of advanced economy countries are not consistent with the common climate goal recorded in the Copenhagen Accord.

Some developing countries have announced significant climate policy initiatives as well. These unilateral actions are designed in part to limit the use of energy in order to reduce dependence on oil imports, but increasingly also to address climate change. For instance, China is developing nuclear and renewable energy sources, implementing tough vehicle efficiency standards, closing inefficient industrial facilities, and burning methane recovered from coal mines and landfills (Helme, 2009). It intends to reduce energy intensity by 20% between 2005 and 2010. In September 2009, President Hu Jintao announced climate policy goals for China for 2020, including reductions in CO_2 emission intensity and increases in forest cover and the use of nonfossil fuels. Brazil has an objective of reducing the rate of deforestation by 70% over the 2006–2017 period, which would lower CO_2 emissions by some 5 billion tons relative to BAU forecasts.

Mexico has announced plans to implement a cap-and-trade program for four industries: electric power, oil refining, steel, and cement. It intends to reduce GHG emissions to half the 2000 level by 2050. South Korea (and perhaps China) is also now beginning to investigate the possibility of a domestic cap-and-trade program.

ALTERNATIVES TO A KYOTO TYPE OF AGREEMENT

A voluminous literature has suggested numerous alternatives to a Kyoto type of agreement. National emission reduction targets could be set by an agreed formula rather than case-by-case negotiations (Frankel, 2007). Developing countries could join in emission reduction commitments once their emissions and GDP per capita exceed certain thresholds (Michaelowa, 2007). Others recommend a shift away from enforceable emission reduction targets. One option would be a harmonized global carbon tax (Cooper, 2006). Other alternatives include a focus on technology research (Barrett, 2007) or a variety of individual policy measures (Pizer, 2007). Groups of nations could join in policy "clubs" to implement common policies. An international body could review the distinct national and regional policies to assess the comparability of efforts across countries and the overall global mitigation results (Victor, 2007).

The approach to enforcement under the Kyoto Protocol is also subject to question. If a country fails to hold its required compliance instruments, it is supposed to make up its excess emissions in the next period along with a 30% penalty. However, the very existence of a second Kyoto-like period now seems in serious jeopardy. If a Kyoto II does emerge, the targets for individual countries will ultimately be decided by each sovereign country for itself.

Stricter compliance penalties could be imposed, including direct monetary penalties, the posting of performance bonds, or trade sanctions. However, countries are not likely to agree to such penalties, and a restriction of international trade could prove harmful to all. Market-based penalties could be imposed, such as the imposition of ex post discounts on the allowances or offset credits of a country, which would have to be paid by buyers of those instruments (Victor, 2001). However, for buyer liability penalties to be effective, carbon markets would need to become more mature than they are today.

An alternative to international enforcement through treaties is reliance on countries to implement actions through domestic laws and regulations. This was the approach suggested by the United States in its submission to the

UNFCCC in May 2009. It may be the default position for the international community if no enforceable treaty takes the place of the Kyoto Protocol. Even if negotiators fail to agree on a top-down approach to climate policies for the post-2012 period, there could be a gradual move to coordination and harmonization of national approaches over time. For instance, whether carbon prices were imposed by taxes in some countries or cap-and-trade programs in others, prices could converge across countries over time. Linkages among cap-and-trade programs would help equalize carbon prices, but arranging for a full linkage of multiple domestic systems could prove problematic, as discussed further.

LINKAGES AMONG CARBON MARKETS

If each country or region has a separate cap-and-trade program, carbon prices are likely to differ. Even if two programs are of comparable stringency, local variations in weather and economic activity, the effectiveness of energy efficiency efforts, program details, and other policies would cause divergences in carbon prices. The differences in prices would mean implementation of expensive emission abatement projects in some countries, whereas cheaper projects fail to go forward in others where prices are lower. The world's overall cost of climate mitigation therefore would be higher than if carbon prices were equalized across the globe.

The Kyoto Protocol provided an incentive for some countries and regions to establish cap-and-trade programs, but countries could also choose other methods to achieve their emission target. The Protocol did generate linkages in carbon trading around the world through its offset mechanisms. However, buying countries have imposed limits on the use of those offsets; indeed, the Protocol itself suggests that they should be used merely to supplement emission reduction efforts. More complete linkages among cap-and-trade systems could promote greater equalization of the prices of carbon instruments. If countries placed no restrictions on the use of each other's allowances for compliance purposes, the markets could be integrated even if the linked programs had slightly different features and administrative arrangements. Linking could also potentially increase the liquidity and depth of carbon markets, making manipulative behavior more difficult. In addition, the ability to link to a larger international carbon market might provide an incentive for smaller developing countries to initiate cap-and-trade programs to control GHG.

Many practical hurdles must be overcome, however, to make linking possible. There will be winners and losers if prices differ across two systems prior to linking. For instance, the equalization of prices will benefit allowance sellers and hurt buyers in the system that previously had the lower prices. To avoid large transfers of capital, a cap-and-trade program may prefer to link only with other programs of comparable stringency.

In addition, cost-containment features tend to be transmitted across linked programs (Jaffe, 2008; Mehling, 2009). Thus, a safety valve in one cap-and-trade system will act as a price ceiling for systems to which it is linked. An allowance reserve will be shared across systems as well. If one program accepts offset credits of questionable quality, the allowance prices in the linked system will also be lower because of those offsets even if the second system does not accept the offsets themselves. To avoid such problems, the cost-containment features of programs could be harmonized prior to linking. However, early harmonization has the disadvantage of precluding further experimentation with design features. Given the limited experience to date, the best practice approach to cap-and-trade it is not yet obvious.

If cap-and-trade programs were only partially linked, the risk to environmental goals from the spread of loose cost-containment features could be alleviated. For instance, limits could be placed on the percentage of a firm's compliance obligation that could be met with allowances from the other system. Alternatively, linking might only be indirect through mutual acceptance of a third system's allowances or offset credits (such as the offset credits from the Kyoto Protocol). Partial or indirect linking would provide some insulation from the cost-containment features of other programs, but it would also limit the amount of price equalization that would occur. Nevertheless, linking with limits may be feasible well before unrestricted linking. It could accelerate movement toward the harmonization and integration of programs that is already under discussion.[1]

Some harmonization may be needed, not only in cap-and-trade design, but also in the regulation of carbon markets. At present, regulatory regimes for commodity trading differ substantially across countries. In the United States, for instance, speculators are subject to limits on their commodity contracts; the purpose is to prevent contract failures and potential manipulation. It has been difficult to close loopholes in these regulations and in the provisions of the underlying Commodity Exchange Act. As a result, energy markets have suffered from the disruptive manipulative activities of the Enron and Amaranth corporations. In Europe, where markets are smaller, no such limitations apply. If carbon markets were linked, trading might migrate to the region with the loosest regulatory regime. Harmonization of

[1] See http://www.icapcarbonaction.com (International Carbon Action Partnership).

approaches could prevent such "regulatory arbitrage" by firms. In addition, with linked systems, coordination among regulators will be needed to investigate possible manipulative behavior across multiple trading systems.

In sum, even though some countries have undertaken strong commitments and developed innovative climate policy approaches, the outlook for a coordinated global regime looks doubtful in the near future. Even if a broad international agreement on climate policy remains elusive, some progress could still occur. Experimentation with new policy designs would be useful, because best practices are not yet clear. Over time, countries with similar policy approaches may explore closer connections. Cap-and-trade programs are now gaining greater interest around the world. As new programs are implemented and design features are harmonized, these programs could forge gradually closer links. If carbon markets eventually become integrated and a uniform carbon price is achieved, an efficient, least-cost solution could emerge to the global climate challenge.

OVERALL REVIEW AND CONCLUSIONS

Lessons from Climate History

As discussed in Part One of the book, natural forces have produced dramatic extremes of climate during the 4.5-billion-year history of the Earth. The breakup of an early supercontinent around 800 million years ago (Mya) may have led to increased rainfall on land and a speedup in the chemical weathering of rocks, thereby removing CO_2 from the atmosphere. The reduced CO_2 levels at a time when solar radiation was weaker evidently led to extensive glaciation. As sea ice spread over the oceans, more of the Sun's light was reflected away, lowering temperatures further. A clustering of the continents near the equator may have helped snow and ice complete their conquest of the planet, perhaps producing a Snowball or Slushball Earth. The ice cover would have shut down chemical weathering, thereby helping prepare the way for its own removal: CO_2 released by volcanoes would then remain in the atmosphere, generating greenhouse warming.

Over most of its life, however, the surface of the Earth was much warmer. During the planet's typical "Greenhouse" climate, no permanent ice existed even at the poles. The latest Greenhouse period lasted from about 250 to 35 Mya. Around 55 Mya, temperatures jumped to an extraordinary peak. A massive dose of GHG was evidently released from a rift vent on the ocean floor between Greenland and the rest of Europe. The estimated carbon emissions were about 2,000 billion tons (Gt), less than half of what we have available in fossil fuel resources today. The pace of emissions was evidently much slower than the current rate, as it took about 10,000 years for the planet to reach a peak warming of about 7°C at that time. The warming and the increased acidity of the oceans evidently caused the extinction of many marine creatures and some species on land as well.

Our Ice House began when Antarctica first developed a permanent ice cover after 35 Mya. The exact cause is controversial, but tectonic forces may have played a key role. The Indian subcontinent began pushing into the rest of Asia at that time, causing the uplift of the Himalayan Mountains and the Tibetan plateau. With the newly exposed rock surfaces, chemical weathering would have accelerated, removing CO_2 from the atmosphere. New snow and ice reflected more sunlight and amplified the cooling trend. Greenland picked up an ice sheet about 7 Mya. Around 3 Mya, the CO_2 levels had apparently dropped to a point where the climate became sensitive to changes in the tilt of the Earth and in the timing of the planet's closest approach to the Sun (the perihelion). A minimal tilt and a January perihelion means less melting of snow during the summer in the Northern Hemisphere, which holds most of the planet's land. At such times, ice sheets have expanded over vast areas of North America and Northern Eurasia. Over the last million years, continental Ice Ages have persisted for intervals of about 100,000 years at a time. They have been interrupted by Interglacial Periods that have generally lasted only one-tenth as long.

During the interglacial period that occurred around 125,000 years ago, the last one preceding ours, the summer radiation in the Northern Hemisphere was especially strong. A sizable fraction of the ice on Greenland apparently melted, despite the fact that the planet's overall temperature was not much different than today. With some feedback response from West Antarctica as well, the level of the oceans was about 5 meters higher than today.

The latest Ice Age reached a peak around 21,000 years ago. The melting of northern ice sheets thereafter was interrupted around 13,000 years ago, when a huge pulse of meltwater drained into the North Atlantic. It reduced the salinity (and density) of surface waters enough to prevent them from sinking; as a result, the ocean conveyor belt shut down. Lacking warm waters from the Western Hemisphere, Europe plunged back into extreme cold until ocean circulation resumed about 1,500 years later.

A controversial theory suggests that human influence on the climate began as early as 8,000 years ago, when CO_2 was released with the clearing of forests for agricultural use. Anthropogenic methane emissions may have contributed noticeably after the initiation of rice farming some 5,000 years ago. The resulting maintenance of high GHG levels may have thwarted the natural end of our interglacial period. The Little Ice Age of 1350 to 1850 may have reflected a resumption of a longer-term cooling trend along with some temporary declines in solar radiation.

With the industrial revolution, the burning of fossil fuels has pushed the atmospheric concentration of CO_2 well above any observed in ice core records for the last 800 millennia. Largely as a result, the planet's temperature has risen about 0.8°C since 1880, putting it at about the interglacial peak reached around 7,000 years ago. The climate effects do not depend on the peak warming reached in a given year, but rather on the average temperatures that will be sustained for decades and centuries.

The Business-as-Usual Outlook

At present, the combustion of fossil fuels produces about 80% of our energy and more than half of our emissions of GHG, mainly in the form of CO_2. Per unit of energy, the release of CO_2 from coal is about 30% more than from oil and 70% more than from natural gas. About 40% of the world's electricity is currently generated from coal and 20% from natural gas. As a liquid fuel, oil is critical for transportation, but conventional sources may be depleted before the end of this century. Producing liquid fuels from tar sands, oil shale, or coal-to-liquids technology currently requires three to five times more energy than extracting oil through conventional means. GHG emissions are also three to five times higher.

Agriculture and forestry currently account for about 30% of our GHG emissions. The largest contributors, aside from the continued clearing of forests, are the release of methane from livestock and of nitrous oxide from cultivated soils. Industry accounts for about 12% of GHG emissions in addition to its consumption of energy. A variety of processes are involved: CO_2 is emitted in producing cement and steel and in refining oil, HFCs in producing refrigerants, and sulfur dioxide in electronic applications. The emissions of methane in the processing of wastes account for the remaining 3% or so of our GHG emissions.

The total anthropogenic emission of key GHGs, when combined in a summary measure, have grown about 1.5% per year since 1970, reaching an estimated CO_2-equivalent level of 44 Gt in 2005. After the world's economy recovers from its current slump, emissions could continue growing at a 1.5% annual rate under BAU policies. The pace of BAU emissions should slow after 2030, however, as the world's population begins to level off and some developing economies reach maturity. The resulting atmospheric concentration of GHG depends importantly on the natural processes that remove extra CO_2 from the air. The ocean takes down CO_2 through diffusion caused by the higher concentration of CO_2 in the atmosphere. On land, CO_2 is removed because of faster growth of plants, which is stimulated by the extra CO_2 in the air. Natural CO_2 takedown will rise as its concentration in the atmosphere increases, but global warming will diminish the size of that response. After accounting for such effects, one benchmark IPCC scenario projected that BAU emissions growth of 1% per year after 2030 would result in a CO_2-equivalent concentration of about 1,250 ppm, more than four times the preindustrial level. This would imply more than 6°C of warming using the IPCC's estimate of the global temperature response to each doubling of CO_2.

Scientists generally do not foresee a global tipping point in climate feedbacks in the BAU outlook. The extreme result of a runaway greenhouse is not a feasible scenario: Earth's transition dynamics to a new climate equilibrium are not that fragile. Furthermore, the amplifying feedbacks of planetary albedo reductions and methane releases from permafrost seem likely to proceed in a fairly linear fashion. Methane hydrates in ocean sediments will not warm enough to be destabilized. The risk of a shutdown in the North Atlantic conveyor belt because of meltwater from Greenland is very low over the next hundred years.

The IPCC projected only a moderate sea level increase of 0.2 to 0.6 meters over this century under BAU policies. The rise would be caused mainly by the thermal expansion of the ocean and the melting of mountain glaciers. All the water in mountain glaciers could raise the ocean by only about a half a meter, and it would take 6°C of warming for thermal expansion to do roughly the same. Despite the limits on these two factors, many scientists consider the IPCC's sea level forecast to be overly optimistic. It omits the potential effects of ice sheet dynamics. Also, since the IPCC report was written, Arctic sea ice and Antarctic ice shelves have suffered unexpectedly large losses. Even taking such effects into account, however, the bulk of the ice sheets on Greenland and Antarctica will not respond to global warming within a few decades. Increases in sea level of more than a meter remain a risk, but more so for the next century than this one. Nevertheless, the GHG emissions of this century could well be the cause of sizable future increases in sea level.

Other projected climate change impacts in this century under BAU policies are not so limited. Thresholds in local climate conditions would likely be crossed, bringing considerable harm to society and to other species. The shrinkage of mountain glaciers would reduce the availability of water during the dry season in many regions. Monsoons may strengthen in Asia and the Sahel, but warmer temperatures will mean greater evaporative losses of soil water in many semiarid areas. Some models predict more frequent El Niño conditions and even an associated drying of the Amazon. Heightened intensity of storms could increase the damages to coastal areas.

Because of CO2 fertilization and the warming of higher-latitude temperate zones, the IPCC expects world food production to increase a bit for modest temperature increases. However, with global warming of more than 3°C and the associated desiccation of semiarid regions, the growth and pollination of crops would fail and world-average yields would begin turning down sharply.

The reductions in water availability, increased damages from storms, and general impairment of food production could lead to lost livelihoods, social unrest, and the migration of large numbers of people.

The effects on human health differ substantially by region. In colder climates, the incidence of cardiovascular illness would be reduced because of more moderate winters. However, warmer temperatures will expand the range of tropical diseases and threaten a substantial net increase in mortality.

Higher temperatures and a reduced pH of the ocean are already causing stress among coral reefs. Loss of coral ecosystems and of the shell-forming plankton at the base of the ocean food chain would cause harm to many species. Our fisheries would also be damaged. The potential for rapid destruction of habitats in polar regions, river deltas, and other areas also threaten the survival of many species.

The Pricing of CO_2

Because the global average temperature changes very slowly, the incremental damage caused by a ton of CO_2 in the beginning of a year is about the same as the damage caused by the last ton in that year. An estimate of the marginal damage from climate change caused by each extra ton of GHG in a given year is called the social cost of carbon (or CO_2). If we knew that social cost, we could add it to the cost of goods that require CO_2 emissions (through a tax or a market price of carbon). With GHG pollution priced for the damage it causes, producers and consumers could find inventive ways to make appropriate adjustments. The natural incentive provided by the price signal would generate creative mitigation activities. Individuals and businesses would seek out efficiency improvements, shifts in fuel sources, altered production processes, and research and development of new technologies for emission abatement. The market price signal would also indicate which mitigation projects are too expensive to be worthwhile. Economic efficiency would be achieved with marginal costs equaling marginal benefits.

Unfortunately, this textbook outcome is not realistic. Although qualitative discussions of the potential damages from climate change are the subject of much publicity, estimates of the monetary value of prospective climate damage vary widely and inspire little confidence. Detailed, comprehensive estimates that include all economic sectors and take account of likely adaptation are generally unavailable. Researchers are divided over basic methodological issues, such as discount rates and adjustments on grounds of equity. The frequently used willingness-to-pay approach can give dramatically different estimates of the value of equivalent damages to health and ecosystems, depending on a country's per capita wealth. Finally, evidence is generally unavailable to help evaluate the costs of displaced people and associated social unrest.

Estimating marginal damages from the emissions in a given year is even more difficult. Widely differing estimates have been made for the social cost of CO_2. In a survey of one hundred different studies, the IPCC (2007) cited values from around zero to $130. This is merely the range of point estimates from different studies; the total uncertainty is wider still. Our inability to quantify damage forecasts in a satisfactory way is a major weakness in the foundations of climate policy.

Climate Goals

Lack of consensus and deep uncertainties regarding the appropriate price of CO_2 motivate a search for an alternative framing objective for climate policy. A global temperature goal would be closely linked with climate outcomes but less controllable than measures of GHG. A goal for the atmospheric concentration of GHG would reflect concerns about both global warming and increased ocean acidity. Targets for emissions would be most closely linked with possible mitigation responses; they have also gained some political traction.

Because the climate system responds slowly, multiyear averages of GHG concentrations and temperatures are of greater concern than the peak levels reached in any particular year. It is therefore preferable to express a quantity goal as a trajectory rather than a single ceiling level. In 2007, the IPCC estimated that the CO_2-equivalent concentration of the atmosphere was about 455 ppm and temperatures about 0.7°C above the preindustrial level. At these concentration and temperature levels, mountain glaciers and polar ice have been melting, and coral ecosystems are threatened. Thus, stabilization of GHG concentrations or global temperatures at current or higher levels is not an appropriate goal for the very long run. Over the next several decades, some increase in concentrations and temperatures may be justified until we develop cheaper technology to reduce emissions. For much longer horizons, however, it may be wise to seek reductions in GHG concentrations and global temperatures even below current levels.

Emission targets are most useful for the near term of a decade or two. Emission goals can be easily translated into specific abatement efforts in the years immediately ahead. However, we have little idea at present how emission goals more than two decades ahead would be achieved. The cost of meeting far-off emission targets is unknown and the alternatives, even including the possibility of geo-engineering, are not well-defined. Moreover, the appropriate level of future GHG emissions will depend on the rates of natural CO_2 removal by plants and the ocean, which remain very uncertain. Finally, the global warming caused by a doubling of CO_2 (the "climate sensitivity" variable), though estimated to be 3°C, could be smaller or much larger. Thus, we should avoid locking in a fixed emission goal many decades ahead. We are likely to be surprised by developments and should therefore build some flexibility into our climate policies.

Policy Mandates

Many of the economic sectors that emit GHG are already subject to regulation for health and safety purposes. New mandates could be imposed or existing standards could be modified for the purpose of achieving climate policy goals. In the transportation sector, standards on vehicle production and fuel composition have been used mainly to limit local pollution hazards and oil imports. They could be tightened further to reduce GHG emissions. Locally enforced standards related to the construction of new homes and commercial buildings could include new provisions to improve energy efficiency. Power generators could be subject to CO_2 emission intensity limits, technology mandates, or Renewal Portfolio Standards that require a minimum proportion of electricity to be supplied from renewable resources. Governments could also invest in research on the climate, on emission abatement technologies, and on geo-engineering possibilities.

From an economic point of view, special rationalizations are needed to justify government interventions that go beyond adjusting market prices for unpriced externalities. Support for basic and applied research helps achieve social benefits that generally exceed the private rewards that are gained. However, picking winners among the alternative technologies for commercial development and deployment is not the usual forte of politicians and bureaucrats. Standards may help overcome information problems in homebuilding and new vehicle planning. Relative to market-based measures, however, specific mandates generally imply a narrow scope of possible responses and therefore a greater cost of achieving an overall emission reduction goal.

Taxes and Cap-and-Trade

Taxes and cap-and-trade programs are market-based policies that can substantially lower the cost of achieving an environmental goal. Tax rates can be designed to rise by formula, depending on behavioral responses and environmental outcomes. Tradable permits can be used to implement a performance standard or a broader GHG emission cap. A cap-and-trade system provides an incentive for a firm to overcomply with a regulation if it can do so cheaply. The firm's unused permits or "allowances" can be sold to other firms that find it more expensive to comply. Therefore, the cheapest emission reductions among all the regulated firms will be implemented.

In a cap-and-trade program, the free distribution of allowances could help affected firms and communities adjust to the new regulation during a transitional period, but it could also result in additional profits for some regulated firms. In competitive markets, output prices will rise to reflect the opportunity cost of using allowances rather than selling them. Thus, firms will recover the cost of allowances in their output prices even if they receive the allowances for free. Large windfall profits were earned by power companies in the early years of the cap-and-trade system used by the European Union to implement the Kyoto Protocol.

A cap rations emissions and, implicitly, the activities that produce emissions. Cap levels are typically set well in advance of their year of application and if the caps turn out to be out of line with economic conditions in the year they take effect, allowance prices could soar or plummet if the program includes no flexibility mechanisms. One common flexibility feature allows firms to retain ("bank") excess allowances for use in later periods. Banking provides a link between current allowance prices and the expected prices in future periods. It can moderate the response of prices to transitory pressures, but it can also cause sharp movements of prices in response to news of future developments. For instance, in the cap-and-trade program of the Acid Rain Program, which provides for banking, allowances prices spiked in 2005 after announcement of tighter program rules that were scheduled to take effect only in 2010.

Offsets are another flexibility feature. They provide an incentive for emission reductions in economic sectors that are difficult to include in a cap-and-trade system. For instance, it may be difficult to measure the total methane released from landfills and dairy farms. However, the methane captured from such sources could earn credits that could be sold to firms in a cap-and-trade system. While offsets can reduce the cost of meeting a given level of emission caps, they are not very helpful in addressing temporary price pressures. Also, it is difficult to ensure that offset projects result in real, additional, and permanent emission reductions. Some evidence suggests possible gaming of even the heavily administered offset program of the Kyoto Protocol.

In U.S. legislative bills, a variety of other flexibility mechanisms have been proposed that have not been widely tested as yet. In one approach, firms could borrow allowances to cover their obligations by agreeing to return the borrowings with interest in a future period. This would help relieve price pressures in the current period at the expense of greater pressures in the period of repayment. In another approach, allowances would be freely issued beyond the cap level if prices reached a safety-valve ceiling. A modification of the safety-valve approach is a limited reserve of allowances that would be released if the market price exceeds a given threshold. A safety-valve ceiling or a price threshold for release of a reserve would be ineffective if set too high. If set too low, environmental goals could be threatened. These mechanisms could also be targets for gaming behavior by market participants.

A managed-price approach is an alternative that could both limit price volatility and remove opportunities for manipulation and excess speculation. In particular, the procedures that the Federal Reserve and other central banks use to manage interest rates could be employed to make carbon prices predictable while still achieving cumulative emission goals. Predictable prices would mean better emission abatement decisions and lower overall costs of the program. They would also eliminate the incentives to manipulate the market, as those efforts would be unsuccessful, or to engage in excess speculation, as prices would not be subject to bubbles. A managed-price approach eliminates the unnecessary uncertainty that occurs when prices fluctuate in response to temporary influences. However, future prices would not be certain, as adjustments would be made to the price path in response to permanent influences to ensure adequate progress toward an intermediate-term (i.e., 2020) emission goal.

Managed prices are a hybrid between a carbon tax and a traditional cap-and-trade program. A fixed-price approach, such as a standard carbon tax, provides certainty about prices. Predictable prices can achieve environmental goals at lower cost than a hard emissions cap because of the flat marginal damage curve from emissions in a given year. However, price certainty leaves uncertain the response of consumers and producers and therefore the emission reductions that are actually achieved. Although emission reductions are not the ultimate goal, they have the advantage of addressing, more directly than a carbon price, the large upside risks of climate change and resulting damages. With a managed-price approach, unnecessary price uncertainty is eliminated and a cumulative emission goal can also be ensured, in part through adjustments as needed in the price path and in part through a makeup of excess cumulative emissions in a subsequent intermediate-run period. Some flexibility would also be advisable regarding the design of a cap-and-trade program. In that light, a managed-price approach could be employed during the early years of a new cap-and-trade program, when it would be especially helpful to avoid risks or suspicions of market manipulation and excess speculation. After several years, the experience could be evaluated and alternative procedures could be employed if appropriate.

Emission caps also have political advantages, both within countries and internationally. Emission caps were the basis of the Kyoto Protocol and they are a key component of negotiations toward a new international agreement to follow Kyoto when it expires in 2012. The creation of an active carbon market through a cap-and-trade system also has the advantage of possible links to existing and planned markets in other countries. The EU has had a cap-and-trade program for GHG since 2005. The United States, Japan, Australia, New Zealand, and even Mexico and Korea have announced intentions to develop one. Some experimentation with different program designs is likely desirable for a while, as the best design for cap-and-trade has not been proved as yet. Over time, however, the features of these national trading programs could be harmonized enough to allow them to be linked. With linking, carbon prices could become equalized around the world, and the common price signal would allow a least-cost solution to the global climate challenge.

Final Comment

As a species, we are just now coming to the realization that, barring asteroid strikes or mega-volcanoes, we can control the future climate of the Earth.

If we deny our power and responsibility, we cannot hurt the planet itself. Indeed, Gaia has put herself through far more trouble than we can cause. Massive eruptions of flood basalts have at times pushed the global average temperature to extremes we will never see and, at other times, the planet may have turned itself into a huge snowball. Moreover, we are not the only creatures to have altered the climate of the Earth. Living things have caused climate change, and even occasional mass extinctions, ever since cyano-bacteria began spewing oxygen into the air billions of years ago.

However, we are the first species to recognize our effects on the climate. Our civilization evolved during the moderate, stable interglacial period of the last ten millennia, but natural forces by now should have nudged us back toward the start of another Ice Age. We may have brought that prospect to a halt. Our GHG emissions may have inadvertently helped us avoid the effects of a down-cycle in orbital factors and secured us interglacial warmth for at least another twenty millennia.

We are currently overdoing the warm spell. Nevertheless, our choices are not one-sided. We face a trade-off between current economic costs and future climate damage, and the risks are difficult to assess. If we fail to take adequate action, future generations will judge us harshly for the severity of the damages caused by our GHG emissions. But we could over-react and spend excessive resources now on avoiding outcomes that may be easier to prevent or adapt to in the future. So far, we have invested very little to reduce what are large risks of damage to the health, peace, and eco-nomic welfare of human society, and potential extinction of many species. Furthermore, overinvestment in mitigating climate change could be fairly quickly reversed, but if policy responses are inadequate, the momentum of natural amplifying feedbacks could be almost impossible to halt. We have surely not done enough to balance the risks in the outlook.

Although we will have to bear mitigation costs that we did not foresee when the industrial revolution began, we need not be overly gloomy about the prospects. After all, we have the resources and the knowledge to con-sciously manage the future climate of the Earth. Since its emergence more than 150,000 years ago, our species has suffered extremes of climate far more severe than what we face in the centuries just ahead. Now, however, we homo sapiens will endure only what we choose.

Appendix

Discount Rates in Climate Analysis

Discount rates are used to compare current and future costs. Confusion sometimes arises because of the failure to distinguish between a discount *rate* and a discount *factor*. To illustrate the difference, suppose you have a government savings bond that will be worth $1,000 next year. Because you need the money today, you sell the bond and only get $935. The discount *factor* is 935/1000 or 0.935. If you waited till next year, you would get the remaining $65. Your rate of return on holding the bond another year would thus be 65/935, which is 7%. That is the discount *rate*.

With a discount factor of 0.935, anything in the far-off future has a minuscule present value. For instance, if you multiply 0.935 by itself a hundred times, the answer is only 0.001. The implication is that $1,000 of climate damages a hundred years from now is worth only $1 today. If a dollar spent on climate investments today would offset less than $1,000 of damages a century ahead, it would make more sense to invest in the stock market, assuming the market keeps earning the average 7% return it has in the past. A $1 investment in stocks at that rate of return would give your heirs $1,000 in a hundred years.

As the historical average real rate of return on the stock market, 7% represents the average rate of return on private sector investments in the economy. It is thus the opportunity cost of investing in a public project like climate mitigation. Indeed, the U.S. government uses that discount rate to evaluate public sector projects. However, some climate analysts argue for a lower discount rate because climate risks are different than the risks of a typical private sector investment (Cline, 1992). If climate uncertainties were uncorrelated with systematic risk in the stock market, you could lower overall risks by combining the two types of investments. That would justify a lower rate of return on climate mitigation than on the stock market. You couldn't accept a return as low as 2%, however, which is the average short-term real interest rate, representing a risk-free return. A risk-free investment provides a guaranteed return in any circumstances and therefore has a zero correlation with stock market risk. If the discount rate were as low as 2%, $1,000 of damages a hundred years from now would be worth $133 today.

Another reason for a lower discount rate is uncertainty about the rate itself. For instance, suppose you were uncertain whether to use a 7% rate or a 2% rate. If the chances were equal that either was right, you would have to average the associated discount *factors* to get the appropriate rate (because it's the *factors* that are used to compute present values for the cost benefit analysis, not the rates per se). The average of .98 and .935 is .9575, equivalent to a discount rate of 4.25%, which is a little less than the average of the rates. The averaging of the discount factors over longer time periods implies an even lower effective discount rate.

The subject becomes even more complex because two different types of discount rates are used in climate studies: one for *costs* and another for social *welfare*. The discount rate for costs (and monetary benefits) is like an interest rate or the rate of return on the stock market, as discussed earlier. But evaluating policy alternatives based only on monetary costs and benefits is a shortcut for true welfare analysis. It works well enough for individual projects that last only up to a few decades. However, for climate policies that affect the entire economy over longer time periods, the appropriate analysis requires measuring changes in overall welfare at each point in time and then discounting those effects to the present. The welfare discount rate (sometimes called the pure rate of time preference) is used for this purpose. It is not something observed, like the return on stocks. In theory, the cost discount rate should equal the welfare discount rate plus a second term related to risk aversion.[1] If people didn't care at all about risk, the two discount rates would be the same. It is possible to estimate the average risk aversion prevailing in society and, combining that estimate with the observed average return on stocks, the welfare discount rate could be found as a residual. Employing such methods, one recent study found a welfare discount rate of 1.5% (Nordhaus, 2007).

It is sometimes argued that we should ignore current social risk preferences and instead use a very low welfare discount rate for ethical reasons. After all, shouldn't we value the welfare of future generations as much as

---

[1]   More precisely, the second term is the relative risk aversion of the representative individual's utility function multiplied by the growth rate of per capita consumption. For a recent review of the economics of discounting in climate studies, see Weitzman (2007).

our own?[2] From such sentiments, as well as the likelihood of heavier climate damages in poorer areas of the world, Stern (2006) called for a low welfare discount rate of 0.1%.

The choice of welfare discount rate is not just a fine point about identifying one component of the observed return on stocks. It affects policy recommendations of how much should be spent today on mitigating future climate damage. It also has implications for future cost discount rates. We don't know what the average return on investments will be far ahead in the future, but we expect it will decline as the world becomes more saturated with capital and the growth of consumption slows. A lower welfare discount rate implies that the return on capital will fall that much further in the decades to come.

[2] Philosophical counterarguments can also be made. Because of continuing growth in per capita income, future generations almost surely will be wealthier than ours. This would be reflected in the measure of welfare at that time, but it would also weaken the case for using a lower welfare discount rate for future generations than we implicitly apply to ourselves later in our own lives, as indicated by observed social risk preferences.

References

Popular Books

Brown, L. (2008), *Plan B 3.0*, W.W. Norton & Company.
Cox, J. (2005), *Climate Crash*, Joseph Henry Press.
Fagan, B. (2004), *The Long Summer: How Climate Changed Civilization*, Basic Books.
Flannery, T. (2005), *The Weather Makers*, Atlantic Monthly Press.
Linden, E. (2006), *The Winds of Change*, Simon and Schuster.
Lovelock, J. (1991), Gaia, The Practical Science of Planetary Medicine.
Romm, J. (2007), *Hell and High Water*, HarperCollins.
Ruddiman, W. (2005), *Plows, Plagues & Petroleum*, Princeton University Press.
Weart, S. (2003), *The Discovery of Global Warming*, Harvard University Press.

Technical Books, Papers, and Articles

Aldy, J. and R. Stavins, ed. (2007), *Architectures for Agreement*, Cambridge University Press.
Alley, R. (2000), "The Younger Dryas Cold Interval as Viewed from Central Greenland," *Quaternary Science Reviews* 19: 213–226.
Alvarez, L., W. Alvarez, F. Asaro, and H. Michel (1980), "Extraterrestrial Cause for the Cretaceous–Tertiary Extinction," *Science* 208: 1095–1108.
Ahman, M. et al. (2005), "The Ten Year Rule," Resources for the Future.
Ambrose, S. (1998), "Late Pleistocene Human Population Bottlenecks, Volcanic Winter, and Differentiation of Modern Humans," *Journal of Human Evolution* 34: 623–651.
An, F. and A. Sauer (2004), "Comparison of Passenger Vehicle Fuel Economy and GHG Emission Standards around the World," PEW Center.
Andres, R., D. Fielding, G. Marland, T. Boden, and N. Kumar (1999), "Carbon Dioxide Emissions from Fossil-Fuel Use, 1751–1950," *Tellus* 51: 759–765.
Archibald, J. and D. Fastovsky (2004), "Dinosaur Extinction," in *The Dinosauria*, edited by Weishampel, D. et al., University of California Press, 672–684.
Barnett, T. et al. (2005), "Penetration of Human-Induced Warming into the World's Oceans," *Science* 309: 284–287.
Barras, J. et al. (2003), "Historical and Projected Coastal Louisiana Land Changes: 1978–2050," Open File Report 03–334, U.S. Geological Survey.

Barrett, S. (2007), "A Multi-track Climate Treaty System," in *Architectures for Agreement*, edited by J. Aldy and R. Stavins, Cambridge University Press.

Berger, A. (1978), "Long-term Variations of Daily Insolation and Quaternary Climatic Changes," *Journal of the Atmospheric Sciences* 35: 2362–2367.

Bernanke, B. et al. (2001), *Inflation Targeting: Lessons from the International Experience*, Princeton University Press.

Betz, R., W. Eichhammer, and J. Schleich (2004), "Designing National Allocation Plans for EU Emissions Trading – A First Analysis of the Outcomes," *Energy & Environment* 15: 375–425.

Blackman, J. and R. Kantamaneni (2003), "EPA's SF6 Emissions Reduction Partnership for Electric Power Systems," Environmental Protection Agency.

Blyth, W. and R. Baron (2003), "Green Investment Schemes: Options and Issues," International Energy Agency.

Bonan, G. (2008), "Forests and Climate Change: Forcings, Feedbacks, and the Climate Benefits of Forests," *Science* 320: 1444–1449.

Bosello, F., R. Roson, and R. Tol (2006), "Economy-Wide Estimates of the Implications of Climate Change: Human health," *Ecological Economics* 58: 579–591.

(2007), "Economy-Wide Estimates of the Implications of Climate Change: Sea Level Rise," *Environmental & Resource Economics* 37: 549–571.

Bottke, W., D. Vokrouhlicky, and D. Nesvorny (2007), "An Asteroid Breakup 160 My Ago as the Probable Source of the K-T Impactor," *Nature* 449: 48–53.

Bowman, D. et al. (2009), "Fire in the Earth System," *Science* 324: 481–484.

BP (2008), "Statistical Review of World Energy."

Brainard, W. (1967), "Uncertainty and the Effectiveness of Policy," *American Economic Review* 57(2): 411–425.

Broecker, W. (1997), "Will Our Ride into the Greenhouse Future Be a Smooth One?" *GSA Today* 7(5): 1–13.

Broecker, W. and T. Stocker (2006), "The Holocene CO_2 Rise: Anthropogenic or Natural?" *Eos* 87(3): 27–29.

Broeke, M. et al. (2009), "Partitioning Recent Greenland Mass Loss," *Science* 326: 984–986.

Burke, E., S. Brown, and N. Christidis (2006), "Modeling the Recent Evolution of Global Drought and Projections for the Twenty-First Century with the Hadley Centre Climate Model," *Journal of Hydrometeorology* 7: 1113–1125.

Burtraw, D. (2008), "Cap, Auction, and Trade," testimony before the House Select Committee on Energy Independence and Global Warming, January 23.

(2007), "Climate Change: Lessons Learned from Existing Cap-and-trade Programs," testimony before the House Committee on Energy and Commerce, March 29.

Burtraw, D., D. Kahn, and K. Palmer (2006), "Dynamic Adjustment to Incentive-Based Policy to Improve Efficiency and Performance," Resources for the Future.

Burtraw, D., K. Palmer, R. Bharvirkar, and A. Paul (2002), "The Effect on Asset Values of the Allocation of Carbon Dioxide Emission Allowances," Resources for the Future.

Buyuksahin, B. et al. (2008), "Fundamentals, Trader Activity, and Derivative Pricing," Commodity Futures Trading Commission.

CAIT (2010), Climate Analysis Indicators Tool, version 7.0, World Resources Institute.

CAN (Climate Action Network)–Europe (2007), "Status of the EU ETS," available at: http://www.climnet.org/EUenergy/ET/ETS_Status.htm#1st

Carlin, A. (2007), "The Inadequacy of Global Climate Change Policy," *Environmental Forum* 24(5): 42–47.

CCAP (Center for Clean Air Policy), 1998a, "US Carbon emissions Trading: Some Options That Include Downstream Sources."

Chan, M. (2009), "Lessons Learned from the Financial Crisis: Designing Carbon Markets for Environmental Effectiveness and Financial Stability," testimony before the Ways and Means Committee, March 26.

Chen, J., C. Wilson, D. Blankenship, and B. Tapley (2009), "Accelerated Antarctic Ice Loss from Satellite Gravity Measurements," *Nature Geoscience* 2: 859–862.

Cheney, E. (1996), "Sequence Stratigraphy and Plate Tectonic Significance of the Transvaal Succession of Southern Africa and Its Equivalent in Western Australia," *Precambrian Research* 79: 3–24.

Church, J. and N. White (2006), "A 20th Century Acceleration in Global Sea-Level Rise," *Geophysical Research Letters* 33: L01602.

Clarke, L. et al. (2006), "Synthesis and Assessment Product," Climate Change Science Program Review, including a data supplement at: http://www.sc.doe.gov/ober/CPDAC/database_scenarios_information.xls.

Cline, W. (1992), The Economics of Global Warming, Institute of International Affairs.

CNA Corporation (2007), "National Security and the Threat of Climate Change," available at: http://www.securityandclimate.cna.org.

Coase, R. (1960), "Problem of Social Cost," *Journal of Law and Economics* 3: 1–44.

Condon, D., A. Prave, and D. Benn, (2002) "Neoproterozoic Glacial-Rainout Intervals: Observations and Implications," *Geology* 30: 35–38.

Cooper, R. (2006), "Alternatives to Kyoto: The Case for a Carbon Tax," working paper, Harvard University.

Corfee-Morlot, J. and N. Hoehne, (2003), "Climate Change: Long-Term Targets and Short-Term Commitments," *Global Environmental Change* 13: 277–293.

Cox, P. et al. (2000), "Acceleration of Global Warming Due to Carbon-Cycle Feedbacks in a Coupled Climate Model," *Nature* 408: 184–187.

Cox, P. et al. (2003), "Amazon Die-Back under Climate-Carbon Cycle Projections for the 21st Century," Hadley Centre technical, note 42.

Cronin, T. et al. (2003), "Medieval Warm Period, Little Ice Age and 20th Century Temperature Variability from Chesapeake Bay," *Global and Planetary Change* 36: 17–29.

DEFRA (2007), "The Social Cost of Carbon and the Shadow Price of Carbon," Department for Environment, Food, and Rural Affairs, Government of the United Kingdom.

Demiralp, S., B. Preslopsky, and W. Whitesell (2006), "Overnight Interbank Loan Markets," *Journal of Economics and Business* 58: 67–83.

de Pater, I. and J. Lissauer (2001), *Planetary Sciences*, Cambridge University Press.

Dept. Finance, Canada (2006), "Oil and Gas Prices, Taxes and Consumers."

Dessler, A. and E. Parson (2006), *The Science and Politics of Global Climate Change*, Cambridge University Press.

Diaz-Pulido, G. et al. (2009), "Doom and Boom on a Resilient Reef: Climate Change, Algal Overgrowth and Coral Recovery," *PLoS ONE* 4(4): e5239.

Dicus, C. and A. Delfino (2003), "A Comparison of California Forest Practice Rules and Two Forest Certification Systems," California Forest Products Commission.

Dinan, T. (2007), "Trade-Offs in Allocating Allowances for CO_2 Emissions," Congressional Budget Office.

Dinan, T. and R. Shackleton (2005) "Limiting Carbon Dioxide Emissions: Prices versus Caps," Congressional Budget Office.

DOE (U.S. Department of Energy) (2006), "The Electricity Delivery System."

Doggett, L. and J. Cooper (2009), "The Safe Markets Development Act" (H.R. 1666).

Dlugokencky, E. et al. (2003), "Atmospheric Methane Levels off: Temporary Pause or New Steady State?" *Geophysical Research Letters* 30: 1992.

Durner, G. et al. (2007), "Predicting the Future Distribution of Polar Bear Habitat in the Polar Basin from Resource Selection Functions Applied to 21st Century General Circulation Model Projections of Sea Ice," United States Geological Survey.

Duxbury, Alyn, Alison Duxbury, and K. Sverdrup (2000), *World's Oceans*, McGraw Hill.

ECCP (European Climate Change Programme) (2006), "EU Action Against Climate Change," available at: http://ec.europa.eu/environment/climat/pdf/eu_climate_change_progr.pdf

Edge, R., T. Laubach, and J. Williams (2004), "Learning and Shifts in Long-Run Productivity Growth," Board of Governors of the Federal Reserve System.

EIA (U.S. Energy Information Agency) (2009), "International Energy Outlook."

Eichengreen, B., A. Rose, and C. Wyplosz (1994), "Speculative Attacks on Pegged Exchange Rates: An Empirical Exploration with Special Reference to the European Monetary System," working paper # W4898, National Bureau of Economic Research.

Eijffinger, S. and J. de Haan (1996), "The Political Economy of Central Bank Independence," Princeton University.

Elderfield, H. and G. Ganssen (2000), "Past Temperature of Surface Ocean Waters Inferred from Foraminiferal Mg/Ca Ratios," *Nature* 405: 442–445.

Elguindi, N. and F. Giorgi (2006), "Projected Changes in the Caspian Sea Level for the 21st Century Based on the Latest AOGCM Simulations," *Geophysical Research Letters* 33: L08706.

Elmendorf, D. (2009), "Flexibility in the Timing of Emission Reductions under a Cap-and-Trade Program," Congressional Budget Office.

EPA (U.S. Environmental Protection Agency) (2007), "Inventory of U.S. Greenhouse Gas Emissions and Sinks: 1990–2005."

EPA (U.S. Environmental Protection Agency) (2001), "The United States Experience with Economic Incentives for Protecting the Environment."

EPICA Community (56 authors) (2004), "Eight Glacial Cycles from an Antarctic Ice Core," *Nature* 429: 623–628.

ETAAC (Economic and Technology Advancement Advisory Committee) (2008), "Technologies and Policies to Consider for Reducing Greenhouse Gases in California."

EU (European Union) (1991), "The Protection of Waters against Pollution Caused by Nitrates from Agricultural Sources," 91/676/EEC.

EU (European Union) (2005), "Winning the Battle against Global Climate Change," press release, February 9.

EU (European Union) Commission (2007), "Limiting Global Climate Change to 2°C," http://www.europa-eu-un.org/Articles/en/Article_6666_en.htm

Fankhauser, S. (1995), Valuing Climate Change – The Economics of the Greenhouse, EarthScan.

FBR (Friedman, Billings, Ramsey) (2006), "Bloom to Come off the Rose: Decline of SO_2 Story Driving BTU Convergence."

Feely, R. et al. (1999), "Influence of El Niño on the Equatorial Pacific Contribution to Atmospheric CO_2 Accumulation," *Nature* 398: 597–601.

Fernandez, L. (2009), "Influence of Temperature and Rainfall on the Evolution of Cholera Epidemics in Lusaka, Zambia, 2003–2006," *Transactions of the Royal Society of Tropical Medicine and Hygiene* 103(2): 137–143.

Fettweis, X. et al. (2008), "A Record Negative Greenland Ice Sheet Surface Mass Balance Rate in 2007," *Geophysical Research Abstracts* 10: EGU2008–0033388.

Fischer, C. and M. Toman (2000), "Environmentally and Economically Damaging Subsidies: Concepts and Illustrations," Resources for the Future.

Fischer, H. et al. (1999), "Ice Core Records of Atmospheric CO_2 around the Last Three Glacial Terminations," *Science* 283: 1712–1714.

Fischer, S. (1995), *The Future of Central Banking*, Cambridge University Press.

Foukal, P., G. North, and T. Wigley (2004), "A Stellar View on Solar Variations and Climate," *Science* 306: 68–69.

Frankel, J. (2007), "Formulas for Quantitative Emission Targets," in *Architectures for Agreement*, edited by J. Aldy and R. Stavins, Cambridge University Press.

Friedlingstein, P. et al. (2001), "Positive Feedback between Future Climate Change and the Carbon Cycle," *Geophysical Research Letters* 28: 1543–1546.

Friedlingstein, P. et al. (2006), "Climate-Carbon Cycle Feedback Analysis: Results from C4MIP Model Intercomparison," *Journal of Climate* 19: 3337–3353.

Friedman, M. (1968), "The Role of Monetary Policy," presidential address to the American Economic Association.

Gordon, R. (1986), *The American Business Cycle; Continuity and Change*, National Bureau of Economic Research.

Goulder, L. and W. Pizer (2008), "The Economics of Climate Change," The New Palgrave Dictionary of Economics.

Hanna, E. et al. (2008), "Increased Runoff from Melt from the Greenland Ice Sheet: A Response to Global Warming," *Journal of Climate*.

Hansen, J. (2007), "Dangerous Human-Made Interference with Climate," testimony before the Select Committee on Energy Independence and Global Warming, U.S. House of Representatives, April 26.

Hansen, J. et al. (2001), "A Closer Look at United States and Global Surface Temperature Change," *Journal of Geophysical Research* 106: 23947–23963.

Hansen, J. et al. (2008), "Target Atmospheric CO_2: Where Should Humanity Aim?" working paper, Columbia University.

Hansen, J., R. Ruedy, J. Glascoe, and M. Sato (1999), "GISS Analysis of Surface Temperature Change," Goddard Institute: pubs.giss.nasa.gov/docs/1999/1999_HansenRuedyG.pdf

Hansen, J., M. Sato, R. Ruedy, K. Lo, D. Lea, and M. Medina-Elizalde (2006), "Global Temperature Change," Proceedings of the National Academy of Sciences, Sept. 25.

Hardin, G. (1968), "The Tragedy of the Commons," *Science* 162: 1243–1248.

Hargrave, T. (1998), "U.S. Carbon Emissions Trading: Description of an Upstream Approach," Center for Clean Air Policy (http://www.ccap.org).

Hartmann, D. (1994), *Global Physical Climatology*, Academic Press.

Harrabin, R. (2007), "CO$_2$ Row Threatens Climate Report," BBC, May 2: http://news.bbc.co.uk/2/hi/science/nature/6615025.stm

Heath, J. et al. (2005), "Rising Atmospheric CO$_2$ Reduces Sequestration of Root-Derived Soil Carbon," *Science* 309: 1711–1713.

Held, I. and B. Soden (2006), "Robust Responses of the Hydrological Cycle to Global Warming," *Journal of Climate* 18: 5686–5699.

Helme, N. (2009), "The Road to Copenhagen and Beyond: Elements of a Global Climate Deal between Developed and Developing Countries," testimony before the Senate Committee on Foreign Relations, April 22.

Helme, N., J. Schmidt, J. Lee, and M. Houdashelt (2006), "Sector-based Approach to the Post-2012 Climate Change Policy Architecture," Center for Clean Air Policy.

Hoffman, P., A. Kaufman, G. Halverson, and D. Schrag (1998), "A Neoproterozoic Snowball Earth," *Science* 281: 1342–1346.

Hope, C. and D. Newbery (2007), "Calculating the Social Cost of Carbon," working paper, Cambridge University.

Houweling, S. et al. (1999), "Inverse Modeling of Methane Sources and Sinks Using the Adjoint of a Global Transport Model," *Journal of Geophysical Research* 104: 26137–26160.

Howell, Katie (2009), "New Chemicals Could Better Capture CO$_2$ from Coal Plants," *Scientific American.*

IEA (International Energy Agency) (2010), "Analysis of the Scope of Energy Subsidies and Suggestions for the G-20 Initiative," International Energy Agency, Organization of Petroleum Exporting Countries, Organization for Economic Cooperation and Development, and the World Bank.

IEA (2009), "World Energy Outlook."

IISD (International Institute for Sustainable Development) (2009), "Summary of the Bangkok Climate Change Talks," *Earth Negotiations Bulletin* 12: 439.

IMF (International Monetary Fund) (2008), "World Economic Outlook."

IPCC (Intergovernmental Panel on Climate Change) (2001), Third Assessment Report, http://www.ipcc.ch

IPCC (Intergovernmental Panel on Climate Change) (2007), Fourth Assessment Report, http://www.ipcc.ch

Jaffe, J. and R. Stavins (2008), "Linkage of Tradable Permit Systems in International Climate Policy Architecture," working paper RWP08–053, Harvard Kennedy School.

Jakosky, B., R. Haberle, and R. Arvidson (2005), "The Changing Picture of Volatiles and Climate on Mars," *Science* 310: 1439–1440.

Jetz, W., D. Wilcove, and A. Dobson (2007), "Projected Impacts of Climate and Land-Use Change on the Global Diversity of Birds," PLoS Biology.

Jirikowic, A. and P. Damon (1994), "The Medieval Solar Activity Maximum," *Climate Change* 26: 309–316.

Jouzel, J. et al. (2007), "Orbital and Millennial Antarctic Climate Variability over the Past 800,000 Years," *Science* 317: 793–796.

Kasting, J. (1988), "Runaway and Moist Greenhouse Atmospheres and the Evolution of Earth and Venus," *Icarus* 74: 472–494.

Kaufman, D. et al. (2009), "Recent Warming Reverses Long-Term Arctic Cooling," *Science* 325: 1236–1239.

Keeling, C. and T. Whorf (2005), "Atmospheric Carbon Dioxide Concentrations at 10 Locations," Carbon Dioxide Information Analysis Center, Oak Ridge National Laboratory.

Keller, G. et al. (2008), "Main Deccan Volcanism Phase Ends Near the K-T boundary: Evidence from the Krishna-Godavari Basin, SE India," *Earth and Planetary Science Letters* 268: 293–311.

Kennett, D. et al. (2009), "Shock-Synthesized Hexagonal Diamonds in Younger Dryas Boundary Sediments," *Proceedings of the National Academy of Sciences* 106: 12623–12628.

Kerr, S. and D. Mare (1997), "Transaction Costs and Tradable Permit Markets: The United States Lead Phasedown" working paper, University of Maryland.

Kidland, F. and E. Prescott (1977), "Rules Rather than Discretion; The Inconsistency of Optimal Plans," *Journal of Political Economy* 85: 473–491.

Kirschvink, J. (1992), "Late Proterozoic low-latitude global glaciation: the Snowball Earth", in *The Proterozoic Biosphere: A Multidisciplinary* Study, edited by J. Schopf and C. Klein, Cambridge University Press.

Kirschvink, J., R. Ripperdan, and D. Evans (1997), "Evidence for a Large-Scale Reorganization of Early Cambrian Continental Masses by Inertial Interchange True Polar Wander," *Science* 25: 541–545.

Kleiven, H. et al. (2008), "Reduced North Atlantic Deep Water Coeval with the Glacial Lake Agassiz Freshwater Outburst," *Science* 319: 60–64.

Knight, F. (1921), *Risk, Uncertainty, and Profit*, Houghton Mifflin.

Knittel, C. (2009), "The Implied Cost of Carbon Dioxide under the Cash for Clunkers Program," working paper, U. of California Energy Institute.

Kriegler, E., J. Hall, H. Held, R. Dawson, and H. Schellnhuber (2009), "Imprecise Probability Assessment of Tipping Points in the Climate System," *Proceedings of the National Academy of Sciences*.

Kohler, P. and H. Fischer (2006), "Simulating Low Frequency Changes in Atmospheric CO_2 during the Last 740,000 Years," *Climate of the Past Discussions* 2: 1–42.

Kopp, R. (2007), "Greenhouse Gas Regulation in the United States," Resources for the Future discussion paper 07–16.

Kopp, R. et al. (2005), "The Paleoproterozoic Snowball Earth: A Climate Disaster Triggered by the Evolution of Oxygenic Photosynthesis," *Proceedings of the National Academy of Sciences* 102: 11131.

Kutzbach, J. and Z. Liu (1997), "Response of the African Monsoon to Orbital Forcing and Ocean Feedbacks in the Middle Holocene," *Science* 278: 440–443.

Kvenvolden, K. (1995) "A Review of the Geochemistry of Methane in Natural Gas Hydrate" *Organic Geochemistry* 23(11–12): 997–1008.

LaJeunnesse, T. et al. (2009), "Outbreak and Persistence of Opportunistic Symbiotic Dinoflagellates during the 2005 Caribbean Mass Coral 'Bleaching' Event," *Proceedings of the Royal Society B*.

Larter, R. (2007), Presentation at a conference at the University of Texas at Austin, March 28.

Le Quere, C. et al. (2008), "Response to Comments on 'Saturation of the Southern Ocean CO2 Sink Due to Recent Climate Change," *Science* 319, Technical comment 570c.

Lea, D., D. Pak, and H. Spero (2000), "Climate Impact of Late Quaternary Equatorial Pacific Sea Surface Temperature Variations," *Science* 289: 1719–1724.

Lear, C., H. Elderfield, and P. Wilson (2000), "Cenozoic Deep-Sea Temperatures and Global Ice Volumes from Mg/Ca in Benthic Foraminiferal Calcite," *Science* 287: 269–282.

Leuliette, E., R. Nerem, and G. Mitchum (2004), "Calibration of TOPEX/Poseidon and Jason Altimeter Data to Construct a Continuous Record of Mean Sea Level Change," *Marine Geodesy* 27: 79–94.

Lenton, T. et al. (2008), "Tipping Elements in the Earth's Climate System," *Proceedings of the National Academy of Sciences* 105: 1786–1793.

Liberman, E. (2003), "A Life Cycle Assessment and Economic Analysis of Wind Turbines Using Monte Carlo Analysis," master's thesis, Air Force Institute of Technology.

Liu, Z. and T. Herbert (2004), "High-Latitude Influence on the Eastern Equatorial Pacific Climate in the Early Pleistocene Epoch," *Nature* 427: 720–723.

Lomborg, B. (2007), "Perspective on Climate Change," testimony before the U.S. Congressional subcommittees, March 21.

Majaess (2008), "New Constraints on the Asteroid 298 Baptistina, the Alleged Family Member of the K/T Impactor," *Journal of the Royal Astronomical Society of Canada*.

Mann, M., R. Bradley, and M. Hughes (1998), "Global-scale Temperature Patterns and Climate Forcing over the Past Six Centuries," *Nature* 392: 779–787.

Mann, M. et al. (1999), "Northern Hemisphere Temperatures during the Past Millenium: Inferences, Uncertainties, and Limitations," *Geophysical Research Letters* 26: 759–762.

Marland, G., T. Boden, and R. Andres (2007), "Global, Regional, and National CO_2 Emissions," Carbon Dioxide Information Analysis Center, U.S. Department of Energy.

Marshak, S. (2005), *Earth: Portrait of a Planet*, second edition, Norton.

McCarthy, J. (2005), "Clean Air Act: A Summary of the Act and its Major Requirements," Congressional Research Service.

McCarthy, J., L. Parker, and R. Meltz (2009), "Clean Air after the CAIR Decision: Back to Square One," Congressional Research Service.

McKerrow, W., C. Scotese, and M. Brasier (1992), "Early Cambrian Continental Reconstructions," *Journal of the Geological Society*, London 149: 599–606.

McKibbon, W. and P. Wilcoxen (2006), "A Credible Foundation for Long Term International Cooperation on Climate Change," Lowy Institute working paper no. 1.06.

McManus, W. (2007), "Economic Analysis of Feebates to Reduce Greenhouse Gas Emissions from Light Vehicles for California," University of Michigan Transportation Research Institute.

Medina-Elizalde, M. and D. Lea (2005), "The Mid-Pleistocene Transition in the Tropical Pacific," *Science* 310: 1009–1012.

Mehling, M. and E. Haites (2009), "Mechanisms for Linking Emissions Trading Schemes," *Climate Policy* 9: 169–184.

Metcalf, G. (2009), "Price Volatility in Climate Change Legislation," testimony before the Ways and Means Committee, March 26.

Michaelova, A. (2007), "Graduation and Deepening," in *Architectures for Agreement* edited by J. Aldy and R. Stavins, Cambridge University Press.

Milkov, A. (2004), "Global Estimates of Hydrate-Bound Gas in Marine Sediments: How Much Is Really Out There?" *Earth-Science Review* 66 (3–4), 183–197.

MIT (Massachusetts Institute of Technology) (2007), "The Future of Coal," available at: http://web.mit.edu/coal

Mullen, L. (2004), "Multiple Impacts," *Astrobiology Magazine*.

Murray, B., R. Newell, and W. Pizer (2009), "Balancing Cost and Emissions Certainty: An Allowance Reserve for Cap-and-Trade," working paper 14258, National Bureau of Economic Research.

Nadel, S. (2006), "Energy Efficiency Resource Standards: Experience and Recommendations," American Council for an Energy-Efficient Economy.

Nemai, R. et al. (2003), "Climate-Driven Increases in Global Terrestrial Net Primary Production from 1982 to 1999," *Science* 300: 1560–1563.

Newell, R., W. Pizer, and J. Zhang (2005), "Managing Permit Markets to Stabilize Prices," *Environment and Resource Economics* 31(2): 133–157.

Norby, R. et al. (2005), "Forest Response to Elevated CO_2 is Conserved Across a Broad Range of Productivity," *Science* 102: 18052–18056.

Nordhaus, W. (2005), "Life after Kyoto: Alternative Approaches to Global Warming Policies," working paper, http://nordhaus.econ.yale.edu/kyoto_long_2005.pdf

(2006a), "The Economics of Hurricanes in the United States," working paper, http://nordhaus.econ.yale.edu/hurr_122106a.pdf

(2006b), "The *Stern Review* on the Economics of Climate Change," working paper, http://nordhaus.econ.yale.edu/SternReviewD2.pdf

(2007), "The Challenge of Global Warming: Economic Models and Environmental Policy," working paper, http://nordhaus.econ.yale.edu

Nordhaus, W. and J. Boyer (2000), *Roll the DICE Again: Economic Models of Global Warming*, MIT Press.

Oreopoulos, L. and R. Davies (1998), "Plane Parallel Albedo Biases from Satellite Observations," *Journal of Climate* 11: 919–944.

Otto-Bliesner, B. et al. (2006), "Simulating Arctic Climate Warmth and Icefield Retreat in the Last Interglaciation," *Science* 311: 1751–1753.

Overpeck, J. et al. (2006), "Paleoclimatic Evidence for Future Ice-Sheet Instability and Rapid Sea-Level Rise," *Science* 311: 1747–1750.

Pagani, M. et al. (2006), "Arctic Hydrology during Global Warming at the Paleocene/ Eocene Thermal Maximum," *Nature* 442: 671–675.

Palmer, K. and D. Burtraw (2007), "The Electricity Sector and Climate Policy," in *Assessing U.S. Climate Policy Options*, Resources for the Future.

Paltsev, J. et al. (2007) "Assessment of U.S. Cap-and-Trade Proposals," working paper, Massachusetts Institute of Technology.

Parry, I. et al. (2007), "Automobile Externalities and Policies," *Journal of Economic Literature* 45(3): 373–399.

Pearce, D. (1993), *Economic Values and the Natural World*, Earthscan.

Pearson, P. and M. Palmer (2000), "Atmospheric Carbon Dioxide Concentrations over the Past 60 Million Years," *Nature* 406: 695–699.

Pearson, P., G. Foster, and S. Wade (2009), "Atmospheric Carbon Dioxide through the Eocene–Oligocene Climate Transition," *Nature* online.

Petit, J. R. et al. (1999), "Climate and Atmospheric History of the Past 420,000 Years from the Vostok Ice Core, Antarctica," *Nature* 399: 429–436.

Petrenko, V. et al. (2009), "$^{14}CH_4$ Measurements in Greenland Ice: Investigating Last Glacial Termination CH_4 Sources," *Science* 324: 506–508.

Pflaumann, U. et al. (1998), "Variations in eolian and carbonate sedimentation, sea-surface temperature, and productivity over the last 3 m.y. at site 958 off northwest Africa," *Proceedings of the Ocean Drilling Program, Scientific Results*, Vol. 159T.

Pierce, J. and P. Adams (2009), "Can Cosmic Rays Affect Cloud Condensation Nuclei by Altering New Particle Formation Rates?" *Geophysical Research Letters* 36.

Pigou, A. (1920), *The Economics of Welfare*, 4th edition – 1932, MacMillan and Co., London.

Pizer, W. (2007), "Practical Global Climate Policy," in *Architectures for Agreement*, edited by J. Aldy and R. Stavins, Cambridge University Press.

Poole, W. (1970), "Optimal Choice of Monetary Policy Instruments in a Small Stochastic Macro Model," *Quarterly Journal of Economics* 84: 197–216.

Previdi, M. and B. Liepert (2008), "Interdecadal Variability of Rainfall on a Warming Planet," *EOS* 89 21: 193–195.

Pritchard, H., R. Arthern, D. Vaughan, and L. Edwards (2009), "Extensive Dynamic Thinning on the Margins of the Greenland and Antarctic Ice Sheets," *Nature* 461: 971–975.

Rasch, P., P. Crutzen, and D. Coleman (2008), "Exploring the Geoengineering of Climate Using Stratospheric Sulfate Aerosols: The Role of Particle Size," *Geophysical Research Letters* 35, L02809.

Rayner, P. et al. (1999), "The Relationship between Tropical CO_2 Fluxes and the El Niño-Southern Oscillation," *Geophysical Research Letters* 26(4): 493–496.

Reddy, V. et al. (2008), "Composition of 298 Baptistina: Implications for K-T Impactor Link," Asteroids, Comets, Meteors conference.

RGGI (Regional Greenhouse Gas Initiative) (2007), Model Rule, http://www.rggi.org

RGGI (2008a), "Design Elements for Regional Allowance Auctions," http://www.rggi.org

(2008b), "Potential Emissions Leakage," http://www.rggi.org

Rieu, R., P. Allen, M. Plotze, and T. Pettke (2007), "Climatic Cycles during a Neoproterozoic 'Snowball' Glacial Epoch," *Geology* 35: 299–302.

Roe, G. and M. Baker (2007), "Why is Climate Sensitivity so Unpredictable," *Science* 318: 629–632.

Rogers, J. (1996), "A History of Continents in the Past Three Billion Years," *Journal of Geology* 104: 91–107.

Royer, Dana L., Robert A. Berner, Isabel P. Montañez, Neil J. Tabor, and David J. Beerling (2004), "CO_2 as a Primary Driver of Phanerozoic Climate," *GSA Today* 14(3): 4–10.

Ruddiman, W. (2001), *Earth's Climate*, W.H. Freeman and Company.

(2006), "Ice-Driven CO_2 Feedback on Ice Volume," *Climate of the Past Discussions* 2: 43–78.

Sabine, C. et al. (2004), "The Oceanic Sink for Anthropogenic CO_2," *Science* 305: 367–371.

Saltzman, M. and S. Young (2005), "A long-lived Glaciation in the Late Ordovician?: Isotopic and Sequence Stratigraphic Evidence from Western Laurentia," *Geology* 33: 109–112.

SCAQMD (South Coast Air Quality Management District) (2008), "Annual RECLAIM Audit Report for the 2006 Compliance Year."

Schmidt, G. (2006), "Calculating the Greenhouse Effect," RealClimate post at: http://www.realclimate.org/index.php/archives/2006/01/calculating-the-greenhouse-effect

Schmidt, P. and G. Williams (2003), "Paleomagnetism of the Lorrain Formation, Quebec, and Implications for the Latitude of Huronian Glaciation," *Geophysical Research Abstracts* 5: 08262.

Scotese, C. (2002), "Earth History," Paleomap project.

Shapiro, R. (2007), "Addressing the Risks of Climate Change: The Environmental Effectiveness and Economic Efficiency of Emissions Caps and Tradable Permits, Compared to Carbon Taxes," working paper.

Shaviv, N. and J. Veizer (2003), "Celestial Driver of Phanerozoic Climate?" *GSA Today* 13: 4–10.

Shepherd, A. and D. Wingham (2007), "Recent Sea-Level Contributions of the Antarctic and Greenland Ice Sheets," *Science* 315: 1529–1532.

Siddall, M., J. Chappell, and E. Potter (2006), "Eustatic Sea Level during Past Interglacials," in *The Climate of Past Interglacials*, Elsevier

Siegenthaler, U. and other EPICA authors (2005a), "Supporting Evidence from the EPICA Dronning Maud Land Ice Core for Atmospheric CO2 Changes during the Past Millennium," *Tellus* 57B: 51–57.

(2005b), "Stable Carbon Cycle – Climate Relationship during the Late Pleistocene," *Science* 310: 1313–1317.

Soden, B. et al. (2005), "The Radiative Signature of Upper Tropospheric Moistening," *Science* 310: 841–844.

Stavins, R. (1994), "Correlated Environmental Uncertainty and Policy Instrument Choice," working paper, Harvard Belfer Center.

(2005), "The Lessons Learned from the SO_2 Trading Program," *Choices* 20: 53–57.

Stehr, H. and R. Sethi (2007), "Status of the CDM," presentation in Bonn, available at: http://cdm.unfccc.int/EB/media/index.html

Stern, N. (2008), "Key Elements of a Global Deal on Climate Change," working paper, London School of Economics.

(2006), "Stern Review: The Economics of Climate Change," U.K. Treasury.

Stewart, R. et al. (2000), The Clean Development Mechanism: Building International Public-Private Partnerships under the Kyoto Protocol, United Nations.

Stewart, R. and J. Wiener (2003), *Reconstructing Climate Policy: Beyond Kyoto*, American Enterprise Institute.

Storey, M., R. Duncan, and C. Swisher (2007), "Paleocene-Eocene Thermal Maximum and the Opening of the Northeast Atlantic," *Science* 316: 587–589.

Taylor, J., ed. (1999), *Monetary Policy Rules*, University of Chicago Press.

Tedesco, M. and A. Monaghan (2009), "An Updated Antarctic Melt Record through 2009 and Its Linkages to High-Latitude and Tropical Climate Variability," *Geophysical Research Letters* 36: L18502.

Tilmes, S., R. Muller, and R. Salawitch (2008), "The Sensitivity of Polar Ozone Depletion to Proposed Geoengineering Schemes," *Science Express*.

Timmermann, A., O. Timm, L. Stott, and L.Menviel (2008), "Austral Spring Insolation Changes Help to Jump-Start Deglacial Temperature Rise in Antarctica," *Journal of Climate*.

Tol, R. (2002), "Estimates of the Damage Costs of Climate Change," *Environmental and Resource Economics* 21: 47–73.

Torsvik, T. (2003), "The Rodinia Jigsaw Puzzle," *Science* 300: 1379–1381.

Trenberth, K. and L. Smith (2005), "The Mass of the Atmosphere: A Constraint on Global Analyses," *Journal of Climate* 18: 864–875.

Tripati, A., C. Roberts, and R. Eagle (2009), "Coupling of CO_2 and Ice Sheet Stability over Major Climate Transitions of the Last 20 Million Years," *Science* 326: 1394–1397.

UN (United Nations) (2006), "World Population Prospects: The 2006 Revision."

UNFCCC (United Nations Framework Convention on Climate Change) (1992), available at: http://unfccc.int/resource/docs/convkp/conveng.pdf

UNFCCC (2009), "Compilation of Information Relating to Possible Quantified Emission Limitation and Reduction Objectives as Submitted by Parties," secretariat document, August 11.

USCAP (2009), "A Blueprint for Legislative Action: Consensus Recommendations for U.S. Climate Protection Legislation," U.S. Climate Action Partnership.

van der Hilst, R. et al. (2007), "Seismostratigraphy and Thermal Structure of Earth's Core-Mantle Boundary Region," *Science* 315: 1813–1817.

Veizer, J., Y. Godderis, and L. M. François (2000) "Evidence for Decoupling of Atmospheric CO_2 and Global Climate during the Phanerozoic Eon," *Nature* 408: 698–701.

Victor, D. (2001), *The Collapse of the Kyoto Protocol and the Struggle to Slow Global Warming*, Princeton University Press.

    (2007), "Fragmented Carbon Markets and Reluctant Nations," in *Architectures for Agreement*, edited by J. Aldy and R. Stavins, Cambridge University Press.

Walsh, C. (2005), "Central Bank Independence," *New Palgrave Dictionary of Economics*.

Wara, M. (2007), "Is the Global Carbon Market Working," *Nature* 445: 595–596.

Weiss, R., R. Jahnke, and C. Keeling (1982), "Seasonal Effects of Temperature and Salinity on the Partial Pressure of Carbon Dioxide in Seawater," *Nature* 300: 511–513.

Weitzman, M. (1974), "Prices vs. Quantities," *Review of Economic Studies* 41(4): 477–491.

Weitzman, M. (2007), "A Review of the Stern Review on the Economics of Climate Change," *Journal of Economic Literature* 45: 703–724.

Weldeab, S., D. Lee, R. Schneider, and N. Andersen (2007), "155,000 Years of West African Monsoon and Ocean Thermal Evolution," *Science* 316: 1303–1307.

Wentz, F., L. Ricciardulli, K. Hilburn, and C. Mears (2007), "How Much More Rain Will Global Warming Bring?" *Science* 317: 233–235.

Werf, G. et al. (2004), "Continental-Scale Partitioning of Fire Emissions during the 1997 to 2001 El Niño/ La Niña period," *Science* 303: 73–76.

Whitesell, W. (2009), "The Safe Markets Development Approach to Cap and Trade," testimony before the Ways and Means Committee, U.S. House of Representatives, March 26.

Whitesell, W. and A. Vanamali (2009), "Norway's Proposal to Auction Assigned Amount Units: Implementation Options," Center for Clean Air Policy.

Wiener, J. (1999), "Global Environmental Regulation: Instrument Choice in Legal Context," *Yale Law Journal* 108: 677–800.

Worldwatch Institute (2006), "American Energy: The Renewable Path to Energy Security."

Zachos, J. et al. (2005), "Rapid Acidification of the Ocean during the Paleocene-Eocene Thermal Maximum," *Science* 308: 1611–1615.

Zachos, J., G. Dickens, and R. Zeebe (2008), "An Early Cenozoic Perspective on Greenhouse Warming and Carbon-Cycle Dynamics," *Nature* 451: 279–283.

Index

Printed in the United States
By Bookmasters